Study Guide

Corinne R. Livesay
Belhaven College

Management

Comprehension, Analysis, and Application

Robert D. Gatewood
Robert R. Taylor
O.C. Ferrell

IRWIN
Chicago • Bogotá • Boston • Buenos Aires • Caracas
London • Madrid • Mexico City • Sydney • Toronto

Printed in the United States of America.

ISBN 0-256-18485-2

1 2 3 4 5 6 7 8 9 0 MG 2 1 0 9 8 7 6 5

PREFACE

This *Study Guide* has many features to help you learn and apply the information in your text, *Management: Comprehension, Analysis, and Application.* Here are some suggestions for using this guide with your text:

- Review the Learning Objectives (listed both in the text and in the *Study Guide*) to give you an understanding of what the authors had in mind when they wrote each chapter.
- Read the Chapter Outline in the *Study Guide* to give you the framework for the learning objectives.
- Skim the list of Key Terms in the *Study Guide* and stop to read those that are unfamiliar. Becoming familiar with the terms before reading the text will make your reading go more quickly.
- Read the Chapter in the text, relating each section to the Chapter Outline. This will help you organize the new material and improve your recall of what you have learned.
- Read the Chapter Recap section of the *Study Guide*.
- Answer the 25 Review Questions in the *Study Guide* (5 true/false, 5 multiple-choice, 5 fill-in-the-blank, 5 matching, and 5 short answer/discussion questions).
- Check your answers with the ones provided after the questions. Mark any you miss and refer to the page number to review the information from which the question was taken.
- Use the accompanying computer diskette, prepared by Gary Gardiner and Brian Hirt, to take a sample quiz for each chapter or to simulate a test by choosing multiple chapters. You may select a multiple-choice exam, a true/false exam, or a combination of each. The self-study scoring system will allow you to measure your improvement and mastery of the subject by tracking your scores on each exam for up to ten separate attempts.

Trying various approaches for your study time and using the tools contained in this *Study Guide* will increase your interest and help you find the most efficient way to learn the material.

In addition, by completing the Student Exercise at the end of each chapter you will be able to apply what you have learned. Here is a listing of the exercise titles, which will give you an overview of the range of activities included:

Chapter 1	Performing Management Functions
Chapter 2	To Tell the Truth
Chapter 3	Career Environment
Chapter 4	Making Decisions about Ethical Issues
Chapter 5	Learning about Other Cultures
Chapter 6	Dealing with Diversity
Chapter 7	Competing on Quality Standards
Chapter 8	Are You Entrepreneurial?
Chapter 9	Understanding Your Attitude toward Goal Setting
Chapter 10	Analyzing McDonald's Strategy

Chapter 11	Matching Your Decision Style with Your Leadership Style
Chapter 12	Identifying Type of Departmentalization
Chapter 13	Rendering Your Decision
Chapter 14	Effective Human Resources Management Can Reduce Workplace Stress
Chapter 15	Building a Really Great Team
Chapter 16	Playing Hard at Work
Chapter 17	A Stewardship Leadership Case Study
Chapter 18	Being Sensitive to Nonverbal Cues
Chapter 19	Making a Change
Chapter 20	Examining Labor Productivity in the Service Sector
Chapter 21	Assessing and Increasing Your Computer Literacy
Chapter 22	Applications to Operations Control

The more you use the various options provided in this *Study Guide,* the more involved you will become in the learning process. As you become more involved, you will move from passive learning to active learning. Every time you sit down to study, you make the decision of how best to spend your time. Active learners comprehend material more quickly and retain greater amounts of information for longer periods of time than do passive learners. The choice is yours.

Corinne R. Livesay

CONTENTS

Study Guide

NOTE TO THE INSTRUCTOR

Austen Press texts are marketed and distributed by Richard D. Irwin, Inc. For assistance in obtaining supplementary material for this and other Austen Press titles, please contact your Irwin sales representative or the customer service division of Richard D. Irwin at (800) 323-4560.

Study Guide

chapter one

The Essence of Management

LEARNING OBJECTIVES

- Define management and describe its purpose in organizations.
- Determine the effect that management actions have on the manager and others in the organization.
- List the major functions of managers.
- Explain the importance of decision making in management activities.
- Describe the many roles managers play in an organization.
- Specify why different managers perform different job activities.
- Review what you can reasonably learn from a textbook about how to perform management activities.
- Evaluate a small-business owner's management skills and propose a future course of action for the firm.

CHAPTER OUTLINE

Introduction

The Nature of Management

The Impact of Management

The Functions of Management

- Planning
- Organizing
- Leading
- Controlling

Management Decision Making

Management Roles

- Interpersonal Roles
- Informational Roles
- Decisional Roles

CHAPTER RECAP

Note: Boldface words are major chapter headings.

Introduction

In order to understand what management is, you must know how management is similar and different across organizations.

The Nature of Management

Management is a set of activities designed to achieve an organization's objectives by using its resources effectively and efficiently in a changing environment. How well a manager coordinates the activities of the organization and uses its resources determines not only how well the organization accomplishes its objectives but also how he or she will be judged in terms of job performance.

The Impact of Management

Because management activities are characterized by interacting with others, decision making, and completing work tasks, management reaches several different groups connected with the organization. The three groups most affected by management activities are the manager, the manager's immediate subordinates, and the manager's organization.

The Functions of Management

The following four management functions usually occur simultaneously in management activities.

Planning is the process of determining what the organization will specifically accomplish and deciding how to accomplish these goals.

Organizing is the activities involved in designing jobs for employees, grouping these jobs together into departments, and developing working relationships among organization units and employees to carry out the plans.

Leading is the act of influencing others' activities to achieve set goals.

Controlling is those activities that an organization undertakes to ensure that its activities lead to achievement of its objectives.

Management Decision Making

Along with the four basic management functions, all managers engage in the decision-making process—gathering information, using information to reach a decision, and implementing the decision. Each of the four management functions requires a manager to make a decisions.

Management Roles

Henry Mintzberg, a noted management professor, described ten specific roles that managers perform, which, in turn, can be grouped into three larger categories:

1. **Interpersonal roles** include figurehead, liaison, and leadership. In this capacity, managers perform activities that involve interacting with others who may be external or internal to the organization and at a higher or lower level than the manager.
2. **Informational roles** include monitor, disseminator, and spokesperson. In this capacity, managers perform activities, such as preparing reports or briefings, that focus on obtaining data important for the decisions the manager needs to make.
3. **Decisional roles** include entrepreneur, disturbance handler, resource allocator, and negotiator. In this capacity, managers perform activities that deal primarily with the allocation of resources in order to reach organizational objectives.

Management Skills

General skills include interpersonal, technical, and conceptual skills.

Specific skills include job knowledge, oral communication, persuasiveness, problem analysis, cooperativeness, tolerance of stress, negotiation, assertiveness, and initiative.

Situational Differences in Management Activities

Although there are many similarities of management activities across organizations, there is a great deal of diversity among their specific tasks. These differences in management activities can be attributed to the following characteristics of organizations: **level of management** (upper, middle, or lower managers), **area of management** (human resource, marketing, finance, or production and operations managers), **organizational size, organizational culture** (the values, beliefs, traditions, philosophies, rules, and heroes that are shared by members of the organization), **industry,** and **for-profit versus nonprofit organizations.**

Can You Learn Management in a Management Class?

You can certainly learn valuable aspects of management in a college or university class. In addition to presenting factual data and relationships among data, formal classes can help you develop conceptual and analytic skills, which are needed by all managers. Also, the discussion of organizational and human behavior principles should serve as important bases for the managerial activities associated with leading.

KEY TERMS

Text page numbers where terms are first defined are in parentheses.

management (4)—a set of activities designed to achieve an organization's objectives by using its resources effectively and efficiently

effectively (4)—having the intended result

efficiently (4)—accomplishing objectives with a minimum of resources

managers (4)—individuals who make decisions about the use of the organization's resources and are concerned with planning, organizing, leading, and controlling the organization's activities in order to reach its objectives

organizations (4)—groups of individuals who work together to achieve desired objectives

resources (5)—the people, equipment, finances, and data an organization uses in order to reach its objectives

planning (6)—the process of determining what the organization will specifically accomplish and deciding how to accomplish these goals

organizing (7)—the activities involved in designing jobs for employees, grouping these jobs together into departments, and developing working relationships among organizational units and employees to carry out the plans

leading (7)—the act of influencing others' activities to achieve set goals

controlling (8)—those activities that an organization undertakes to ensure that its activities lead to achievement of its objectives

interpersonal roles (10)—activities that involve interacting with others who may be external or internal to the organization and at a higher or lower level than the manager

informational roles (11)—activities, such as reports or briefings, that focus on obtaining data important for the decisions the manager needs to make

decisional roles (12)—activities that deal primarily with the allocation of resources in order to reach organizational objectives

interpersonal skills (13)—those management skills, such as communication, conflict resolution, and leading, that are necessary to work with others

technical skills (14)—the knowledge and ability to accomplish the specialized activities of the work group

conceptual skills (14)—the intellectual abilities to process information and make accurate decisions about the work group and the job task

upper managers (17)—those who make decisions about the overall performance and direction of the organization

middle managers (17)—those who receive broad statements of strategy and policy from upper-level managers and develop specific objectives and plans

lower (first-line) managers (17)— those concerned with the direct production of items or delivery of service

human resource managers (18)—managers concerned with developing and carrying out programs used to make decisions about employees, such as selection, training, and compensation

marketing managers (18)—managers who develop programs that provide information about the company's goods or services and encourage potential customers to purchase these

finance managers (18)—managers concerned with the value of the organization's assets and various investment strategies that would increase net worth

production and operations managers (18)—managers who schedule and monitor the work process that turns out the firm's goods and services

organizational culture (19)—the values, beliefs, traditions, philosophies, rules, and heroes that are shared by members of the organization

for-profit companies (20)—companies owned either privately by one or more individuals or publicly by stockholders

nonprofit organizations (20)—institutions such as governments, churches, and universities that cannot retain earnings over expenses, do not have equity interests, and cannot be bought or sold

REVIEW QUESTIONS

True/False

Indicate whether the following statements are true or false.

___ 1. The three groups most affected by management activities are the manager, the manager's immediate subordinates, and the manager's organization.

___ 2. In the management role category Mintzberg called *liaison*, the manager acts as a public official for the company at formal activities.

___ 3. In general, conceptual skills require a high level of intellectual ability in information processing and decision making.

___ 4. Managers exhibit the specific skill of *initiative* when they clearly and consistently express a point of view on a topic being discussed.

___ 5. Nonprofit organizations must pay taxes on profits and may be bought and sold.

Multiple Choice

Select the best answer for each question.

___ 6. An activity that seems to be important for the effective performance of all the major management functions is:
   a. evaluating negative and positive employee performance
   b. dividing the organization into sensible departments
   c. gathering and processing appropriate information
   d. staffing the company with competent employees
   e. leading the organization to a common objective

___ 7. In which of Mintzberg's management role categories is the manager both protecting and using the unit's assets: money, time, material and equipment, human resources, data, and reputation?
   a. negotiator
   b. disturbance handler
   c. monitor
   d. resource allocator
   e. disseminator

___ 8. Which of the following is an example of technical skills?
   a. The accounting manager must know current tax reporting regulations.
   b. A manager reviews an employee's work performance.
   c. A manager tries to determine whether an employee's poor performance is a result of drug or alcohol addiction.
   d. A manager responds to a hostile environmental group concerning the use of chemicals.
   e. A manager discusses a customer's complaint about a perceived deficiency in a product.

____ 9. Which statement is true of upper managers?
   a. They are concerned with the direct production of items or delivery of service.
   b. Examples of their job titles are product manager, department head, plant manager, and quality control manager.
   c. Technical skills are especially important to upper managers.
   d. They train and monitor the performance of their subordinates.
   e. They spend most of their time planning and leading.

____ 10. When managers communicate the basic beliefs that define success of employees in the organization, they are focusing on which component of organizational culture?
   a. heroes
   b. rites and rituals
   c. cultural network
   d. symbols
   e. values

Fill in the Blank

11. ____________ is a set of activities designed to achieve an organization's objectives by using its resources effectively and efficiently.
12. ____________ involves determining what the organization will accomplish and deciding how to accomplish these goals.
13. ____________ refers to those activities undertaken to ensure that actions lead to achievement of the organization's objectives.
14. The knowledge and ability to accomplish the specialized activities of a work group are the ____________ skills of the manager.
15. ____________ skills, the intellectual abilities to process information and make accurate decisions about the work group and the job process, usually become more important as a manager moves higher in the organization.

Matching

Place the corresponding letter of the word or phrase with each definition or description. Each word or phrase can be used only once.

   a. upper managers
   b. organizing
   c. leading
   d. marketing managers
   e. organizational culture

____ 16. The values, beliefs, traditions, philosophies, rules, and heroes that are shared by members of the organization

____ 17. Those who make decisions about the overall performance and direction of the organization

____ 18. Those who develop programs that provide information about the firm's goods and services and encourage potential customers to purchase them

____ 19. Assigning duties to subordinates and developing an established working relationship among members of the work unit

____ 20. This management function requires a knowledge of human behavior

Short Answer/Discussion Questions

21. Peter Drucker developed two phrases to describe management efficiency and effectiveness: "doing the right thing" and "doing things right." Which phrase would you associate with "effective," and which phrase would you associate with "efficient"?
22. Identify the three broad steps into which management decision making can be broken down.
23. Under the three general roles of management (interpersonal, informational, and decisional), list the ten specific roles that are associated with each general role.
24. Examine the list of nine specific skills related to managerial job performance on p. 16 of the text. Based on your assessment of your ability in each skill area, identify each skill as either "Very Competent," "Somewhat Competent," or "Not Competent." What can you do to increase your skill competence in those areas in which you gave yourself the lowest rating?
25. List three facts you learned in the "Careers Corner" box on p. 22 that you didn't know before you read the feature.

ANSWERS TO REVIEW QUESTIONS

Text page numbers where the answers can be found are included in parentheses.

1. True (5)
2. False (11)
3. True (14)
4. False (16)
5. False (20)
6. c (8)
7. d (13)
8. a (14)
9. c (17)
10. e (19)
11. management (4)
12. planning (6)
13. controlling (8)
14. technical (14)
15. conceptual (14)
16. e (19)
17. a (17)
18. d (18)
19. b (7)
20. c (7)
21. effective (doing the right things) and efficient (doing things right). (4)
22. information gathered, using information to make decisions, and implementing decisions. (9)
23. interpersonal (figurehead, liaison, leadership), informational (monitor, disseminator, spokesperson), and decisional (entrepreneur, disturbance handler, resource allocator, negotiator). (10–13)
24. Self-assessments will vary; however, you can take action to improve all of these skill areas by seeking out opportunities in this course and others you take to learn more about these skills and to practice them. You can also identify those people in your life whom you think are very competent in skill areas where you need help and observe how they practice their skill and ask them questions that can help you learn more about how you can increase your competence.
25. Answers will vary. (p. 22)

STUDENT EXERCISE

Performing Management Functions

You learned the four major functions managers perform in Chapter 1. Here you will broaden your perspective of how these functions usually occur simultaneously in management activites.

Directions

1. Imagine you are the supervisor in each scenario described below and you have to decide which management function(s) you would use in each.
2. Mark your answers using the CODE below.
3. Compare your answers with those at the end of the exercise.

CODE	SUPERVISORY FUNCTION	BRIEF DEFINITION
P	PLANNING	the process of determining what the organization will specifically accomplish and deciding how to accomplish these goals
O	ORGANIZING	the activities involved in designing jobs for employees, grouping these jobs together into departments, and developing working relationships among organizational units and employees to carry out the plans
L	LEADING	the act of influencing others' activities to achieve set goals
C	CONTROLLING	those activities that an organization undertakes to ensure that its activities lead to achievement of its objectives

NO.	SCENARIO	ANSWER
1.	Your group's work is centered around a project that is due in two months. Although everyone is working on the project, you have observed your employees involved in what you believe is excessive socializing and other time-filling behaviors. You decide to meet with the group to have them help you break down the project into smaller subprojects with mini-deadlines. You believe this will help keep the group members focused on the project and that quality of the finished project will then reflect the true capabilities of your group.	

2	Your first impression of the new group you'll be managing is not too great. You tell your friend at dinner after your first day on the job: "Looks like I got a babysitting job instead of a management job."	
3	You call a meeting of your work group and begin it by letting them know that a major procedure the work group has been using for the past two years is being significantly revamped, and your department will have to phase in the change during the next six weeks. You proceed by explaining to them the reasoning your boss gave you for this change. You then say, "Let's take the next five to ten minutes to let you voice your reactions to this change." After ten minutes elapse with the majority of comments being critical of the change, you say: "I appreciate each of you sharing your reactions; and I, too, recognize that *all* change creates problems. The way I see it, however, is that we can spend the remaining 45 minutes of our meeting focusing on why we don't want the change and why we don't think it's necessary or we can work together to come up with viable solutions to solve the problems that implementing this change will most likely create." After about five more minutes of comments being exchanged, the consensus of the group is that the remainder of the meeting needs to be focused on how to deal with the potential problems the group anticipates having to deal with as the new procedure is implemented.	
4	You are preparing for the annual budget allocation meetings to be held in the plant manager's office next week. You are determined to present a strong case to support your department getting money for some high-tech equipment that will help them do their jobs better. You will stand firm against any suggestions of budget cuts in your area.	
5	Early in your career you learned an important lesson about employee selection. One of the nurses on your floor unexpectedly quit. The other nurses were putting pressure on you to quickly fill the position because they were overworked even before the nurse left, and now things were really bad. After a hasty recruitment effort, you made a decision based on insufficient information. You ended up regretting your quick decision during the three months of problems that followed until you finally had to discharge the new hire. Since then, you have never let anybody pressure you into making a quick hiring decision.	

ANSWERS TO STUDY EXERCISE

1. planning (deciding how to accomplish the goals)
   organizing (a form of designing jobs for employees)
   leading (seeking to influence your employees' activities)
   controlling (ensuring that activities lead to achievement of objectives)
2. planning (you will need this function to get your group headed in the right direction)
   organizing (trying to get this group of employees to carry out the plans will be a challenge)
   leading (influencing them will be a high priority)
   controlling (you will, no doubt, have to work closely with this group until you can develop them into a group of self-starters)
3. planning (deciding how to accomplish the new goal of making the change)
   organizing (you will need to determine what new relationships should be developed in order to successfully implement the change)
   leading (you have already used your influence to get your group to move toward making the change—and will undoubtedly need to do more throughout the change process)
   controlling (you will need to monitor what's happening to make sure things stay on track)
4. leading (you will need to use your influence to get what your department needs)
   controlling (the budgeting process is part of this function)
5. controlling (your monitoring the performance of the new employee led to your making needed corrections—discipline and eventually discharge—and your new selection system helps to ensure that your work group will achieve its objectives)

chapter two

The Development of Management Thought

LEARNING OBJECTIVES

- Specify the major cultural changes that preceded the development of modern management practice and thought.
- Explain the major theories within the classical approach to management.
- Examine some of the major contributions to the development of the behavioral approach to management.
- Describe the systems approach to management theory and identify the early contributors to this perspective.
- Relate the significance of the contingency approach within the study and practice of management.
- Summarize how current management knowledge and practices are a result of the work and ideas of many management scholars and practitioners over the past century.
- Apply the management theories discussed in this chapter to a manager's efforts to revitalize a small business.

CHAPTER OUTLINE

Introduction

A Cultural Framework for the Development of Management Theory
- The Protestant Ethic
- Capitalism and Division of Labor
- The Industrial Revolution
- The Productivity Problem

The Development of Management Theories

The Classical Approach
- Scientific Management
- Principles of Scientific Management
- Assumptions of Scientific Management
- Criticisms and Contributions of Taylor
- The Gilbreths
- Henry Gantt
- Morris L. Cooke

CHAPTER RECAP

Note: Boldface words are major chapter headings.

Introduction

The topic of this chapter is how management developed into what it is today. You will learn about two major aspects of the history of management thought: (1) the major developments within the history of Western civilization that stimulated the evolution of the practice and study of management; and (2) the development of major perspectives of management thought and some of the important contributors to the various perspectives.

A Cultural Framework for the Development of Management Theory

Four major developments in Western culture set the stage for the systematic study and teaching of management that began during the late 1800s and early 1900s: (1) the Protestant ethic, (2) capitalism and the division of labor, (3) the Industrial Revolution, and (4) the productivity problem.

The first development came about as a result of the challenge led by Martin Luther and John Calvin to the bleak philosophy of life widely held during the Middle Ages (A.D. 600 to A.D. 1500). This new interpretation of the purpose of life became known as the **Protestant ethic** (or work ethic), which held that instead of merely waiting on earth for release into the next world, people should pursue an occupation and engage in high levels of worldly activity so that they will fulfill their calling. Society interpreted the Protestant ethic as a mandate for people to work hard, use their wealth wisely, and to live self-denying lives. This created a new age of self-determination, self-control, and individualism.

Another major societal change that occurred following the Middle Ages was the move from feudalism to **capitalism and division of labor**. The basic tenets of capitalism as described in Adam Smith's *The Wealth of Nations* are:

1. Natural laws of supply and demand and free competition within the marketplace will efficiently regulate the flow of resources within a society.
2. All individuals should have the right to accumulate wealth.
3. All individuals should have the right to private ownership of property.
4. Division of labor—the simple idea of breaking an entire job into its components and assigning each task to an individual worker—would lead to great gains in productivity.

The final development needed to launch the world toward large-scale business and industrialization was the refinement of the use of the steam engine and the ensuing **Industrial Revolution**. Techniques for mass-production of standardized products, made from interchangeable parts in a factory system using steam-powered machines, were the hallmarks of the American manufacturing system in the late 1800s.

Instead of steady progress, a certain degree of chaos existed in industry at the dawn of the twentieth century, due to changes in philosophies of life, economic structures, and manufacturing systems. Three issues formed the basis of the **productivity problem**:

1. A technical and behavioral problem of meshing workers and machines.
2. General inexperience in the operation of organizations and factories of the size needed to achieve the economies of scale inherent in mass production and distribution.
3. Widespread lack of both management and trained managers. Bringing together raw materials, capital, and labor on a large scale with power-driven machines could no longer be accomplished without the presence of management. Management was the missing link to future productivity gains.

The Development of Management Theories

One commonly accepted system of grouping management theories categorizes the major perspectives from which to study management as (1) the classical approach, (2) the behavioral approach, (3) the systems approach, and (4) the contingency approach.

The Classical Approach

The classical approach to management stresses the manager's role in a formal hierarchy of authority and focuses on the tasks, machines, and systems needed to accomplish the task efficiently. This approach to management thought emerged in the late 1800s and early 1900s and has two components: scientific management and administrative management.

Scientific management focuses on improving operational efficiencies through the systematic and scientific study of work methods, tools, and performance standards. After almost 26 years of investigating the problems of low productivity, Frederick W. Taylor, who is often called the "father of scientific management", devised the **principles of scientific management**, which described the role of management as: (1) develop the "one best way to perform any task"; (2) scientifically select, train, teach, and develop each worker; (3) cooperate with workers and provide an incentive to ensure that the work is done according to the "one best way;" and (4) divide the work and the responsibility equally between management and the workers.

The three **assumptions of scientific management** are: (1) employers and employees have mutual interests associated with economic gain; (2) man is a rational being and economically motivated; and (3) for every man willing to work hard, there was a job for which he was ideally suited.

The criticisms of Taylor revolved around (1) whether the scientific management's efficiency methods led to exploitation of workers by getting them to produce more and causing large work-force reductions; (2) whether Taylor failed to give credit to others for the work they did; and (3) whether Taylor fabricated some of the data reported in his studies. Despite the criticisms, Taylor's **contributions** are very evident in current areas of management study and practice known as the quantitative approach, management science, and production/operations management.

Some other major contributors to scientific management include **Frank and Lillian Gilbreth**, who used time and motion studies to improve workplace conditions and worker efficiency; **Henry Gantt**, who was a passionate advocate of workplace democracy and humanitarian management; and **Morris L. Cooke**, who attempted to apply the gospel of efficiency in higher education, in government agencies, and in the management of World War I.

The second component of the classical approach to management theory is **administrative management**, which focuses on the need to organize and coordinate the workings of the entire organization instead of dwelling on organizing the work of individual workers, as in scientific management. Two important contributors to administrative management were **Henri Fayol,** whose main contributions include defining the functions of management, developing a comprehensive list of general principles of management, and espousing the necessity of teaching management; and **Max Weber**, who formed the theory of a bureaucracy as a means of large organizations operating more efficiently.

The main **contribution of the classical approach to management theory** can be described as providing the basic theory that forms the main roots of the study and practice of management as we know it today.

The Behavioral Approach

During the early 1900s, the theories of management began to emphasize understanding the importance of human behavior, needs, and attitudes within formal organizations. Contributors to this view of management, known as the behavioral approach, included **Mary Parker Follett**, whose ideas of shared power and human cooperation earned her an international reputation as a political and business philosopher; **the Hawthorne studies**, which concluded that human relations and the social needs of workers are a crucial aspect of business management; **Abraham H. Maslow**, who advocated a humanistic approach to management, taking the innate nature and needs of human beings into account in management theories and practices; and **Douglas McGregor**, who believed that manager's individual assumptions about human nature and behavior (Theory X or Theory Y) determined how they managed their employees.

The Systems Approach

The systems approach views organizations and the environments within which they operate as sets of interrelated parts to be managed as a whole in order to achieve a common goal. Two systems theorists are Chester Barnard and W. Edwards Deming. **Chester Barnard's** cooperative systems theory (formal organizations are necessary so that individuals can accomplish tasks that they could not accomplish working on their own) and acceptance theory of authority (in formal organizations authority flows up because the decision as to whether an order, or communication, has authority lies with the person who receives the communication) formed the basis of his view that organizations must be managed so that they can adjust effectively to a constantly changing external environment. One of **W. Edwards Deming's** major contributions was to integrate emphasis on quantitative methods and efficiency with the psychological and social dimensions of the work environment into an approach in which all dimensions of the formal organization and its environment are considered as part of one system.

The Contingency Approach

The contingency approach, characterized by the phrase "it depends," is considered to be an outgrowth of the systems approach and has inspired research and promoted understanding about bridging the gap between theory and practice.

Management Theory: Past, Present, and Future

Each major approach to management theory studied in this chapter has added significantly to our current knowledge about management. The ideas embedded in each approach have also changed, in some respects, the way managers think and act. Contemporary managers and managers of the future benefit most from understanding and applying selected aspects of each approach.

KEY TERMS

Text page numbers where terms are first defined are in parentheses.

social forces (32)—the relationship of people to each other within a particular culture

economic forces (32)—the relationship of people to resources

political forces (32)—the relationship of individuals, their rights, and their property to the state

Protestant ethic (33)—an interpretation of the purpose of life, stating that, instead of merely waiting on earth for release into the next world, people should pursue an occupation and engage in high levels of worldly activity so that they will fulfill their calling

capitalism (33)—an economic system wherein the natural laws of supply and demand and free competition within the marketplace will efficiently regulate the flow of resources within a society

division of labor (33)—the idea of breaking down an entire job into its component parts and assigning each specific task to an individual member; also called specialization

management theory (35)—a systematic statement, based on observations, of how the management process might best occur, given stated underlying principles

classical approach (36)—an approach to management that stresses the manager's role in a formal hierarchy of authority and focuses on the task, machines, and systems needed to accomplish the task effectively

scientific management (36)—a theory within the classical approach that focuses on improvement of operational efficiencies through the systematic and scientific study of work methods, tools, and performance standards

soldiering (37)—systematic slowdown in work by laborers with the deliberate purpose of keeping their employers ignorant of how fast the work can be done

quantitative approach (38)—a viewpoint of management that emphasizes the application of mathematical models, statistics, and structured information systems to support rational management decision making

management science (38)—the field of management that includes the study and use of mathematical models and statistical methods to improve the effectiveness of managerial decision making

administrative management (40)—the universality of management as a function that can be applied to all organizations

bureaucracy (42)—a theory of management by office or position, rather than by person, based on rational authority

behavioral approach (43)—a view of management that emphasizes understanding the importance of human behavior, needs, and attitudes within formal organizations

Hawthorne studies (44)—a group of studies that provided the stimulus for the human relations movement within management theory and practice

human-relations movement (45)—a practice whereby employees come to be viewed as informal groups of their own, with their own leadership and codes of behavior, instead of as unrelated individual workers assigned to perform individual tasks

Theory X (45)—the assumption that people are naturally lazy, must be threatened and forced to work, have little ambition or initiative, and do not try to fulfill any need higher than security needs at work

Theory Y (46)—the assumption that people naturally want to work, are capable of self-control, seek responsibility, are creative, and try to fulfill higher-order needs at work

systems approach (46)—an approach to management theory that views organizations and the environments within which they operate as sets of interrelated parts to be managed as a whole in order to achieve a common goal

system (46)—an arrangement of related or connected parts that form a whole unit

closed system (47)—an organization that interacts little with its external environment and therefore receives little feedback from or information about its surroundings

open system (47)—an organization that interacts continually with its environment and therefore is well informed about changes within its surroundings and its position relative to these changes

subsystem (47)—any system that is part of a larger one

entropy (47)—the tendency of systems to deteriorate or break down over time

synergy (47)—the ability of the whole system to equal more than the sum of its parts

acceptance theory of authority (48)—the theory that, in formal organizations, authority flows up because the decision as to whether an order, or communication, has authority lies with the person who receives the communication

contingency approach (49)—an approach to management theories that emphasizes identifying the key variables in each management situation, understanding the relationships among these variables, and recognizing the complex system of cause and effects that exists in each and every managerial situation

Theory Z (51)—a management theory involving increased concern for quality of work-life, job security, group decision making, cooperation between groups, informal control mechanisms, and concern for work-family issues

REVIEW QUESTIONS

True/False

Indicate whether each of the following statements is true or false:

___ 1. Of the social, economic, and political forces that have influenced our ideas about management, economic forces refer to the relationship of individuals, their rights, and their property to the state.

___ 2. Adam Smith acknowledged that the dysfunctional aspect of division of labor was that a lifetime spent doing a very specialized, narrow job could result in boredom and lack of intellectual and/or social development.

___ 3. Frank Gilbreth's thesis was published as a book *The Psychology of Management.*

___ 4. Mary Parker Follett's ideas of shared power and human cooperation earned her an international reputation as a political and business philosopher.

___ 5. Cooperative systems and the acceptance theory of authority were two aspects of Chester Barnard's view of how organizations must be managed so that they can adjust effectively to a constantly changing external environment.

Multiple Choice

Select the best answer for each question.

___ 6. Which issue listed below was **not** among the developments in Western culture that set the stage for the systematic study and teaching of management?
   a. the Protestant ethic
   b. the stagnation of technological innovation
   c. capitalism and the division of labor
   d. the Industrial Revolution
   e. the productivity problem

___ 7. What is/are the assumption(s) of scientific management?
   a. Employers and employees have mutual interests associated with economic gain.
   b. Man is a rational being and economically motivated.
   c. For every man willing to work hard, there was a job for which he was ideally suited according to his mental and physical traits and abilities.
   d. all of the above
   e. a and b only

___ 8. Whose concern for devotion to service in the business system and call for "morality in the habits of industry" made him a pioneer in the area of business ethics and corporate social responsibility as they are studied in management today?
   a. Henry Gantt
   b. Morris L. Cooke
   c. Max Weber
   d. Elton Mayo
   e. Douglas McGregor

___ 9. The functional definition of management and the comprehensive list of general principles of management are attributed to:
   a. W. Edwards Deming
   b. Mary Parker Follett
   c. Henri Fayol
   d. Chester Barnard
   e. both b and c

___ 10. Which one of the following was not associated with the Hawthorne studies that provided the stimulus for the human-relations movement?
   a. The Western Electric Company's Hawthorne plant in Cicero, Illinois, in 1924.
   b. Researchers from MIT conducted experiments with several different groups of factory operators.
   c. George Pennock sought professional advice from two professors, Claire Turner of MIT and Elton Mayo of Harvard University.
   d. Scholars have criticized the studies as having too many uncontrolled variables to permit valid conclusions.
   e. Many other lengthy tests conducted in the workplace to study actual worker behavior prompted the researchers to go to the Hawthorne plant.

Fill In The Blank

11. The ______________ held that people should pursue an occupation and engage in high levels of worldly activity so that they will fulfill their calling rather than wait on earth for release into the next world.
12. Another name for division of labor is ____________.
13. ____________ is the systematic slowdown in work by laborers with the deliberate purpose of keeping their employers ignorant of how fast the work can be done.
14. According to Weber, ______________ is a theory of management by office or position, rather than by person, based on rational authority.
15. Theory ___ is the belief that man naturally wants to work, is capable of self-control, seeks responsibility, is creative, and tries to fulfill higher-order needs at work.

Matching

Match the following people with the approach to management theory with which they are associated. One answer will not be used and two answers will be used twice.

a. The classical approach
b. The behavioral approach
c. The systems approach

___ 16. Mary Parker Follett

___ 17. W. Edwards Deming

___ 18. Frederick W. Taylor

___ 19. Abraham H. Maslow

___ 20. Henri Fayol

Short Answer/Discussion Questions

21. According to Adam Smith's *The Wealth of Nations*, what are the four basic tenets of capitalism?
22. List the three issues that formed the basis of the productivity problem.
23. What connection exists between the rise of the factory system, where people left their homes to work in the factories, to the current trend of more than 24 million Americans (that's 20 percent of the entire adult work force) who have chosen self-employment and are leaving the workplace to work at home? The same connection exists between the rise of the factory system and increasing numbers of employees who telecommute at least part of their workweek by working out of their home offices.
24. Name and briefly describe the two components of the classical approach to management.
25. What was the role of management, according to Frederick Taylor's principles of scientific management?

ANSWERS TO REVIEW QUESTIONS

Text page numbers where the answers can be found are included in parentheses.

1. False (32)
2. True (34)
3. False (38–39)
4. True (44)
5. True (48)
6. b (32)
7. d (37–38)
8. a (39)
9. c (40)
10. e (44)
11. Protestant ethic (33)
12. specialization (33)
13. soldiering (37)
14. bureaucracy (42)
15. Y (46)
16. b (43)
17. c (48)
18. a (36)
19. b (45)
20. a (40)
21. (1) Natural laws of supply and demand and free competition within the marketplace will efficiently regulate the flow of resources within a society. (2) All individuals should have the right to accumulate wealth. (3) All individuals should have the right to private ownership of property. (4) Division of labor—the simple idea of breaking an entire job into its components and assigning each task to an individual worker—would lead to great gains in productivity. (33)
22. (1) the technical and behavior problem of meshing workers and machines, (2) general inexperience in the operation of organizations and factories to make large volumes of a product at a lower cost per item, (3) the widespread lack of both management and trained managers. (34–35)
23. The text discussed how the increased capital requirements for power-driven machinery made it impossible for most individuals to buy and install machinery at home. Instead, workers had to travel to the machine's home. (34) Today, with increased computing power at lower and lower prices, com-

puters are within reach of many people. Therefore, millions are leaving the formal workplace, using computer and communication technology to start home businesses or to work in an office from home.

24. The two components are scientific management, which focuses on improvement of operational efficiencies through the systematic and scientific study of work methods, tools, and performance standards; and administrative management, which emphasizes the universality of management as a function that can be applied to all organizations—large, small, for-profit, not-for-profit, political, religious, or any other. (36 and 40)
25. The role of management is to (1) develop the "one best way to perform any task"; (2) scientifically select, train, teach, and develop each worker; (3) cooperate with workers and provide an incentive to ensure that the work is done according to the "one best way"; and (4) divide the work and the responsibility equally between management and the workers.(37)

STUDENT EXERCISE

To Tell the Truth

This chapter introduced you to more than 20 people who made contributions to the development of management thought. Some of those "history makers" are placed in groups of three below. Beneath each of their names is a quotation that they could have said about themselves.

Directions

1. Identify within each group, which one of the "speakers" has misstated some information about him- or herself.
2. Circle the name of the person within each group who is **not** telling the truth in some portion of the quotation.
3. Underline the statement within the quotation that is inaccurate.

Group 1		
Chester Barnard	Morris L. Cooke	Mary Parker Follett
"I am associated with the systems approach because I devised a theory of managing organizations as cooperative systems."	"I am one of the four men originally authorized to teach W. Edwards Deming's work on continuous improvement and zero defects."	"I strongly believe that work groups are one of the primary sources of influence on worker behavior—more so even than management's control and reward systems."

Group 2		
Henri Fayol	W. Edwards Deming	Elton Mayo
"My theory for devising a pure form of organization based on rationality, called bureaucracy, was published in a monograph, *General and Industrial Management*, in 1916."	"One of my first jobs in the 1920s was at Western Electric's Hawthorne plant in Chicago."	"George Pennock, the assistant works manager at the Western Electric plant, sought my professional advice on interpreting the results of experiments conducted at his plant."

Group 3		
Frank and Lillian Gilbreth "Among our contributions to the scientific management movement are Lillian's book *The Psychology of Management* and my use of motion picture technology to analyze and classify therbligs."	William Ouichi "My Theory Z involves increased concern for quality of work-life, job security, group decision making, cooperation between groups, informal control mechanisms, and concern for work-family issues."	Henry Gantt "If it were not for me, scientific management might have been lost in a storm of criticism. My work laid the foundation for the ~~development of the concept of self-managed work groups.~~"

Group 4		
Max Weber "I saw the issue of size as the major challenge to the progress of industry. Therefore, I developed the ~~concepts of closed and open systems.~~"	Abraham Maslow "Anybody who has ever taken a management course has probably heard of my hierarchy of human needs theory. I advocated taking the basic innate nature and needs of human beings into account in management theories and practices."	Adam Smith "I described in detail the outcome and advantages of division of labor in the first three chapters of my book *The Wealth of Nations.*"

Group 5		
Frederick W. Taylor "After working in the steel mills of Philadelphia, I chose to disagree with the common belief of my day that the productivity problem was due to the pure laziness of common laborers. Instead, I believed that the lack of productivity was management's fault."	James Watt "In 1765, I developed the first workable ~~printing press~~ that, after further refinement, became one of the key players in the development of the factory system and what is now known as the Industrial Revolution."	Douglas McGregor "My Theory X and Theory Y concepts were based, in part, on my belief that effective management required a thorough understanding and consideration of human nature and human behavior."

ANSWERS TO STUDENT EXERCISE

Group One
Morris L. Cooke
W. Edwards Deming's work on continuous improvement and zero defects." (supposed to be Taylor's management methods)

Group Two
Henri Fayol
My theory for devising a pure form of organization based on rationality called bureaucracy (this theory is Max Weber's) Note: W. Edwards Deming's quotation is correct if you look at Table 2.2 "Did You Know..."

Group Three
Henry Gantt
development of the concept of self-managed work groups (should be area of business ethics and corporate social responsibility)

Group Four
Max Weber
concepts of closed and open systems (should be theory of bureaucracy)

Group Five
James Watt
printing press (should be steam engine)

chapter three

Environmental Factors of Management

LEARNING OBJECTIVES

- Define the term *environment*.
- Formulate the components of the general environment, task environment, and internal environment.
- Examine the major factors in the general environment.
- Analyze the major factors in the task environment.
- Specify the major factors in the internal environment.
- Explain the stakeholder approach to viewing the environment.
- Distinguish the major ways that an organization can attempt to manage its environment.
- Specify why the external environment is important for organizations.
- Assess the environmental forces affecting an actual business.

CHAPTER OUTLINE

Introduction

The Nature of the Environment

The General Environment
- The Sociocultural Dimension
- The Political-Legal Dimension
- The Technological Dimension
- The Economic Dimension
- The Global Dimension

The Task Environment
- Suppliers
- Customers
- Substitutes
- Competitors
- Potential New Competitors

The Internal Environment
- Owners
- Managers
- Employees
- Boards of Directors

Stakeholder View of the Environment
- Identifying Stakeholders
- Chester's Bar: The Nard
- Gathering Information about Stakeholders in the Environment
- Techniques for Interacting with the Environment

The Importance of the External Environment
- Environmental Change: Two Stories
- Constraints on Viewing the Environment
- Dimensions of the External Environment

CHAPTER RECAP

Note: Boldface words are major chapter headings.

Introduction

Knowledge of the environment in which a business operates is essential. Managers must constantly be aware of factors both inside and outside the firm that affect their decisions and actions and must be able to determine what factors of the organization's world affect its operation and how these factors may be successfully addressed.

The Nature of the Environment

The environment refers to all those factors that affect the operation of the organization. The three aspects of the organizational environment are (1) the general environment, (2) the task environment, and (3) the internal environment.

The General Environment

The general environment refers to broad factors that influence all organizations, but in varying degrees. The forces that comprise the general environment can be categorized into five groups:

1. **The sociocultural dimension** includes the demographics and the values of the society within which an organization operates.
2. **The political-legal dimension** is composed of the political, legal, and regulatory elements that define the nature of the relationship between various areas of government and the organization.
3. **The technological dimension** is the knowledge and process of changing inputs (resources, labor, and money) to outputs (goods and services).

4. **The economic dimension** reflects the overall condition of the complex economies throughout the world.
5. **The global dimension** refers to those factors in other countries that affect the organization.

The Task Environment

The task environment includes a firm's competitors in industry as well as those parties that have a direct influence on the industry and the firm. The following five factors have a major effect on the overall profitability and competitive position of the firm within its industry:

1. **Suppliers** are the organizations and individuals who provide resources to other organizations.
2. **Customers** are those who purchase an organization's goods and/or services.
3. **Substitutes** are goods and services that may be used in place of those furnished by a given business.
4. **Competitors** are other organizations that produce similar, or in some cases identical, goods or services.
5. **Potential new competitors** are companies not currently operating in a business's industry but which have a high potential for entering the industry.

The Internal Environment

The internal environment refers to all the factors that make up the organization. Some of the broad factors of the internal environment are owners, managers, employees, and boards of directors.

Owners can have various degrees of influence and power with an organization. Examples of owners include an entrepreneur of a small firm, stockholders in a corporation, or institutional investors.

Managers can be identified as strategic or institutional, technical, and operational.

One important way **employees** can be classified is as unionized or nonunionized.

The **board of directors** is elected by stockholders and is charged with ensuring that the corporation is being managed so as to increase stockholder wealth. The board typically approves major strategic decisions and hires key personnel, such as the CEO.

Stakeholder View of the Environment

A stakeholder is a person or group that can affect, or is affected by, an organization's goals or the means to achieve those goals. Primary stakeholders are those who have a formal and/or contractual relationship with the firm, such as customers, suppliers, and employees. Secondary stakeholders are the groups that have a less formal connection to the organization, such as environmentalists, community activists, and the media.

Identifying stakeholders is the first step of interacting with the environment. A stakeholder map is a representation of the organization's stakeholders and their stakes. A stake can be of three basic types: equity interest (stockholder or lender), market interest (buyers or suppliers), and influencing interest (government or interest group).

Chester's Bar: The Nard presented on pages 73–74 of the text illustrates how one manager created a stakeholder map.

Once the stakeholder map has been determined, the next step is to **gather information about stakeholders in the environment**. Techniques organizations can use to collect information systematically and accurately include customer surveys, economic forecasting, trend analysis, and the Delphi method.

After the manager has identified the relevant stakeholders and collected information about future trends involving these stakeholders, the final step is to develop **techniques for interacting with the environment**. Some of the more common means of interacting effectively with the environment include (1) public relations, (2) boundary spanning, (3) lobbying, (4) negotiation, (5) alliances, and (6) organizational restructuring.

The Importance of the External Environment

Managers must perceive the threats and opportunities to the organization presented in the external environment and react accordingly.

Environmental change: two stories presents the story of how GM surpassed Ford as the world's largest auto manufacturer because of GM's appropriate responses to changes in consumer demands. The second story relates how McDonald's saw and responded to the trends in the environment, which contributed to its standing today as the biggest fast-food restaurant chain in the world.

The following **constraints on viewing the environment** identify the common problems in receiving and using information about the external environment: (1) limited capability, (2) lack of information, (3) superfluous information, and (4) current organizational constraints.

There are two **dimensions of the external environment** that differ among organizations: degree of homogeneity (from simple to complex) and degree of change (from stable to changing).

KEY TERMS

Text page numbers where terms are first defined are in parentheses.

environment (60)—all of those factors that affect the operation of the organization

external environment (60)—all of the factors outside the organization that may affect its managers' actions

general environment (60)—the broad, complex factors that affect all organizations

task environment (61)—those factors that have a direct effect on a specific organization and its managers, including customers, suppliers, competitors, substitutes, and potential new entrants to the industry

internal environment (61)—all factors that make up the organization, such as the owners, management, employees, and board of directors

sociocultural dimension (62)—the aspect of the general environment that includes the demographics and the values of the society within which an organization operates

political-legal dimension (62)—within the general environment, the nature of the relationship between various areas of government and the organization

technological dimension (64)—within the general environment, the knowledge and process of changing inputs (resources, labor, and money) to outputs (goods and services)

economic dimension (65)—the overall condition of the complex economies throughout the world

global dimension (65)—pertaining to the general environment, those factors in other countries that affect the organization

suppliers (66)—organizations and individuals who provide resources to other organizations

customers (66)—those who purchase an organization's goods and/or services

substitutes (67)—goods or services that may be used in place of those furnished by a given business

competitors (68)—other organizations that produce similar, or in some cases identical, goods or services

potential new competitors (68)—companies not currently operating in a business's industry but which have a high potential for entering the industry

stakeholder (72)—a person or group that can affect, or is affected by, an organization's goals or the means to achieve those goals

primary stakeholders (72)—those who have a formal and/or contractual relationship with the firm, such as customers, suppliers, and employees

secondary stakeholders (72)—groups that have a less formal connection to the organization, such as environmentalists, community activists, and the media

stakeholder map (73)—a representation of the organization's stakeholders and their stakes

REVIEW QUESTIONS

True/False

Indicate whether the following statements are true or false.

T 1. Recent trends in American business indicate that many organizations are "flattening" the organizational hierarchy and eliminating many of the technical managers.

T 2. Stockholders elect the corporate board of directors, who represent the stockholders and are charged with ensuring that the corporation is being managed so as to increase stockholder wealth.

F 3. A stake can be of three basic types: an equity interest, a market interest, or a boundary spanning interest.

T 4. The degree of change dimension of the external environment refers to the extent that the external environment is relatively stable or relatively dynamic.

F 5. Increased uncertainty in the external environment usually corresponds to more levels of management, fewer employees involved in decision making, and more policies and procedures.

Multiple Choice

Select the best answer for each question.

d 6. The aging of the population of the United States is an example of the:
a. task environment
b. organizational environment
c. legal environment
d. general environment
e. global environment

e 7. Which of the following is **not** a main reason why businesses react negatively to a new government regulation?
a. It will increase the cost of doing business
b. It will limit the business's decision options
c. It means extra costs and effort in order to comply
d. It will normally increase paperwork
e. It will expose the business's unethical behavior

c 8. A good or service that may be used in place of those produced by a business is usually called a:
a. synthetic good
b. competitive good
c. substitute good
d. technological improvement
e. counterfeit good

a 9. A reality or fact of life in many corporations is that:
 a. the CEO manipulates the board of directors
 b. the directors do not know their legal responsibilities
 c. the board of directors runs the show
 d. stock owners are usually large institutions
 e. stakeholders do not play an important role

b 10. The fast-food chain that first saw the environmental trend that hurried families needed a place where they could obtain a quick meal was:
 a. Domino's Pizza
 b. McDonald's
 c. Burger King
 d. Wendy's
 e. Hardees

Fill in the Blank

11. Suppliers are organizations and individuals who provide resources to other organizations.
12. Other organizations that produce similar, or in some cases identical, goods or services are called competitors.
13. A stakeholder is a person or group which can affect, or is affected by, an organization's goals or the means to achieve those goals.
14. Companies not currently operating in a business's industry but which have a high potential for entering the industry are known as potential new competitors.
15. Secondary stakeholders are those groups that have a less formal connection to the organization, such as environmentalists, community activists, and the media.

Matching

Place the corresponding letter of the five general environment forces with the correct description of each. Each answer can be used only once.

 a. global dimension
 b. political-legal dimension
 c. sociocultural dimension
 d. economic dimension
 e. technological dimension

e 16. the knowledge and process of changing inputs (resources, labor, and money) to outputs (goods and services)

c 17. includes the demographics and the values of the society within which an organization operates

b 18. the nature of the relationship between various areas of government and the organization

a 19. those factors in other countries that affect the organization

d 20. the overall condition of the complex economies throughout the world

Short Answer/Discussion Questions

21. Briefly describe how each of the three elements of the general environment's political-legal dimension affect or are affected by businesses.
22. List the four barriers that affect a potential new competitor's decision about entering an industry.
23. What four organizational processes exist for collecting information about stakeholders in the environment?
24. Identify three of the more common actions that an organization may take to interact effectively with the environment.
25. Discuss the common problems in receiving and using information about the external environment.

ANSWERS TO REVIEW QUESTIONS

Text page numbers where the answers can be found are included in parentheses.

1. True (70)
2. True (71)
3. False (73)
4. True (82)
5. False (83)
6. d (61)
7. e (63)
8. c (67)
9. a (71)
10. b (79)
11. suppliers (66)
12. competitors (68)
13. stakeholder (72)
14. potential (68)
15. secondary (72)
16. e (64)
17. c (62)
18. b (62)
19. a (65)
20. d (65)
21. (a) political element—businesses seek to influence the forming of public policy; (b) legal element—businesses use the judicial branches of government to resolve disputes between parties; (c) regulatory element—regulatory agencies apply federal regulations and laws that greatly affect organizational operations. (63)
22. high entrance costs, economies of scale, lack of access to distribution channels, and lack of technical expertise. (68–69)
23. customer surveys, economic forecasting, trend analysis, and the Delphi method. (75)
24. Six were mentioned in the text: public relations, boundary spanning, lobbying, negotiation, alliances, and organizational restructuring. (76–78)
25. limited capability (human beings are restricted in their cognitive ability to receive, process, and store information); lack of information (it is often difficult to obtain the information necessary to make a thoughtful decision); superfluous information (in today's information-rich society, organizations may receive too much information); and current organizational constraints (some situations may prevent an organization from properly evaluating the environment). (79–81)

STUDENT EXERCISE

Career Environment

You have spent a great deal of time in this chapter examining the factors in the internal, task, and general environments that affect managers' decisions and actions. This exercise will give you a chance to look at a new aspect of the internal environment that directly influences your career choices.

Among the preparations you should make when choosing prospective employers are determining your career goals and finding out whether a potential employer's career environment suits your goals. Where you work will generally be characterized by a career environment that describes the primary incentives the organization provides to attract and keep its employees.

Marketing Career Environment—emphasizes monetary rewards
Bureaucratic Career Environment—provides advancement and power
Professional Career Environment—emphasizes opportunities for meaningful work and autonomy

Various departments within an organization will typically have different career environments. For example, the sales department may be characterized by a market career environment; and research and development department may offer its employees a professional career environment.

Directions

In order to help you determine your preferred career environment, rank each statement below by placing a "2" in the box next to the statement that comes *closest* to expressing your opinion of what would attract you most about a new job. Place a "1" in the box by the statement that comes next closest and a "0" in the box that is least closest. When you have completed all your rankings, transfer the numbers to the appropriate boxes in the equation. Adding each row of boxes will show you the relative importance of each of the three career environments. The higher the score, the greater the preference you have for that career environment.

1. A new job would be most attractive to me if it provided:
   - ☐ a. frequent salary increases
   - ☐ b. ample say in organizational direction and plans
   - ☐ c. an opportunity to do meaningful work
2. A new job would be most attractive to me if it provided:
   - ☐ a. increased responsibility
   - ☐ b. a performance-based incentive plan
   - ☐ c. challenging work
3. A new job would be most attractive to me if it provided:
   - ☐ a. an atmosphere of innovation and creativity
   - ☐ b. ample promotion potential
   - ☐ c. a chance to share in organizational profits (profit sharing)

4. A new job would be most attractive to me if it provided:
   - ☐ a. liberal benefits and perks
   - ☐ b. autonomy and independence
   - ☐ c. greater status in the organization
5. A new job would be most attractive to me if it provided:
   - ☐ a. opportunities for personal development and growth
   - ☐ b. a liberal stock purchase plan
   - ☐ c. greater control over people and things
6. A new job would be most attractive to me if it provided:
   - ☐ a. an attractive pension plan
   - ☐ b. considerable flexibility and reduced controls
   - ☐ c. a higher level of status
7. A new job would be most attractive to me if it provided:
   - ☐ a. rapid advancement potential
   - ☐ b. freedom to explore new ideas and approaches
   - ☐ c. a liberal annual bonus
8. A new job would be most attractive to me if it provided:
   - ☐ a. frequent cost of living increases
   - ☐ b. a clearly defined career path
   - ☐ c. a variety of tasks and projects

1a		2b		3c		4a		5b		6a		7c		8a			
☐	+	☐	+	☐	+	☐	+	☐	+	☐	+	☐	+	☐	=	☐	MARKET
1b		2a		3b		4c		5c		6c		7a		8b			
☐	+	☐	+	☐	+	☐	+	☐	+	☐	+	☐	+	☐	=	☐	BUREAUCRATIC
1c		2c		3a		4b		5a		6b		7b		8c			
☐	+	☐	+	☐	+	☐	+	☐	+	☐	+	☐	+	☐	=	☐	PROFESSIONAL

APPLICATION

Now that you've determined in which career environment you would most likely find satisfaction, here are some sample questions you can ask a prospective employer to get information relating to each of the career environments. Depending on which of these three career environments is most suited to your career aspirations, you will want to get information during the interview process that will help you see if there is a good fit between what the prospective employer provides and what your needs are.

Marketing Career Environment

- Do you have a merit pay system? If so, how does it work?
- What is the complete financial package available (bonus, perks, stock options, pension, etc.)?
- How often are salaries reviewed (annually, semiannually, etc.)?

Bureaucratic Career Environment

- Does your organization have formal succession and career planning systems? If so, how do they work?
- What is the career path for the job for which I'm interviewing?
- What is your company's policy on internal promotion?
- What is the ratio of internal promotion to external recruitment in this organization?

Professional Career Environment

- What is the reporting structure of the department I'll be working in? (Highly structured, multi-level organizations tend to be more bureaucratic and, as a result, more controlling than organizations with fewer levels and looser reporting relationships.)
- What types of reports and other control mechanisms are required within this department or division? (Time reports, time clocks, and work measurement are indicators of a "high control" organization.)
- What is the management philosophy of this company? Division? Department?

Source: Matt Hennecke, "Finding a Corporate Culture to Suit Your Career Goals," Management Education Consulting Company of America (MECCA), 40 W 919 Elodie Drive, Elburn, Illinois 60119.

chapter four
Management Ethics and Social Responsibility

LEARNING OBJECTIVES

- Define business ethics and explain its importance to management.
- Detect some of the ethical issues that may arise in management.
- Specify how personal moral philosophies, organizational relationships, and opportunity influence decision making in management.
- Examine how managers can try to foster ethical behavior.
- Define social responsibility and discuss its relevance to management.
- Debate an organization's social responsibilities to owners, investors, employees, and consumers, as well as to the environment and the community.
- Determine the ethical issues confronting a hypothetical business.

CHAPTER OUTLINE

Introduction
- What Is Business Ethics?
- Why Is Ethics Important in Management?

Recognizing Ethical Issues in Management
- Ethical Issues in Management
- Making Decisions about Ethical Issues

The Ethical Decision-Making Process
- The Role of Moral Philosophies in Ethical Behavior
- Work Relationships
- The Role of Opportunity

Improving Ethical Behavior

The Nature of Social Responsibility
- Arguments for and against Social Responsibility
- Evolution of Social Responsibility

Social Responsibility Issues
- Relations with Owners and Investors
- Employee Relations
- Consumer Relations
- Environmental Issues
- Community Relations
- Social Audits

CHAPTER RECAP

Note: Boldface words are major chapter headings.

Introduction

This chapter addresses ethics and social responsibility, two of the most important areas in establishing management trust and respect.

What Is Business Ethics?

Business ethics refers to moral principles and standards that define acceptable behavior in business. The public, government regulators, interest groups, competitors, and an individual's personal morals and values determine what is acceptable behavior in business.

Why is ethics important in management? Ethical considerations exist in nearly all management decisions. Well-publicized incidents of unethical activity strengthen the public's perception that ethical standards and trust in business need to be raised.

Recognizing Ethical Issues in Management

Learning to recognize ethical issues is the most important step in understanding ethics in management. The "line" between an issue and an ethical issue is the point at which accepted rules no longer serve and the decision maker is faced with the responsibility of weighing moral rules and making a choice. In management, the decision often requires weighing monetary profit or personal interests against what the individual, work group, or organization considers honest and fair.

Ethical issues in management—managers have an obligation to ensure that their ethical decisions are consistent with company standards, codes of ethics, and policies, as well as community and legal standards. Examples of ethical issues arise from organizational relationships, operations and communications, and employee relations.

Making decisions about ethical issues—once a person has recognized an ethical issue and can openly discuss it with others, he or she has begun the ethical decision-making process. Table 4.1 lists some questions to consider in determining whether an action is ethical.

The Ethical Decision-Making Process

To better understand the significance of ethics in management decisions, it is helpful to examine the following factors that influence how a person makes ethical decisions:

The role of moral philosophies in ethical behavior. A moral philosophy is a set of principles that describe what a person believes is the right way to behave. Moral philosophies can be divided into two categories: (1) the utilitarian philosophy seeks the greatest satisfaction for the largest number of individuals; and (2) ethical formalism focuses on human rights and values and on the intentions associated with a particular behavior.

Work relationships. Because employees' perception of the ethics of their coworkers influences their behavior, work groups represent the most important factor affecting daily ethical decisions.

The role of opportunity. Opportunity to engage in unethical behavior has been found to be a better predictor of unethical behavior than one's personal beliefs or the beliefs of peers.

Improving Ethical Behavior

Establishing and enforcing ethical standards and policies can help reduce unethical behavior by prescribing which activities are acceptable and which are not and by removing the opportunity to act unethically. Codes of ethics and ethics-related corporate policy foster appropriate behavior by limiting the opportunity to behave unethically through the use of punishments for violations of the rules and standards. Encouraging whistle blowing, when employees expose an employer's wrongdoing, is another way to foster ethical behavior.

The Nature of Social Responsibility

While ethics relates to an individual's values and moral standards and the resulting decisions he or she makes, social responsibility is a broader concept that concerns the impact of an organization's activities on society. The four dimensions of social responsibility are economic, legal, ethical, and voluntary (illustrated in Figure 4.3 on p. 105).

Among the four **arguments for social responsibility** listed in the text is the argument that it sidetracks managers from the primary objective of business—earning profits. **Among the five arguments against social responsibility** listed is that, since business helped to create many of the social problems that exist today, it should play a significant role in solving them, especially in the areas of pollution reduction and toxic waste cleanup.

The evolution of social responsibility can be traced from the rule for consumers of *caveat emptor* (let the buyer beware) to government intervention that resulted in the creation of new laws and federal agencies designed to protect consumers and to police industry. Then the public began to demand that individuals, government, and business take greater responsibility for their actions. The trend continues today, with more and more businesses adopting socially responsible management techniques, manufacturing processes, charitable donation policies, and otherwise trying to respond to the demands of society.

Social Responsibility Issues

Among the many social responsibility issues, organizations must consider their **relations with owners and investors** (a business must maximize the owners' investment in the firm), **employee relations** (providing a safe workplace, paying adequately, keeping employees informed, listening to their grievances, and treating them fairly), **consumer relations** (provide satisfying, safe products and respect their rights as consumers), **environmental issues** (animal rights and pollution), **and community relations** (responsibilities to the general welfare of the communities and societies in which they operate).

Social Audits

To determine whether it is adequately meeting the demands of society as well as its own social responsibility objectives, an organization can measure its performance through a voluntary social audit. The social audit is a systematic examination of the objectives, strategies, organization, and performance of the social responsibility function. Used effectively, the social audit provides a tool for managers to help their firms become better citizens by contributing positively to society.

KEY TERMS

Text page numbers where terms are first defined are in parentheses.

business ethics (92)—moral principles and standards that define acceptable behavior in business

ethical issue (94)—an identifiable problem, situation, or opportunity that requires a person or organization to choose among several actions that may be evaluated as ethical or unethical

moral philosophy (99)—a set of principles that describe what a person believes is the right way to behave

utilitarian philosophy (99)—a philosophy where believers seek the greatest satisfaction for the largest number of individuals

ethical formalism (99)—a philosophy that focuses on human rights and values and on the intentions associated with a particular behavior

codes of ethics (102)—formalized rules and standards that describe and delineate what the organization expects of its employees

whistle blowing (103)—the act of an employee's exposing an employer's wrongdoing; typically such reporting is to outsiders, such as the media or government regulatory agencies

social responsibility (105)—the obligation a business assumes to maximize its positive impact and minimize its negative impact on society

consumerism (108)—the activities undertaken by independent individuals, groups, and organizations to protect their rights as consumers

social audit (112)—a systematic examination of the objectives, strategies, organization, and performance of the social responsibility function

REVIEW QUESTIONS

True/False

Indicate whether the following statements are true or false.

T 1. Ethics is the study of morals and values and focuses on the standards, rules, and codes of conduct that govern the behavior of individuals and groups.

F 2. Business ethics and the study of ethical decisions stay within a framework of legal issues.

T 3. Learning to recognize ethical issues is the most important step in understanding ethics in management.

T 4. The greater the reward and the less the punishment for unethical behavior, the greater is the likelihood that unethical behavior will recur.

F 5. Air pollution results from the dumping of residential and industrial waste, strip mining, forest fires, and poor forest conservation.

Multiple Choice

Select the best answer for each question.

a 6. According to the Harris Poll, which of the following groups is perceived by the public as having the highest ethical standards?
   a. small-business owners
   b. business executives
   c. lawyers
   d. members of Congress
   e. journalists

c 7. In the United States, if a businessperson brought an elaborately wrapped gift to a prospective client on their first meeting, it might be viewed as:
   a. appropriate
   b. normal
   c. a bribe
   d. a thoughtful gift
   e. expected

b 8. Surveys by the Michael Josephson Ethics Institutes reveal that about what percentage of middle managers have written deceptive internal reports?
   a. under 10 percent
   b. 20 to 30 percent
   c. about 50 percent
   d. 70 to 80 percent
   e. over 90 percent

d

b 9. Unethical activity in the savings and loan industry may have resulted from:
   a. poor ethics
   b. personal moral philosophies
   c. organizational roles
   d. opportunity
   e. codes of ethics

e

b 10. Which of the following is **not** one of the four rights highlighted in John F. Kennedy's 1962 consumer bill of rights?
   a. right to safety
   b. right to be informed
   c. right to choose
   d. right to be heard
   e. right to privacy

Fill in the Blank

11. Believers of the utilitarian philosophy seek the greatest satisfaction for the largest number of individuals.
12. The ethical formalism philosophy focuses on human rights and values and on the intentions associated with a particular behavior.
13. When an employee exposes an employer's wrongdoing to the media or a government regulatory agency, this is called whistle blowing.
14. Consumerism is the label given to the activities undertaken by independent individuals, groups, and organizations to protect their rights as consumers.
15. Organizations conduct a Social Audit when they systematically examine the objectives, strategies, organization, and performance of the social responsibility function.

Matching

Identify whether the arguments listed are for or against social responsibility. One answer will be used twice, and one answer will be used three times.

a. argument for social responsibility
b. argument against social responsibility

a 16. Businesses helped to create many of the social problems that exist today.

b 17. Many people believe that social problems are the responsibility of government agencies and officials, who can be held accountable by voters.

a 18. Businesses have the financial and technical resources to help solve social problems.

b 19. Participation in social programs gives businesses greater power, perhaps at the expense of particular segments of society.

a 20. Socially responsible decision making by business organizations can prevent increased government regulation.

Short Answer/Discussion Questions

21. List and discuss two of the three management areas where managers face ethical issues.
22. Name the three factors that influence how a person makes ethical decisions.
23. Identify and describe the four dimensions of social responsibility.
24. Discuss the evolution of social responsibility.
25. Select two from the many social responsibility issues that managers face and briefly describe them.

ANSWERS TO REVIEW QUESTIONS

Text page numbers where the answers can be found are included in parentheses.

1. True (92)
2. False (93)
3. True (94)
4. True (101)
5. False (110)
6. a (94)
7. c (95)
8. b (96)
9. d (101)
10. e (109)
11. utilitarian (99)
12. ethical formalism (99)
13. whistle blowing (103)
14. consumerism (108)
15. social audit (112)
16. a (106)
17. b (106)
18. a (106)
19. b (106)
20. a (106)
21. Examples of ethical issues arise from (1) organizational relationships—examples include maintaining confidentiality in personal relationships; meeting obligations, responsibilities, and mutual agreements; and avoiding undue pressure that may force others to behave unethically; (2) operations and communications—examples include writing deceptive internal reports, covering up safety defects or not being honest about the true quality of products; and (3) employee relations—testing procedures that may violate an individual's rights, disclosing personnel records, basing performance appraisals on favoritism and political opportunism, and using unethical strategies for motivating employees. (96–98)
22. (1) individual moral philosophy, (2) work relationships, and (3) opportunity. (99)
23. (1) economic responsibilities—being profitable; (2) legal responsibilities—obeying the law and playing by the rules of the game; (3) ethical responsibilities—being ethical; doing what is right, just, and fair; avoiding harm; (4) voluntary responsibilities—being a "good corporate citizen," contributing to the community and quality of life. (Figure 4.3, p. 105)
24. The evolution of social responsibility can be traced from the rule for consumers of *caveat emptor* (let the buyer beware) to government intervention that resulted in the creation of new laws and federal agencies designed to protect consumers and police industry. Then the public began to demand that individuals, government, and business take greater responsibility for their actions. The trend continues today, with more and more businesses adopting socially responsible management techniques, manufacturing processes, charitable donation policies, and otherwise trying to respond to the demands of society. (107)
25. Among the many social responsibility issues, organizations must consider their relations with owners and investors (a business must maximize the owners' investment in the firm), employee relations (providing a safe workplace, paying adequately, keeping employees informed, listening to their grievances, and treating them fairly), consumer relations (provide satisfying, safe products and respect their rights as consumers), environmental issues (animal rights and pollution), and community relations (responsibilities to the general welfare of the communities and societies in which they operate). (107–112)

STUDENT EXERCISE

Making Decisions about Ethical Issues

This exercise supplements the "Strengthen Your Skills" exercise in the textbook at the end of Chapter 4. That exercise and this one are designed to help you practice your decision-making skills when you are presented with ethical dilemmas.

Background

The five mini-cases in this exercise are disguised versions of actual cases experienced by employees at Martin Marietta Corporation, a Fortune 100 company employing approximately 56,000 employees. Martin Marietta's industry classifications include aerospace (primary), applied research, basic scientific research, computer equipment, computer software, defense, electrical equipment, electronics, information services, marketing research, materials, optics, and robotics/factory automation.

This exercise is designed to teach the solving of ethical dilemmas that occur almost every day in every kind of business. It is also designed to create controversy. It is structured to bring out more than just one company's policies—to allow the participants to argue multiple approaches to ethical dilemmas. For example, is there only one answer—regardless of the circumstances? Or are there modifying influences? Right is right, but what is right?

Ethics is dynamic. No one solution is always correct nor is another solution always wrong. Some solutions will appeal to some while other solutions will appeal to others.

Instructions

Every mini-case poses four solutions. In some cases, only one solution is correct; in others, more than one is correct. But which is most correct? In a few mini-cases, none of the posed answers are correct. But one will be the best selection from the options listed.

None of the posed answers can be changed. You must pick the one that you can best justify—based on company policies (that you'd expect a company like Martin Marietta to have), your experiences, your education, your ethical training, and your beliefs.

MINI-CASE 1

Two of your subordinates routinely provide their children with school supplies from the office. How do you handle this situation?

Potential Answers

A. Lock up the supplies and issue them only as needed and signed for.
B. Tell these two subordinates that supplies are only for office use.
C. Report the theft of supplies to the head of security.
D. Send a notice to all employees that office supplies are for office use only and that disregard will result in disciplinary action.

MINI-CASE 2

Your operation is being relocated. The personnel regulations are complex and might influence your employees' decisions about staying on the "team." Relocating with no experienced staff would be very difficult for you. What do you tell your employees about their options?

Potential Answers

A. State that the relocation regulations are complex. You won't go into them right now; however, "everything probably will come out OK in the end."
B. Suggest that they relocate with you, stating that a job in hand is worth an unknown in the bush.
C. Present them with your simplified version of the regulations and encourage them to "come along."
D. Only tell them you'd like them to relocate with you and conserve the team that has worked so well together.

MINI-CASE 3

A friend of yours wants to transfer to your division, but he may not be the best qualified for the job. You do have an opening; and one other person, whom you do not know, has applied. What do you do?

Potential Answers

A. Select the friend you know and in whom you have confidence.
B. Select the other person who you are told is qualified.
C. Request a qualifications comparison of the two from human resources.
D. Request human resources to extend the search for additional candidates before making the selection.

MINI-CASE 4

Your new employee is the niece of the vice president of finance. Her performance is poor, and she has caused trouble with her coworkers. What do you do?

Potential Answers

A. Call her in and talk to her about her inadequacies.
B. Ask human resources to counsel her and put her on a performance improvement plan.
C. Go see her uncle.
D. Since maybe it is only the "newness" of the job, give her some time to come around.

MINI-CASE 5

After three months you discover that a recently hired employee who appears to be very competent falsified her employment application in that she claimed she had a college degree when she did not. As her supervisor, what do you do?

Potential Answers

A. You're happy with the new employee, so you do nothing.
B. Discuss the matter with human resources to determine company policy.
C. Recommend she be fired for lying.
D. Weight her performance, length of service, and potential benefit to the organization before making any recommendation to anyone.

ANSWERS, POINT VALUES, AND RATIONALE

You may disagree with the values of some of the answers, but do you always agree with the penalties in football? Or that fine line in baseball that distinguishes a strike from a ball?

Case No.	Answer	Points	Rationale
1	A	–5	Is an example of locking everybody up; therefore, there can be no more crime. Not an efficient way to work either.
	B	10	Is directed at solving the immediate problem. But is this only the tip of an iceberg? Are there more pilferers?
	C	–5	While technically correct—is overkill.
	D	10	Is a solution aimed at the immediate problem and any continuing problem. A reiteration of company policies for comprehensive understanding.
2	A	–5	Could end up misleading your employees as you are promising something over which you have no control.
	B	–5	Is a threat; it's the "fear" approach and does nothing to build teamwork.
	C	5	As long as your "simplified version" is not misleading.
	D	–5	Is not being fair to your employees.
3	A	–5	May not be in the best interest of the company.
	B	5	Told by whom? If by human resources, it may be a good answer.
	C	5	More clearly defines your immediate options.
	D	10	Is favored if you believe there may be someone out there who has even better qualifications than either your friend or the only applicant.

4	A	10	As difficult as it may be for you to do, this is how the problem should be handled.
	B	5	Fails to involve you personally. It is your problem first.
	C	–5	Could solve no problem, yet might develop a new one for you.
	D	–5	Bad news never gets better with time. Guidance, counseling, training, or something else is needed.
5	A	–10	But if she lied that time, will she lie again?
	B	10	You're on your way to a solution.
	C	5	This is normally what happens to liars.
	D	0	Were she a long-term employee who had already proved her performance and proved she never lied again, consideration is commendable—but she is not that person.

How did you do? -30 is the worst score possible; +45 is the best score possible.

Permission granted by the author of *Gray Matters: The Ethics Game,* George Sammet, Jr., Vice President, Office of Corporate Ethics, Martin Marietta Corporation, Orlando, Florida, to use these portions of *Gray Matters: The Ethics Game* ©1992. If you would like more information about the complete game, call 1-800-3ETHICS.

chapter five

Managing in a Borderless World

LEARNING OBJECTIVES

- Analyze the factors within the global trade environment that influence business.
- Specify the different levels of organizational involvement in international trade.
- Summarize the various trade agreements and alliances that have developed worldwide and how they influence business activities.
- Determine how global business affects management.
- Assess the opportunities and problems facing a small business considering expanding into international markets.

CHAPTER OUTLINE

Introduction

The Global Business Environment
- The Sociocultural Environment
- The Political-Legal Environment
- The Economic Environment
- International Trade Facilitators

Levels of Organizational Involvement in Global Business
- Exporting and Importing
- Trading Companies
- Licensing and Franchising
- Contract Manufacturing
- Joint Ventures
- Direct Investment
- Multinational Corporations

Regional Trade Alliances and Agreements
- The North American Free Trade Agreement (NAFTA)
- The European Economic Community
- The Pacific Rim Nations
- Eastern Europe and the Commonwealth of Independent States (CIS)
- Managing Global Business

CHAPTER RECAP

Note: Boldface words are major chapter headings.

Introduction

Global business (globalization) is a strategy in which organizations treat the entire world or major regions of it as the domain for conducting business. Falling political barriers and advancing communications and transportation technology are enabling many companies to sell their products overseas as well as in their own countries. As cultural and other differences among nations narrow, the trend toward the globalization of business is becoming increasingly important.

The Global Business Environment

Managers considering international business must research the following aspects of each country's environment:

The sociocultural environment defines what is acceptable and unacceptable behavior in a given society. Cultural differences among countries include variations in language, body language, personal space, perception of time, national and religious holidays, and customs regarding respect for authority.

The political-legal environment includes such considerations as the relative stability of the political environment, the laws that govern the process of doing business in other nations, and tariffs and trade restrictions.

The economic environment includes the level of economic development as well as exchange rates in the country in which the organization is considering doing business.

International trade facilitators exist to help managers get involved in and succeed in global markets. These include the General Agreement on Tariffs and Trade (GATT), the World Bank, and the International Monetary Fund (IMF).

Levels of Organizational Involvement in Global Business

The degree of commitment of resources and effort required in international trade increases according to the level at which a business involves itself in global trade. Here are seven different types of organizational involvement in global business:

1. **Exporting** (the sale of goods and services to foreign markets enabling organizations of all sizes to participate in global business) and **importing** (the purchase of goods and services from a foreign source).
2. **Trading companies** (organizations that acquire goods in one country and sell them to buyers in another country).
3. **Licensing** (a trade agreement in which one company—the licensor—allows another country—the licensee—to use its company name, products, brands, trademarks, raw materials, and/or production processes in exchange for a fee) and **franchising** (a form of licensing in which a company—the franchiser—agrees to provide a franchisee elements associated with the franchiser's business, in return for a financial commitment and the agreement to conduct business in accordance with the franchiser's standard of operations).
4. **Contract manufacturing** (a company hires a foreign company to produce a specified volume of its product to specification).

5. **Joint venture** (agreement by which a company that wants to do business in another country may find a local partner to share the costs and operation of the business).
6. **Direct investment** (purchase of overseas production and marketing facilities).
7. **Multinational corporations** (corporations that operate on a worldwide scale, without significant ties to any one nation or region).

Regional Trade Alliances and Agreements

Various regional trade alliances and specific markets have created both difficulties and opportunities for organizations engaging in global business. In this section, you will learn about four such alliances and agreements:

1. **The North American Free Trade Agreement (NAFTA)** went into effect on January 1, 1994, and effectively merged Canada, the United States, and Mexico into one market of about 374 million consumers, eliminating most tariffs and trade restrictions on agricultural and manufactured products among the three countries over a period of 15 years.
2. **The European Economic Community** represents the merging of 13 European nations to form one of the largest single world markets—the European Community (EC), with more than 340 million consumers.
3. **The Pacific Rim Nations** include Japan, China, South Korea, Taiwan, Singapore, Hong Kong, the Philippines, Malaysia, Indonesia, Australia, and Indochina.
4. **Eastern Europe and the Commonwealth of Independent States (CIS)** are experiencing changing economic conditions that provide many business opportunities for American, European, and Asian firms.

Managing Global Business

Competing in an increasingly global economy provides both challenges and opportunities for today's managers as they engage in the planning, organizing, leading, and controlling functions.

KEY TERMS

Text page numbers where terms are first defined are in parentheses.

global business (globalization) (124)—a strategy in which organizations treat the entire world or major regions of it as the domain for conducting business

international business (124)—the buying, selling, and trading of goods and services across national boundaries

cartel (128)—a group of firms or nations that agree to act as a monopoly and not compete with each other

Webb-Pomerene Export Trade Act (128)—legislation allowing selected American firms desiring international trade to form monopolies in order to compete with foreign cartels

Foreign Corrupt Practices Act (128)—legislation outlawing direct payoffs to and bribes of foreign governments or business officials by American companies

import tariff (128)—a tax levied by a nation on goods bought outside its borders and imported into the country

exchange controls (129)—restrictions on the amount of a particular currency that may be bought or sold

quota (130)—the maximum number of units of a particular product that may be imported into a country

embargo (130)—the suspension of trade in a particular product by the government

dumping (130)—the sale of products, by a country or business firm, at less than what it costs to produce them

infrastructure (131)—the physical facilities that support a country's economic activities, such as highways, utilities, schools, hospitals, communication systems, and commercial distribution systems

exchange rate (131)—the ratio at which one nation's currency can be exchanged for another nation's currency or for gold

General Agreement on Tariffs and Trade (GATT) (131)—legislation, first signed by 23 nations in 1947, providing a forum for tariff negotiations and a place where international trade problems can be discussed and resolved

World Bank (133)—financial organization established and supported by the industrialized nations to loan money to underdeveloped and developing countries; formally known as the International Bank for Reconstruction and Development

International Monetary Fund (IMF) (133)—organization established to promote trade among member nations by eliminating trade barriers and fostering financial cooperation

exporting (134)—the sale of goods and services to foreign markets, enabling organizations of all sizes to participate in global business

importing (134)—the purchase of goods and services from a foreign source

countertrade agreements (134)—the bartering of a product for other products instead of for currency

trading company (136)—an organization that acquires goods in one country and sells them to buyers in another country

licensing (136)—a trade agreement in which one company (the licensor) allows another country (the licensee) to use its company name, products, brands, trademarks, raw materials, and/or production processes in exchange for a fee, or royalty

franchising (137)—a form of licensing in which a company (the franchiser) agrees to provide a franchisee elements associated with the franchiser's business, in return for a financial commitment and the agreement to conduct business in accordance with the franchiser's standard of operations

contract manufacturing (137)—occurs when a company hires a foreign company to produce a specified volume of its product to specification

joint venture (137)—an agreement by which a company that wants to do business in another country may find a local partner (occasionally, the host nation itself) to share the costs and operation of the business

strategic alliance (137)—a relatively new form of international joint venture formed to create competitive advantage on a worldwide basis

direct investment (138)—the purchase of overseas production and marketing facilities

outsourcing (138)—a form of direct investment that involves transferring manufacturing or other functions to countries where labor and supplies are less expensive

multinational corporation (MNC) (139)—a corporation, such as IBM or Exxon, that operates on a worldwide scale, without significant ties to any one nation or region

REVIEW QUESTIONS

True/False

Indicate whether the following statements are true or false.

F 1. The Foreign Corrupt Practices Act allows selected American firms desiring international trade to form monopolies to compete with foreign cartels.

F 2. A common reason for establishing an embargo is to prohibit dumping.

T 3. The United States has a lower percentage of its household spending going for food than does India.

T 4. The World Bank loans its own funds or borrows funds from member countries to finance projects ranging from road and factory construction to the building of medical and educational facilities.

T 5. MNCs are more than simple corporations; they often have more assets than some of the countries in which they do business.

Multiple Choice

Select the best answer for each question.

b 6. A strategy in which organizations treat the entire world or major regions of it as the domain for conducting business defines:
   a. national business
   b. global business
   c. international business
   d. local business
   e. regional business

c 7. Most businesspeople engaged in international trade underestimate the importance of:
   a. trade barriers
   b. language barriers
   c. social and cultural differences
   d. import quotas
   e. infrastructure

e 8. A group of nations or companies that band together to act as a monopoly is known as a:
   a. joint venture
   b. franchisee
   c. strategic alliance
   d. countertrade agreement
   e. cartel

e 9. All of the following are examples of infrastructure except:
   a. air fields
   b. communication systems
   c. schools and hospitals
   d. utilities and power plants
   e. shopping malls

a 10. Which of the following has experienced a great deal of political and economic turmoil, creating both opportunities and challenges for businesses?
   a. Eastern Europe and the Commonwealth of Independent States
   b. Canada
   c. The European Community
   d. The Pacific Rim
   e. GATT

Fill in the Blank

___11. An import TARIFF is a tax levied by a nation on goods bought outside its borders and imported into the country.

___12. The maximum number of units of a particular product that may be imported into a country is called a Quota.

___13. The Exchange Rate is the ratio at which one nation's currency can be exchanged for another nation's currency or for gold.

___14. Exporting enables organizations of all sizes to participate in global business by selling goods and services to foreign markets.

___15. Franchising is a form of licensing in which a company (the franchiser) agrees to provide a franchisee elements associated with the franchiser's business, in return for a financial commitment and the agreement to conduct business in accordance with the franchiser's standard of operations.

Matching

Match the appropriate level of organizational involvement in global business with the appropriate description of each level. Each answer can be used only once.

   a. trading company
   b. contract manufacturing
   c. joint venture
   d. direct investment
   e. multinational corporation (MNC)

d 16. the purchase of overseas production and marketing facilities

a 17. an organization that acquires goods in one country and sells them to buyers in another country

c 18. an agreement by which a company that wants to do business in another country may find a local partner (occasionally, the host nation itself) to share the costs and operation of the business

b 19. occurs when a company hires a foreign company to produce a specified volume of its product to specification

e 20. a corporation, such as IBM or Exxon, that operates on a worldwide scale, without significant ties to any one nation or region

Short Answer/Discussion Questions

21. Briefly describe the three environments managers should research about a country in order to help them choose an appropriate level of involvement and operating strategies.
22. What do the letters in IMF stand for and what is its purpose?
23. What is the name for the most committed or highest level of international business involvement?
24. What do the letters in NAFTA stand for, and which countries make up this market?
25. Name as many of the 11 Pacific Rim nations as you can.

21.) 1.) Socialcultural Environment
2.) political - legal Environment
3.) Economic Environment

22.) IMF ⇒ International Monetary Fund → agreement among members - eliminating trade barriers - fostering financial cooperation

23.) Multinational Corporation

24.) NAFTA ⇒ NORTH AMERICAN FREE TRADE AGREEMENT

25.) PACIFIC RIM ⇒ JAPAN, China, SOUTH Korea, Taiwan, Singapore, Hong Kong, Philippines, Malaysia, Indonesia, Australia, Indochina

ANSWERS TO REVIEW QUESTIONS

Text page numbers where the answers can be found are included in parentheses.

1. False (128)
2. False (130)
3. True (131)
4. True (133)
5. True (139)
6. b (124)
7. c (125)
8. e (128)
9. e (131)
10. a (142–143)
11. tariff (128)
12. quota (130)
13. exchange rate (131)
14. exporting (134)
15. franchising (137)
16. d (138)
17. a (136)
18. c (137)
19. b (137)
20. e (139)
21. The sociocultural environment (includes differences in variations in language, body language, personal space, perception of time, customs regarding respect for authority, and observances of national and religious holidays and local customs); the political-legal environment (the relative stability of the political environment, both the international laws and the laws of the other nations, and various tariffs and trade restrictions); and the economic environment (the level of economic development and currency exchange rates). (125–131)
22. International Monetary Fund; IMF promotes trade among member nations by eliminating trade barriers and fostering financial cooperation. (133–134)
23. multinational corporation (MNC). (139)
24. North American Free Trade Agreement; Canada, the United States, and Mexico. (140)
25. Japan, China, South Korea, Taiwan, Singapore, Hong Kong, the Philippines, Malaysia, Indonesia, Australia, and Indochina. (142)

STUDENT EXERCISE

Learning about Other Cultures

This exercise supplements the "Strengthen Your Skills" exercise in the textbook at the end of Chapter 5. That exercise and this one are designed to help you understand and appreciate that you are part of a complex world where your culture is different from, not better than, others.

One training tool that companies, such as Allstate Insurance, Kraft, General Foods, 3M Company, and Proctor & Gamble, are using to help their employees understand people from other cultures is the board game *DIVERSOPHY™—Understanding the Human Race.** The game, among many other features, contains a set of 60 *diversiSMARTS™* cards that develop your knowledge of facts about other cultures.

Here are five questions taken from the *diversiSMARTS™* cards. See how many you know.

___ 1. Being on time is of highest importance to people from:
  a. the United States
  b. Japan
  c. the Philippines

___ 2. This city was singled out by the United Nations as the world's most diverse city. Over 100 languages are spoken in:
  a. Los Angeles
  b. New York
  c. Toronto

___ 3. When communicating, Italians and Hispanics from traditional backgrounds tend to stand:
  a. further from the other person than most Euro-Americans stand
  b. closer
  c. at the same distance

___ 4. It's Chinese New Year. Name as many of the 12 animals that represent a Chinese year as you can.

___ 5. People who grew up in the United States may start conversations with new acquaintances with the question:
  a. "What do you do for a living?"
  b. "Where is your family from?"
  c. "Where do you live?"

The answers are given on page 60.

Whether you missed more than two answers, or got all five answers correct, you should have a lifelong interest in learning more about other cultures. Select two items from the list below that you can do (or at least start) within the next week:

- Find someone from another culture in your neighborhood, in one of your classes, at your fitness center, or at a concert or sporting event and take the initiative to strike up a conversation and show a genuine interest in getting to know the other person.
- Select a culture you are interested in and immerse yourself in that culture. Read novels, look at art, take courses, see plays.
- Look into the possibility of traveling abroad with a group from your college—for example, as a member of a performing arts group, a humanitarian mission group, or as part of a college course studying abroad.
- Study a foreign language.
- The next time you are going to go to a restaurant, instead of choosing that old familiar favorite, use the Yellow Pages to find a restaurant that serves ethnic food you have never tried before.
- Take in the sights and sounds of other cultures at an ethnic festival.

ANSWERS TO *diversiSMARTS*™ QUESTIONS

1. b. Japan. The Japanese consider punctuality very important as a sign of respect.
2. c. Toronto
3. b. Closer. Traditional Italian and Hispanic cultures typically observe a closer "personal space" than most Euro-American peoples.
4. Rat, ox, tiger, hare, dragon, snake, horse, sheep, monkey, fowl, dog, and pig
5. a. "What do you do for a living?" Americans tend to define people by their line of work more than most people from other countries do.

chapter six

The Dynamics of Diversity

LEARNING OBJECTIVES

- Define cultural diversity and explain why it has become so important in business.
- Examine some of the significant cultural groups in the American work force and discuss some issues of concern to each.
- Determine the benefits and problems associated with cultural diversity in the work force.
- Assess different organizational approaches to managing work-force diversity.
- Explain how work-force diversity is created, maintained, and valued by a truly multicultural organization.
- Propose a plan for turning a company into a multicultural organization.

CHAPTER OUTLINE

Introduction

What Is Cultural Diversity?
    Understanding the Characteristics of Cultural Diversity

Cultural Groups in the American Work Force
    Minorities
    Women
    Persons with Disabilities

Benefits and Problems of Diversity in the Work Force
    The Benefits of Cultural Diversity
    Problems Associated with Cultural Diversity

Approaches to Managing Work-Force Diversity
    Assimilation
    Affirmative Action
    Multicultural Organizations

Creating the Multicultural Organization
    Step One: Setting the Stage
    Step Two: Education and Implementation
    Step Three: Maintaining Diversity

CHAPTER RECAP

Note: Boldface words are major chapter headings.

Introduction

The focus of this chapter is on the increasing importance of cultural diversity in the work force.

What Is Cultural Diversity?

Cultural diversity refers to differences in age, gender, race, ethnicity, nationality, and ability.

Understanding the characteristics of cultural diversity means that you recognize and accept differences involving primary characteristics of diversity, which are inborn characteristics that cannot be changed, and secondary characteristics of diversity that can be changed.

Cultural Groups in the American Work Force

Minorities, women, and the disabled have traditionally been denied the opportunities for experience in organizations that would enable them to assume leadership roles in corporate America.

Minorities, such as blacks, Hispanics, Asians, and Native Americans all face equality issues in the workplace. **Women**, too, are underrepresented and underpaid relative to men. As with cultural minority groups, the nearly 15 million **persons with disabilities** face barriers to entry and success in the work force.

Benefits and Problems of Diversity in the Work Force

As the U.S. population becomes increasingly diverse, serving the disparate needs of different cultural groups will become particularly important. There are a number of **benefits** to fostering and valuing workforce diversity, including the following:

1. More productive use of a company's human resources.
2. Reduced conflict among different cultural groups as they learn to respect each other's differences.
3. More productive working relationships among employees from different culture groups.
4. Increased commitment to and sharing of organization goals among culturally diverse employees.
5. Increased innovation and creativity as culturally diverse employees bring new, unique perspectives to decision-making and problem-solving tasks.
6. Enhanced ability to serve the needs of an increasingly diverse customer base.

The most significant **problems associated with cultural diversity** include prejudice (negative attitudes and feelings toward others because of their membership in a different cultural group), discrimination (negative behaviors toward people from other cultural groups), and conflict (the tension or friction between culture groups that stems from a lack of understanding by one group of the values, attitudes, and behaviors of the other).

Approaches to Managing Work-Force Diversity

Over the years, businesses have tried three different approaches to managing cultural diversity:

1. **Assimilation**—organizational practices that force minority groups to accept the norms and values of a majority group.

2. **Affirmative action programs**—policies designed to increase job opportunities for minority groups through analysis of the present pool of workers, identification of areas where women and minorities are underrepresented, and establishment of specific hiring and promotion goals along with target dates for meeting those goals.
3. **Multicultural organizations**—companies that value their culturally diverse employees as assets and that develop and implement policies designed to promote cultural diversity and equality.

Creating the Multicultural Organization

Managing cultural diversity involves recruiting, managing, and retaining highly qualified employees from an increasingly diverse pool of workers. Going beyond affirmative action plans to a multicultural organization that creates and values work-force diversity involves a series of three complex and integrated steps.

Step one: setting the stage includes getting support and involvement from top management, going beyond affirmative action programs, upholding diversity through communication, and adopting and communicating a pluralistic vision.

Step two: education and implementation includes awareness training, developing employee support, diversifying work groups and providing coaching, altering benefit plans and tying rewards to behaviors, and creating a structure that supports diversity.

Step three: maintaining diversity requires following up to ensure that cultural diversity remains a high-priority organizational value.

KEY TERMS

Text page numbers where terms are first defined are in parentheses.

cultural diversity (153)—differences in age, gender, race, ethnicity, nationality, and ability

primary characteristics of diversity (153)—inborn characteristics, such as age, gender, race, ethnicity, abilities, and sexual orientation, that cannot be changed

secondary characteristics of diversity (154)—characteristics, such as work background, marital status, and education, that can be changed

prejudice (163)—negative attitudes and feelings toward others because of their membership in a different cultural group

discrimination (163)—negative behaviors toward people from other cultural groups

cultural conflict (165)—the tension or friction between culture groups that stems from a lack of understanding by one group of the values, attitudes, and behaviors of the other

assimilation (165)—organizational practices that force minority groups to accept the norms and values of a majority group

affirmative action programs (166)—policies designed to increase job opportunities for minority groups through analysis of the present pool of workers, identification of areas where women and minorities are underrepresented, and establishment of specific hiring and promotion goals along with target dates for meeting those goals

reverse discrimination (167)—the result of a company's policies that force it to consider only minorities or women instead of hiring the person who is best qualified

multicultural organizations (168)—companies that value their culturally diverse employees as assets, and that develop and implement policies designed to promote cultural diversity and equality

REVIEW QUESTIONS

True/False

Indicate whether the following statements are true or false.

____ 1. Today, blacks represent the fastest growing minority group in the United States.

____ 2. In terms of occupations, women tend to be concentrated in low-paying clerical, sales, and teaching jobs.

____ 3. The problems and work-related barriers faced by the nation's mentally and physically disabled persons are primarily culture based.

____ 4. Awareness training programs are an important component of setting the stage to create a multicultural organization.

____ 5. An important part of maintaining cultural diversity within an organization is the realization that valuing diversity is a never-ending process.

Multiple Choice

Select the best answer for each question.

____ 6. The black population in the United States tends to be concentrated in the:
   a. Southwest
   b. Northwest
   c. Midwest
   d. Northeast
   e. Southeast

____ 7. The minority group associated with the names Hopi, Navajo, Seminole, and Sioux is called:
   a. Caucasian
   b. Asian
   c. Hispanic
   d. Creole
   e. Native American

____ 8. According to the U.S. Census Bureau, on average, women currently earn how many cents for every $1 earned by men?
   a. 90 cents
   b. 85 cents
   c. 70 cents
   d. 65 cents
   e. 60 cents

Lyndon B Johnson

a 9. Which statement is **not** true about affirmative action?
   a. Affirmative action began in 1972 as Richard M. Nixon issued the first in a series of presidential directives.
   b. The biggest gains from affirmative action have gone to women.
   c. There are growing signs that affirmative action programs do not go far enough.
   d. While affirmative action programs help to minimize prejudice and discrimination, they tend to create a great deal of group conflict within the organization.
   e. While affirmative action represents a great advance over assimilation in managing cultural diversity, it still falls short in many respects.

c 10. Which of the following activities is **not** part of Step Two (education and implementation) of creating a multicultural organization?
   a. awareness training
   b. developing employee support
   c. adopting and communicating a pluralistic vision
   d. diversifying work groups and providing coaching
   e. altering benefit plans and tying rewards to behaviors

Fill in the Blank

11. Secondary characteristics of diversity include those characteristics that can be changed.
12. The negative attitudes and feelings toward others because of their membership in a different cultural group is called discrimination.
13. Cultural Conflict is the term used to describe the tension or friction between culture groups that stems from a lack of understanding by one group of the values, attitudes, and behaviors of the other.
14. Organizational practices that force minority groups to accept the norms and values of a majority group is called assimilation.
15. Reverse Descrimination occurs when a company's policies force it to consider only minorities or women instead of hiring the person who is best qualified.

Matching

Place the corresponding letter of the characteristic type with each characteristic. One answer will be used twice; the other answer will be used three times.

a. primary characteristic of diversity
b. secondary characteristic of diversity

a 16. gender
a 17. ethnicity
b 18. education
b 19. income
(a) b 20. abilities

Short Answer/Discussion Questions

21. List four minority groups represented in the U. S. workplace.
22. Identify three benefits to fostering and valuing work-force diversity.
23. Discuss the assumptions on which assimilation is based.
24. Discuss the assumptions on which multicultural organizations are based.
25. Name the three steps involved in creating a multicultural organization.

ANSWERS TO REVIEW QUESTIONS

Text page numbers where the answers can be found are included in parentheses.

1. False (156)
2. True (157)
3. False (159)
4. False (171)
5. True (174)
6. e (155)
7. e (157)
8. e (167)
9. a (166)
10. c (171–172)
11. secondary (154)
12. prejudice (163)
13. cultural conflict (165)
14. assimilation (165)
15. reverse discrimination (167)
16. a (153)
17. a (153)
18. b (154)
19. b (154)
20. a (153)
21. blacks, Hispanics, Asians, and Native Americans. (155–157)
22. More productive use of a company's human resources; reduced conflict and more productive working relationships among employees from different cultural groups; increased commitment to and sharing of organizational goals; increased innovation and creativity; and enhanced ability to serve the needs of an increasingly diverse customer base. (162)
23. Diversity is an organizational weakness and a threat to the organization's effectiveness; minority groups who are uncomfortable with the majority group's values are oversensitive; members of minority groups want to be and should be more like the majority group; equal treatment of employees means the same treatment for all employees; and managing work-force diversity means changing the people, rather than the organization. (165)
24. Work-force diversity represents a competitive advantage in meeting the needs of an increasingly diverse customer base and in recruiting the best-qualified employees; because deriving benefits from diversity is a long-term process, the organization is in a constant state of transition; and valuing diversity involves changing the organization to adapt to the changing needs of people, rather than changing the people. (168)
25. (1) setting the stage; (2) educating and implementing; (3) maintaining diversity. (170)

STUDENT EXERCISE

Dealing with Diversity

This exercise supplements the "Strengthen Your Skills" exercise in the textbook at the end of Chapter 6. Both exercises are designed to help you focus on the importance of using good judgment in dealing with everyday workplace situations and raising your awareness about diversity topics.

As you learned in the "Strengthen Your Skills" exercise, one training tool that companies such as Herman Miller, McDonald's Corporation, Miami Herald Publishing, and Philip Morris Corporation are using to help their employees to handle encounters with people different from themselves is the board game *DIVERSOPHY™—Understanding the Human Race.*[1] In *DIVERSOPHY™* players take turns rolling dice and moving game pieces around a multicolored board that has a pattern resembling a racetrack. Colored squares along the paths correspond to colored cards. When landing on these squares, players read a corresponding card and follow directions. This game addresses such broad diversity issues as race, gender, age, sexual orientation, and physical abilities by providing four types of challenges.[2]

- The green *diversiSMARTS™* cards develop your knowledge and awareness of other people. (The "Strengthen Your Skills" exercise in Chapter 5 and the exercise in the Student Study Guide and Exercise Book gave you a chance to try some of the *diversiSMARTS™* cards.)
- The yellow *diversiCHOICE™* cards put you in everyday work situations and help you learn how to choose culturally appropriate behaviors.
- The blue *diversiSHARE™* cards provide a forum to dialogue and share personal background and experiences.
- The red *diversiRISK™* cards allow you to experience situations of cultural diversity.

This exercise will give you a chance to sample 4 of the 60 cards available in the yellow *diversiCHOICE™* category.[3]

Instructions

1. Read each situation that is described, examine your choices, and select the best way to deal with the situation.
2. After completing all four questions, compare your answers with those provided on the back of the *diversiCHOICE™* cards as shown at the end of the exercise.

The Case of Keeping It All in the Family

You own a small, growing high-tech assembly operation and employ workers from Latin and Middle Eastern backgrounds. You feel continually under pressure to find jobs for both their near and distant relatives. You should:

A. explain how the legal and professional restraints prevent you from doing favors

B. suggest the relatives apply for work opportunities both in your organization and elsewhere

C. discourage them by refusing to listen or by changing the subject

[1] © 1992 MULTUS INC., 46 Treetop Lane, Suite #200, San Mateo, CA 94402 (415) 342-2040. Permission granted to adapt this material from *DIVERSOPHY™—Understanding the Human Race* for this exercise.

[2] MULTUS INC. has also introduced two additional sets of 180 cards each. One set is on gender, sexual harassment, and sexual orientation; the other is on global negotiation.

[3] Besides a multitude of corporations using *DIVERSOPHY™* to train their employees on diversity issues, many universities and colleges are using the game as well. For more information, contact MULTUS INC., at 46 Treetop Lane, Suite #200, San Mateo, CA 94402 (415) 342-2040.

The Case of the Mentee Blunder

You are a white male manager mentoring a minority individual. Your mentee has made a blunder that has caused your boss to come down rather hard on you. As a result, you:

A. tell your mentee exactly what has happened and what you expect him or her to do the next time
B. avoid upsetting your mentee by taking the heat yourself but resolving to supervise him or her more carefully in the future
C. remove the mentee from situations in which he or she is likely to get into similar problems with upper management

The Case of the Young Image

The people in your organization are all under 30. You like this young image and feel it sells your product.

A. You are justified in not hiring older people because they may not fit in
B. You may want to hire older people for inside work to create a balance in your staff
C. You should disregard these considerations and base your hiring solely on objective, job-related criteria, without respect to age

The Case of Accent Interference

You find it hard to understand an employee whose accent is very different from yours. You have asked this person to repeat twice. What should you do next?

A. Apologize for not understanding and politely ask him or her to repeat again, perhaps in other words
B. Look for a translator and ask him or her to speak in his or her native language
C. Get on with the conversation; the context will clarify what you have not understood

ANSWERS

The Case of Keeping It All in the Family

B. You will keep goodwill and probably find some very good employees, too. A is only a partial answer: you must explain fair hiring practices, especially to employees whose relatives do not measure up, but most will quickly acculturate to this fact of U.S. work life. C will probably cause ill-will among people who expect their employer to be interested in their concerns.

The Case of the Mentee Blunder

A. Tell your mentee exactly what has happened and what you expect him or her to do the next time. This is the most empowering response. Many mentors fail their minority mentees by either failing to give them useful feedback as in B, out of fear that the mentee will find their criticism sexist or racist, or, even worse, by overprotecting them as in C.

The Case of the Young Image

C. You should disregard these considerations and base your hiring solely on objective, job-related criteria, without respect to age. It is the only legally correct answer.

The Case of Accent Interference

A. "So sorry to ask you to repeat again, but I really want to understand..." is the best approach. A translator as in B, may not help; differently accented English may be the person's native language. C sometimes works, but is risky.

chapter seven

Managing for Total Quality

LEARNING OBJECTIVES

- Define total quality management and trace its development.
- Summarize the TQM philosophies of Deming, Juran, and Crosby.
- Explain how quality relates to consumers through the marketing function.
- Discuss the relationship between quality and strategy in the organization.
- Examine some of the tools available to help improve quality.
- Recommend how managers can implement the TQM philosophy in their organizations.
- Compare the Japanese approach to quality with the American approach.
- Describe the importance of national and international awards for quality improvements.
- Propose a course of action for a small business that has just won a prestigious quality award.

CHAPTER OUTLINE

Introduction

What Is Total Quality Management?
- The Evolution of the TQM Concept

Three Masters of Quality: Deming, Juran, and Crosby
- W. Edwards Deming
- Joseph Juran
- Philip Crosby

Quality and the Consumer

Quality and Strategy
- A TQM Strategy Begins at the Top
- Obstacles to Effectively Adopting TQM
- TQM and Commitment

Tools for Improving Quality

Implementing an Effective TQM Program
- The Implementation Process
- Quality by Listening
- Generating Quality throughout the Organization

Quality in Japanese Firms
- Genichi Taguchi
- Quality Function Deployment
- Quality Circles
- Training of Japanese Employees

National and International Recognition of Quality

Quality in the Twenty-First Century

CHAPTER RECAP

Note: Boldface words are major chapter headings.

Introduction

This chapter highlights one approach to improving the quality of goods and services in an organization—total quality management.

What Is Total Quality Management?

Total quality management (TQM) is a management view that strives to create a customer-centered culture that defines quality for the organization and lays the foundation for activities aimed at attaining quality-related goals. The concept of TQM rests largely on five principles: quality work the first time, focus on the customer, strategic holistic approach to improvement, continuous improvement as a way of life, and mutual respect and teamwork.

The evolution of the TQM concept can be traced to Japan's post-World War II rebuilding process and its embracing of Joseph M. Juran's and W. Edwards Deming's ideas—ideas such as building quality into processes and using line-workers to solve process problems through the use of applied statistics. U.S. companies largely ignored their concepts during the 1950s and 1960s, relying instead on quality control departments as the primary means of ensuring quality. The systems of the 1970s emphasized only the manufacturing processes. When they realized they were not competing effectively with the more efficient Japanese, U.S. companies began applying quality considerations throughout their organizations rather than just to production.

Three Masters of Quality: Deming, Juran, and Crosby

W. Edwards Deming encouraged the use of statistical techniques to measure production quality and identify changes necessary to improve quality. He argued that a commitment to quality requires a transformation of the entire organization, and he developed a 14-point system to achieve that commitment.

Joseph Juran believes that while statistical techniques are useful tools in helping to achieve quality goals, quality must move well beyond statistical analysis. He emphasizes, instead, consumer perceptions of quality, defining quality as "fitness for use."

Philip Crosby takes a more practical approach, asserting that high quality is relatively easy and inexpensive in the long run. Crosby is responsible for zero defects programs that emphasize "doing it right the first time." He also developed four "Absolutes of Quality Management": (1) quality must be viewed as conformance to specifications; (2) it should be achieved through the "prevention" of defects rather than inspection after the production process; (3) management needs to demonstrate that a higher standard of performance can lead to perfection through zero defects; and (4) quality should be measured by the price of nonconformity.

Quality and the Consumer

Because quality is best defined by the end user, the concept of quality must be expanded to include not only "objective" measures of the good or service, but also the "subjective" interpretations of buyers.

Quality and Strategy

Organizations embrace a quality strategy for two main reasons: (1) the company's founders typically hold strong views concerning the importance of quality and (2) companies respond to economic downturns or competitive pressures by adopting a customer-focused strategy.

To be effective, **a TQM strategy must begin at the top.** If employees see TQM as mere symbolism and not substance, they will not be inclined to support it. Organizations must overcome **obstacles to effectively adopting TQM**—obstacles such as costs for new equipment, materials, and additional labor that are sometimes required to implement TQM processes. A **commitment to quality** can become a key element of any company's strategy.

Tools for Improving Quality

There are seven major tools and techniques that can help a company accomplish the goal to improve quality: (1) flowchart, (2) cause-and-effect diagram, (3) histogram, (4) Pareto chart, (5) control charts, (6) scatter diagrams, and (7) checksheets.

Implementing an Effective TQM Program

Managers must take an active role in changing an organization to a total quality management system.

The implementation process, according to Juran, involves seven steps: (1) achieve a breakthrough in attitudes, (2) identify a few key projects, (3) organize for a breakthrough in knowledge, (4) conduct the analysis, (5) design a plan to overcome the resistance to change, (6) institute the change, and (7) institute controls to monitor the results.

Quality by listening—managers can utilize their human resources by fostering an environment that is open to suggestions and creativity. Companies must also listen to suggestions and complaints from customers, whether they are internal or external to the company, that will improve product/service quality and enhance customer satisfaction.

Generating quality throughout the organization is possible once management and employees are involved and customers and suppliers have been considered. Managers and employees must determine which approach is best suited to meet the needs of customers and the resources of the company. The appropriate tools and techniques can help improve performance in processes and human resources.

Quality in Japanese Firms

Genichi Taguchi is a key Japanese contributor to the quality revolution in Japan. He emphasizes designing products that will achieve high quality despite environmental fluctuations, while improving the process design of the manufacturing process rather than the process-control technologies. Through continuous improvements in the design phase of a product, both consumers and manufacturers benefit through higher-quality products at lower costs.

Quality function deployment, which originated in 1972 at Mitsubishi's Kobe shipyard, is a set of planning and communication routines that focus and coordinate skills within an organization, first through design, then through the manufacturing and marketing of products.

Quality circles are groups of managers and employees, representing production tasks, who meet periodically to discuss proposals to seek continuous improvements in the production system. Quality circles help improve employee development and involvement while improving a company's competitiveness in the marketplace.

The training of Japanese employees is very important in implementing quality processes throughout Japanese companies. Thus, many firms have implemented extensive training programs that can take as long as six months to properly train their workers.

National and International Recognition of Quality

Among the awards made to American and Japanese firms to recognize their quality improvement efforts are the United States' Malcolm Baldrige National Quality Award, Japan's Deming Prize, and the Shingo Prize for Excellence in Manufacturing.

Quality in the Twenty-First Century

As U.S. firms move toward the coming century, they must integrate a quality emphasis into all aspects of their operations, not just in their mission statements and objectives. Managers should emphasize tangible quality improvements, not just slogans. Quality, not just superior marketing, will likely determine the winners and losers in the coming century.

KEY TERMS

Text page numbers where terms are first defined are in parentheses.

quality (182)—the degree to which a good or service meets the demands and requirements of the marketplace

total quality management (182)—a management view that strives to create a customer-centered culture that defines quality for the organization and lays the foundation for activities aimed at attaining quality-related goals

error-free production (183)—a manufacturing process consisting of maintaining machinery and equipment, quality inspection checks, and well-trained employees

cost-of-quality (COQ) accounting system (187)—a system that permits managers to calculate precisely the costs and savings associated with their quality efforts

zero defects (187)—a program that emphasizes "doing it right the first time," with 100 percent acceptable output

flowchart (193)—a tool that diagrams a process from start to finish, identifying those aspects of the process that need improvement

cause-and-effect diagram (193)—a method for analyzing process dispersion that relates causes and effects; also known as fishbone analysis

histogram (193)—a graphic summary of data that enables a user to interpret patterns that are difficult to see in a simple table of numbers

Pareto chart (194)—a diagram that graphically illustrates the frequencies of key factors that contribute to poor quality

control charts (194)—diagrams that display data over time as well as computed variations in those data

scatter diagrams (194)—illustrations allowing management to evaluate the relationship between two variables, using one variable to make a prediction about another variable or characteristic

checksheets (194)—data-recording forms that have been designed to allow managers to enter data on the form and simultaneously analyze trends in the data

quality loss function (QLF) (199)—the idea that a product that fails to meet consumer expectations results in a measurable loss to society

quality function deployment (QFD) (199)—a set of planning and communication routines that focus and coordinate skills within an organization, first through design, then through the manufacturing and marketing of products

quality circles (199)—groups of managers and employees, representing production tasks, who meet periodically to discuss proposals to seek continuous improvement in the production system

REVIEW QUESTIONS

True/False

Indicate whether the following statements are true or false.

___ 1. General Motors was the first American company that W. Edwards Deming worked with.

___ 2. Philip Crosby's 14-point program is more philosophical than practical.

___ 3. Bob Galvin, chairman of Motorola, demonstrates his commitment to quality by responding to one customer complaint a day.

___ 4. A quality award that can be given either to a U.S. or Japanese company is the Shingo Prize for Excellence in Manufacturing.

___ 5. Many American companies still have a discouraging tendency to use political pressure, "Buy American" campaigns, and slick marketing campaigns to succeed domestically and internationally.

Multiple Choice

Select the best answer for each question.

___ 6. American companies tended to view quality and the quality concept during the 1950s and 1960s as:
- a. one department inspecting finished products for quality
- b. a fad that would quickly pass away
- c. a holistic, companywide, and necessary process
- d. a very promising new concept that they should investigate
- e. something that would work only in Japan

___ 7. Which of the following is a **misstatement** of one of Deming's "Fourteen Points"?
- a. Teach and institute leadership.
- b. Eliminate numerical quotas for production. Instead, learn and institute methods for improvement.
- c. Understand the purpose of inspection, for improvement of processes and reduction of cost.
- d. Use a moderate level of fear in the motivational process.
- e. Encourage education and self-improvement for everyone.

___ 8. Which of the following is **not** one of the key elements of a quality program, as identified by Joseph Juran?
- a. Quality needs to be improved at a faster rate.
- b. It must be initiated at the bottom of the organization.
- c. Top management must support quality and monitor it.
- d. Top management must be in charge.
- e. Employees must be trained in quality management.

___ 9. While time and costs are often viewed as deterrents to the adoption of TQM, some companies can gain payoffs in as little as a month's time by doing such things as:
   a. holding motivational seminars
   b. improving customer service
   c. replacing the chief executive officer
   d. printing a good TQM brochure
   e. getting rid of the union contract

___10. Investing in quality programs is perhaps best viewed by companies as a:
   a. short-term loser
   b. fad of the 1990s
   c. Japanese strategy
   d. long-term commitment
   e. necessary outlay of dollars

Fill in the Blank

11. __________ __________ __________ involves creating a customer-centered culture that defines quality for the organization and lays the foundation for activities aimed at attaining quality-related goals.
12. __________ __________ is a manufacturing process consisting of maintaining machinery and equipment, quality inspection checks, and well-trained employees.
13. __________ __________ is a program that emphasizes "doing it right the first time," with 100 percent acceptable output.
14. According to __________ __________ __________, products should be designed to reflect consumer demands, requiring the coordination and collaboration of all areas of the company from the design engineers to the marketing department.
15. A __________ __________ consists of managers and employees, representing production tasks, who meet periodically to discuss proposals to seek continuous improvement in the production system.

Matching

Place the corresponding letter of the tools for improving quality with each definition or description. Each answer can be used only once.

   a. cause-and-effect diagram
   b. histogram
   c. Pareto chart
   d. scatter diagrams
   e. checksheets

___16. a graphic summary of data that enables a user to interpret patterns that are difficult to see in a simple table of numbers

___17. illustrations allowing management to evaluate the relationship between two variables, using one variable to make a prediction about another variable or characteristic

___18. a diagram that graphically illustrates the frequencies of key factors that contribute to poor quality

___19. data-recording forms that have been designed to allow managers to enter data on the form and simultaneously analyze trends in the data

___20. a method for analyzing process dispersion that relates causes and effects; also known as fishbone analysis

Short Answer/Discussion Questions

21. The concept of TQM rests largely on what five principles?
22. Who are the three "masters" of quality?
23. List two of the five company examples used under the discussion of the quality imperative that companies understand how consumers define quality in both the goods and services offered.
24. Based on a study by the Forum Corporation, list the two main reasons why organizations embrace a quality strategy.
25. According the text section, "Quality by Listening," who is it that managers should be listening to?

21.) 1.) Quality work the 1st Time
2.) focus on the Customer
3.) strategic holistic approach to improvement
4.) Continuous improvement as a way of life
5.) mutual Respect and teamwork

22) 1. W. edward Deming
2. Joseph Juran
3. philip Crosby

23.) 1.) Caterpillar
2.) Toyota

24.) 1.) Co. founders want it
2.) economic downturn / competitive pressures

25.) Employees & Customers

ANSWERS TO REVIEW QUESTIONS

Text page numbers where the answers can be found are included in parentheses.

1. False (185)
2. False (188)
3. True (196)
4. True (201)
5. True (202)
6. a (183)
7. d (186-187)
8. b (187)
9. b (191)
10. d (198)
11. total quality management (182)
12. error-free production (183)
13. zero defects (187)
14. quality function deployment (QFD) (199)
15. quality circles (199)
16. b (193)
17. d (194)
18. c (194)
19. e (194)
20. a (193)
21. quality work the first time, focus on the customer, strategic holistic approach to improvement, continuous improvement as a way of life, and mutual respect and teamwork. (182)
22. W. Edwards Deming, Joseph M. Juran, and Philip Crosby. (184)
23. Caterpillar (customer surveys), Toyota ("The Toyota Touch"), Wal-Mart (no-hassles return policy), L. L. Bean (replacement of products), and Saturn (total refunds for vehicles within 30 days if the customer is not fully satisfied). (189)
24. (a) The company's founders typically hold strong views concerning the importance of quality; and (b) many companies respond to economic downturns or competitive pressures by adopting a customer-focused strategy (190)
25. employees and customers. (197–198)

STUDENT EXERCISE

Competing on Quality Standards

You read in this chapter about the seven quality criteria of the U.S.'s Malcolm Baldrige National Quality Award. This exercise will give you a chance to learn more about the criteria that American companies compete on to win this award. You will also learn about the companies that have won this award since it was created by Congress in 1987. Remember that this national quality award is a means (1) to recognize quality improvement efforts by U.S. companies and (2) to foster greater competitiveness in the areas of excellence and high standards.

Quality Criteria

To help you learn more about the quality criteria, match the items listed below with the items left blank under the examination categories.

a. management of supplier performance
b. competitive comparisons and benchmarking
c. leadership system and organization
d. customer relationship management
e. employee education, training, and development
f. product and service quality results
g. strategy deployment

1995 Examination Categories/Items[1]

			Point Values	
1.0	Leadership			90
	1.1	Senior Executive Leadership	45	
	1.2	_____	25	
	1.3	Public Responsibility and Corporate Citizenship	20	
2.0	Information and Analysis			75
	2.1	Management of Information and Data	20	
	2.2	_____	15	
	2.3	Analysis and Use of Company-Level Data	40	
3.0	Strategic Planning			55
	3.1	Strategy Development	35	
	3.2	_____	20	
4.0	Human Resource Development and Management			140
	4.1	Human Resource Planning and Evaluation	20	
	4.2	High Performance Work Systems	45	
	4.3	_____	50	
	4.4	Employee Well-Being and Satisfaction	25	
5.0	Process Management			140
	5.1	Design and Introduction of Products and Services	40	
	5.2	Process Management: Product and Service Production and Delivery	40	
	5.3	Process Management: Support Services	30	
	5.4	_____	30	
6.0	Business Results			250
	6.1	_____	75	
	6.2	Company Operational and Financial Results	130	
	6.3	Supplier Performance Results	45	

7.0	Customer Focus and Satisfaction			250
	7.1	Customer and Market Knowledge	30	
	7.2	______	30	
	7.3	Customer Satisfaction Determination	30	
	7.4	Customer Satisfaction Results	100	
	7.5	Customer Satisfaction Comparison	60	
	TOTAL POINTS			1,000

Where to find out more: You can obtain individual copies free of charge of the full document that describes in detail the above award criteria. Request your copy of the *Malcolm Baldrige National Quality Award Criteria* from:

Malcolm Baldrige National Quality Award
National Institute of Standards and Technology
Route 270 and Quince Orchard Road
Administration Building, Room A537
Gaithersburg, MD 20899-0001
Telephone: 301-975-2036

Quality Companies

Here is a list of recent award winners, together with telephone numbers (when available) you may call to get more information about the company's quality programs. Please note: (1) The first year that awards were given was 1988; and (2) although two awards may be given in each category each year, there are some years when there are fewer than six winners.

Recent Malcolm Baldrige National Quality Award Winners
(telephone numbers provided where available)

Year	*Manufacturing*	*Service*	*Small Business*
1994	•none awarded	•AT&T Consumer Communications Services (800-473-5047) •GTE Directories Corporation (214-453-7985)	•Wainwright Industries, Inc. (314-278-5850)
1993	•Eastman Chemical Company (800-695-4322, Extension 1150)	•none awarded	•Ames Rubber Corporation (201-209-3200)
1992	•AT&T Network Systems Group (201-606-2488) •Texas Instruments Inc., Defense Systems & Electronics Group (FAX 214-480-4880)	•AT&T Universal Card Services (904-954-8897) •The Ritz-Carlton Hotel Company (404-237-5500)	•Granite Rock Company (408-761-2300)

Year	*Manufacturing*	*Service*	*Small Business*
1991	•Solectron Corporation (408-956-6768) •Zytec Corporation (612-941-1100, Extension 104)	•none awarded	•Marlow Industries, Dallas, Texas
1990	•Cadillac Motor Car Company (313-556-9050) •IBM Rochester (507-253-9000)	•Federal Express Corporation (901-395-4539)	•Wallace Co., Inc. (713-237-3700)
1989	•Milliken & Company (803/573-2003) •Xerox Corporation, Business Products & Systems (412-778-5008)	•none awarded	•none awarded
1988	•Motorola Inc. (708-576-5516) •Westinghouse Electric Corp., Commercial Nuclear Fuel Division (412-778-5008)	•none awarded	•Globe Metallurgical, Inc. (614-984-2361)

ANSWERS TO EXERCISE

1. 2 c
2. 2 b
3. 2 g
4. 3 e
5. 4 a
6. 1 f
7. 2 d

chapter eight

Entrepreneurship and Small Business

LEARNING OBJECTIVES

- Define entrepreneurship and small business.
- Summarize the importance of small business in the U.S. economy and the reasons certain fields attract small business.
- Analyze why small businesses succeed and fail.
- Specify how you would go about starting a small business and what resources you would need.
- Determine why many large businesses are trying to "think small."
- Critique a small business's strategy and make recommendations for its future.

CHAPTER OUTLINE

Introduction

The Nature of Entrepreneurship and Small Business
- Defining Small Business
- The Role of Small Business in the American Economy
- Industries That Attract Small Business

Reasons for Small-Business Success
- Independence and Autonomy
- Taking Advantage of Market Opportunities

Causes of Small-Business Failure
- Undercapitalization
- Managerial Inexperience or Incompetence
- Poor Control Systems

Starting a Small Business
- The Business Plan
- Forms of Business Ownership
- Financial Resources
- Approaches to Starting a Small Business
- Help for Small-Business Managers
- Entrepreneurship in Large Businesses

CHAPTER RECAP

Note: Boldface words are major chapter headings.

Introduction

Small businesses are the heart of the U.S. economic and social system because they offer opportunities and express the freedom that people have to make their own destinies.

The Nature of Entrepreneurship and Small Business

Entrepreneurship is the process of creating and managing a business to achieve desired objectives. The entrepreneurship movement is accelerating, with many new smaller businesses emerging.

Defining small business. Although there is no generally accepted definition, in this book small business is defined as any business that is not dominant in its competitive area and does not employ more than 500 people.

The role of small business in the American economy. Ninety-nine percent of all U.S. firms are classified as small businesses, and they account for over 40 percent of the U.S. gross national product. Small businesses are largely responsible for fueling job creation, innovation, and opportunities for minorities and women.

Industries that attract small business. Small businesses are found in nearly every industry, but retailing, wholesaling, services, and manufacturing are especially attractive to entrepreneurs because they are relatively easy to enter and require low initial financing. The growth of small businesses in computer and information processing, scientific measurement equipment, medical goods, electronic components, and chemical and allied products suggests that small business is moving into the high-technology area at a rapid pace.

Reasons for Small-Business Success

Entrepreneurs go into business for themselves for many reasons, but most say it is so that they can use their skills and abilities, gain control of their life, build for their family, and simply enjoy the challenge.

Independence and autonomy are linked to success and are probably the leading reasons that entrepreneurs choose to go into business for themselves.

Taking advantage of market opportunities is a major reason behind many small business start-ups as well as a factor in predicting success.

Causes of Small-Business Failure

According to the Small Business Administration, 24 percent of all new businesses fail within two years, and 63 percent fail within six years. Three major causes of small-business failure are listed below:

1. **Undercapitalization**—The shortest path to failure in business is the lack of funds to operate a business normally.
2. **Managerial inexperience or incompetence**—A person who is good at creating great product ideas and marketing them may lack the skills and experience to make good management decisions in hiring, negotiating, finance, and control.
3. **Poor control systems**—If the firm's control systems do not alert the manager that there are such problems as cash flow, excess inventory, high defect rates, or declining sales, it may be difficult or impossible to survive.

Starting a Small Business

To start a business, an entrepreneur must first have an idea. Then the entrepreneur must develop or make decisions about each of the following elements:

1. **The business plan** is a meticulous statement of the rationale for the business and a step-by-step explanation of how it will achieve its goals. Table 8.4 on page 224 of the text lists the components of a business plan.
2. **Forms of business ownership** addresses the need for the entrepreneur to decide on an appropriate legal form of business ownership, of which there are three basic ones: sole proprietorship, partnership, and corporation.
3. **Financial resources** for financing business ventures come from the small-business owner's contribution, equity financing, and debt financing.
4. **Approaches to starting a small business** include starting from scratch, buying an existing business, and franchising.
5. **Help for small-business managers** includes entrepreneurial training programs, college courses and seminars, information from local chambers of commerce and the U.S. Department of Commerce, and the Small Business Administration.

Entrepreneurship in Large Businesses

In an attempt to capitalize on small-business success in introducing innovative new products, more and more of even the largest companies are trying to instill a spirit of entrepreneurship. In these large firms, intrapreneurs, like entrepreneurs, take responsibility for, or "champion," developing innovations of any kind *within* the larger organization.

KEY TERMS

Text page numbers where terms are first defined are in parentheses.

entrepreneur (210)—a person who creates a business or product, manages his or her resources, and takes risks to gain a profit

entrepreneurship (210)—the process of creating and managing a business to achieve desired objectives

small business (211)—any business that is not dominant in its competitive area and does not employ more than 500 people

Small Business Administration (SBA) (211)—an independent agency of the federal government that offers managerial and financial assistance to small businesses

undercapitalization (221)—the lack of funds to operate a business normally

business plan (223)—a meticulous statement of rationale for the business and a step-by-step explanation of how it will achieve its goals

sole proprietorships (225)—businesses owned and managed by one individual; the most popular form of business organization

partnership (226)—an association of two or more persons who carry on as co-owners of a business for profit

general partnership (226)—a complete sharing in the management of a business, with each partner having unlimited liability for the business's debts

limited partnership (226)—an association of at least one general partner, who assumes unlimited liability, and at least one limited partner, whose liability is limited to his or her investment in the business

corporation (226)—a separate legal entity, or body, created by the state, having assets and liabilities that are distinct from those of the owners of the corporation

stock (226)—shares of a corporation that can be bought, sold, given as gifts, or inherited

venture capitalists (228)—persons or organizations that agree to provide some funds for a new business in exchange for an ownership interest, or stock

franchise (229)—a license to sell another's products or to use another's name in a business, or both

franchiser (229)—the company that sells a franchise

franchisee (229)—the purchaser of a franchise

intrapreneurs (234)—individuals who, like entrepreneurs, take responsibility for, or "champion," developing innovations of any kind within the larger organization

REVIEW QUESTIONS

True/False

Indicate whether the following statements are true or false.

___ 1. The generally accepted definition of small business is "any business that is not dominant in its competitive area and does not employ more than 500 people."

___ 2. Women own or control roughly 6.5 million small businesses (about one-third) and are starting new small businesses at twice the rate of men.

___ 3. According to the Small Business Administration, 58 percent of all new businesses fail within two years.

___ 4. Many financial institutions base their decision of whether or not to loan a small business money on its business plan.

___ 5. Small businesses may obtain funding from their suppliers in the form of equity financing.

Multiple Choice

Select the best answer for each question.

___ 6. One of the reasons many small wholesaling businesses succeed is that they have:
   a. the patience and perseverance that big companies do not have
   b. a nationwide or even global reach in distribution
   c. entrepreneur owners who are highly motivated to succeed
   d. the flexibility to solve distribution problems for large businesses
   e. access to quick sources of capital for growth

___ 7. A corporation is a separate legal entity, or body, created by the state. Which of the following is **not** true of a corporation?
   a. It is liable for its debts.
   b. External capital is more difficult to raise than in other forms of business.
   c. It has many of the same rights, duties, and powers as a person.
   d. It may own property.
   e. It can sue and be sued.

___ 8. Which of the following forms of Small Business Administration financial assistance is usually made only to businesses that do not qualify for loans from financial institutions?
   a. indirect loans
   b. guaranteed loans
   c. participation loans
   d. minority enterprise investment loans
   e. direct loans

____ 9. Franchising in the United States began in which of the following industries?
   a. fast food
   b. maid services
   c. hotel
   d. soft drink
   e. sewing machine

_C_ 10. SCORE and ACE are two volunteer agencies funded by the Small Business Administration for the purpose of:
   a. developing new sites for prospective businesses
   b. obtaining the government approvals that are required
   c. advising small businesses
   d. regulating new business applications
   e. screening prospective entrepreneurs

Fill in the Blank

11. A person who creates a business or product, manages his or her resources, and takes risks to gain a profit is a/an _Entrepreneur_.
12. When a business lacks sufficient funds to operate a business normally, it is suffering from _undercapitalization_.
13. A _Business_ _plan_ is a meticulous statement of rationale for the business and a step-by-step explanation of how it will achieve its goals.
14. Persons or organizations that agree to provide some funds for a new business in exchange for an ownership interest, or stock, are called _venture_ _Capitalists_.
15. _Intrapreneurs_ take responsibility for, or "champion," developing innovations of any kind within the larger organization.

Matching

Place the corresponding letter of the forms of business ownership with each definition or description. Each answer can be used only once.

   a. corporation
   b. sole proprietorships
   c. general partnership
   d. partnership
   e. limited partnership

_d_ 16. an association of two or more persons who carry on as co-owners of a business for profit

_b_ 17. the most popular form of business organization

_a_ 18. a separate legal entity, or body, created by the state, having assets and liabilities that are distinct from those of the owners

_e_ 19. an association of at least one general partner, who assumes unlimited liability, and at least one limited partner, whose liability is limited to his or her investment in the business

_c_ 20. a complete sharing in the management of a business, with each partner having unlimited liability for the business's debts

Short Answer/Discussion Questions

21. Under the text section, "The Role of Small Business in the American Economy," the authors identified three specific areas in which small businesses play a large role. What are they?
22. Traditionally, small businesses have been strongest in low-technology areas such as retailing and wholesaling. Today, however, we are seeing the growth of small businesses in high-technology areas. Name two of the high-tech areas that small business is moving into at a rapid pace.
23. Name three of the many reasons cited for why small business entrepreneurs succeed.
24. What are the three major causes of small-business failure?
25. List the six fundamental components of a business plan.

21.) 1.) fueling Job creation
2.) innovation
3.) opportunities for minorities and women

22.) 1.) Computer and information processing
2.) medical goods

24.) 1.) undercapitalization
2.) managerial inexperience or Incompetence
3.) poor control Systems

23.) 1. Independence and autonomy
2. Taking advantage of market opportunities

25.) 1.) Summary
2.) Situation analysis
3.) Strengths, weaknesses, Opportunities, and Threats
4.) Business Resources
5.) Financial Projections and Budgets
6.) Controls & evaluations

ANSWERS TO REVIEW QUESTIONS

Text page numbers where the answers can be found are included in parentheses.

1. False (211)
2. True (214)
3. False (220)
4. True (223)
5. False (228)
6. d (216)
7. b (226)
8. e (228–229)
9. e (229)
10. c (233)
11. entrepreneur (210)
12. undercapitalization (221)
13. business plan (223)
14. venture capitalists (228)
15. intrapreneurs (234)
16. d (226)
17. b (225)
18. a (226)
19. e (226)
20. c (226)
21. fueling job creation, innovation, and opportunities for minorities and women. (211)
22. computer and information processing, scientific measurement equipment, medical goods, electronic components, and chemical and allied products (215)
23. They are often obsessed with their vision of success and are willing to work hard and long hours; the ever-present risk of failure may place a degree of excitement and concern on each decision; the small business is more flexible in responding to the marketplace through innovative products and staying close to the customer; they can make decisions without consulting multiple levels and departments within the organization; flexibility and rapid decision making mean that new product development can occur more rapidly in small businesses than in larger ones. (218)
24. undercapitalization, managerial inexperience or incompetence, and poor control systems. (220-223)
25. summary; situation analysis; strengths, weaknesses, opportunities, and threats; business resources; financial projections and budgets; and controls and evaluation (224)

STUDENT EXERCISE

Are You Entrepreneurial?

After reading about both the successful and unsuccessful entrepreneurs in this chapter, you may be wondering if you have what it takes to be among the successful entrepreneurs. J. A. Hornady's research of entrepreneurs resulted in his identifying 25 characteristics of successful entrepreneurs.[1] Those 25 characteristics provided the basis for the development of this self-assessment.

Directions

1. After reading column two, "Ways to Exhibit This Characteristic," check the appropriate box to indicate whether that trait describes you "almost never," "sometimes," "usually," or "almost always."
2. Complete the scoring section at the end of the chart.
3. Read the "Indications from Scoring" section.

Characteristic	Ways to Exhibit This Characteristic	This Describes Me			
		Almost Never	Sometimes	Usually	Almost Always
Ability to get along with people	• Considerate of and sensitive to others' needs and feelings • Understand what makes people tick • Maintain control when dealing with difficult people and situations				
Ability to take calculated risks	• Develop a well-thought-out "game plan" that will move resources toward accomplishment of goals				
Creativity	• Imaginative • Think "outside the box" to find innovative solutions to problems				
Determination	• Persistent in pursuing your goals				
Diligence	• Work to complete objectives, avoiding procrastination • Take the initiative to do what needs to be done without having to be told				
Dynamism	• Forceful and vigorous • Make choices and take action that leads to change				

Characteristic	Ways to Exhibit This Characteristic	This Describes Me			
		Almost Never	**Some-times**	**Usually**	**Almost Always**
Energy	• Vital and intense in your pursuits • Willing to work long and hard hours				
Flexibility	• Adapt to changing circumstances • Like being able to choose where and when to work				
Foresight	• Look and plan ahead • Know where you're going • Have concern for the future				
Independence	• Willing to stand alone • Not overly influenced by opinions of others				
Initiative	• Face and deal with difficulties and problems rather than withdrawing from or avoiding them • Productive				
Knowledge of the market	• Work to comprehend the economics of the industry you're in or hope to get into • Exercise good judgment in decisions and actions • Reason deductively and inductively				
Knowledge of product and technology	• Develop technical expertise beyond your formal education • Think strategically • Reason analytically				
Leadership	• Exemplify a strong desire to lead • Willing to accept responsibility • Desire to influence others				
Need to achieve	• Desire to get ahead • Work long hours with high energy and enthusiasm • Exhibit tenacity to overcome obstacles				
Optimism	• Motivate others by your attitude and by what you say and do • Positive about the future • Dynamic, uplifting, enthusiastic				

[1] J. A. Hornady. "Research about Living Entrepreneurs." C. A. Kent, D. L. Sexton, & K. H. Vesper, *Encyclopedia for Entrepreneurship* (Englewood Cliffs, NJ: Prentice Hall, Inc. (1982).

Characteristic	Ways to Exhibit This Characteristic	This Describes Me			
		Almost Never	Some-times	Usually	Almost Always
Perceptiveness	• Intuitive • Able to get to the "bottom line" in complex situations				
Perseverance	• Always working to accomplish goals in many areas of your life • Possess a "stick-to-it-iveness" in pursuing important goals				
Positive responses to challenges	• Choose to emphasize the positives, even in negative situations • See problems as opportunities				
Profit orientation	• Take actions that are best for the organization, even if those actions are unpopular with employees				
Resourcefulness	• Capable of acting effectively in difficult situations • Find a way to get something done when others believe it can't be done				
Responsiveness to criticism	• Appreciate and utilize opiions that differ from your own				
Responsiveness to suggestions	• Seek counsel from others before making decisions • Respect others' ideas				
Self-confidence	• Believe in your ability to get the job done • Remain calm and confident in times of crisis • Gain the trust of others by being sure of your own actions • Be assertive and decisive				
Versatility	• Capable of doing many things competently				
Total checks in each column					
Multiply by		x 1	x 2	x 3	x 4
Total in each column					

GRAND TOTAL POINTS (add total points from all four columns)

Indications from score:

90–100	Exceptional indications of entrepreneurial flair—you share most of the characteristics common to highly successful entrepreneurs
75–89	Above average indications of entrepreneurial flair— you share many of the characteristics common to highly successful entrepreneurs
50–74	Average indications of entrepreneurial flair—you share some of the characteristics common to highly successful entrepreneurs
0–49	Based on this analysis, it appears your chances of successfully starting an entrepreneurial business are marginal

chapter nine

Developing Organizational Plans

LEARNING OBJECTIVES

- Discuss the benefits that planning can bring to an organization.
- List the steps in planning.
- Describe the nature of an organization's mission and goals and how they influence planning.
- Recognize and enumerate the various types of goals that an organization tries to meet.
- Determine the various levels of plans that organizations develop and explain how these levels are related.
- Formulate actions that managers can take to improve the effectiveness of planning.
- Describe management by objectives and explain how it can be used to coordinate planning within the organization.
- Evaluate the goals and plans of a business.

CHAPTER OUTLINE

Introduction

The Nature of Planning

The Benefits of Planning
- Focus
- Coordination
- Motivation

Steps in Planning
- Creating the Mission Statement
- Assessing the Current Situation
- Stating Goals
- Evaluating the Gap between Current Position and Goals
- Specifying Assumptions about the Future
- Creating the Plan
- Implementing the Plan
- Evaluating the Results of the Plan

CHAPTER RECAP

Note: Boldface words are major chapter headings.

Introduction

Planning is an essential element of successful management.

The Nature of Planning

Planning involves determining what the organization will specifically accomplish and deciding how to accomplish these goals. All managers are involved in planning for the future, but different levels or types of managers will be more concerned with different time frames. Typically, top management is concerned with the firm's long-term future, while first-line supervisors focus on daily and weekly planning.

The Benefits of Planning

Planning can benefit organizations by forcing them to focus, helping to coordinate activities and people, and motivating employees and managers.

Focus. When managers answer basic questions about the firm's operations and customers, they help individuals in an organization gain a common understanding of the firm and its purposes.

Coordination. Proper planning provides a means for coordinating the activities of groups and individuals.

Motivation. Frequently, the effects of focus and coordination arising from planning can lead to higher performance levels as organizational members recognize the firm's overall goals.

Steps in Planning

Listed below are the eight steps in the planning process:

1. **Creating the mission statement.** A mission statement is a formal written declaration of the organization's mission that contains all, or at least most, of the following: the firm's philosophy, its primary products and markets, the intended geographic scope, and the nature of the relationships between the firm, its stakeholders, and society. A clear understanding of the mission reduces the

ambiguity that employees may have about where the organization is trying to go and how they can help it get there.

2. **Assessing the current situation.** Before a company can make any plan, it must be aware of its present situation by determining (a) the extent of the organization's resources; financial assets, employee skills, technology, and data about the work process, and (b) the firm's working relationship with its suppliers, financial backers, and consumers.
3. **Stating goals.** To be stated correctly, a goal must contain several components: the attribute sought, the target to be achieved, an index to measure progress, and a time frame. Organizations develop three types of goals: (a) strategic goals, (b) tactical goals, and (c) operational goals. Four difficulties inherent in goal setting are: different stakeholders' goals are often in conflict with one another; unpredictable changes can make the plans impossible to carry out; organizational reward structures can overemphasize short-term performance; and good planning requires courage and risk taking.
4. **Evaluating the gap between current position and goals.** This step helps management determine whether the changes needed to close the gap are major or minor and whether it is necessary to develop a plan that will require a dramatic amount of time, effort, and resources.
5. **Specifying assumptions about the future.** If the present status of the organization or its external environment is expected to change in an unpredictable fashion, then planning becomes more difficult and complex. In general, organizations that cannot assume stability plan for shorter time periods and review and redesign plans more often than organizations that can assume stability.
6. **Creating the plan.** The process of creating a plan can be broken down into four basic steps: determining alternatives, evaluating alternatives, selecting an alternative, and specifying the steps.
7. **Implementing the plan.** This is the step where the organization goes from the "thinking" mode to the "doing" mode by carrying out the steps specified in the plan.
8. **Evaluating the results of the plan.** A well-done assessment of the outcomes that resulted from the plan provides valuable feedback.

Levels of Planning

Strategic plans address the general business actions outlined in the strategic goals and will be discussed in Chapter 10. Tactical plans relate to the tactical goals that are concerned with specific people, activities, and resources. The operational plans specify how the operational goals will be met as they relate to the steps the organization must follow at its service, delivery, or production levels.

Tactical plans. Four characteristics of tactical plans are that they are: (1) concerned with specific people, activities, and resources; (2) most commonly associated with the various functional areas of a business, such as marketing, operations, finance, R&D, and human resources; (3) normally designed for a relatively shorter time period than are strategic plans; and (4) usually designed and implemented by middle-level managers.

Operational plans. Two ways to categorize operational plans are as single-use plans (programs, projects, and budgets) or standing plans (policies, rules, and procedures).

Effective Planning

The chances that planning can be successful will increase if (1) sufficient information about all levels of planning should be conveyed to organizational members; (2) organizations create contingency plans that will allow them to react quickly to changes in environmental conditions; and (3) those involved in implementing the plan have input into developing the plans.

Management by Objectives (MBO) and Planning

MBO can be used to link together the three levels of plans—strategic, tactical, and operational.

Steps in the MBO process. First, top executives develop the strategic goals that become the foundation for the other parts of MBO. Second, the strategic plans and goals provide the framework upon which all planning for the functional areas are built. At this stage, middle-level managers are identifying tactical goals and developing tactical plans that are linked to the strategic goals. This process continues to move down the organization with more individuals and those at lower levels of the organization becoming involved. Finally, as MBO reaches the final levels of the company, operational plans are developed and closely linked with other plans.

Effectiveness of MBO. Although there is much evidence of the effectiveness of MBO in terms of improving organizational performance, it is also a time-consuming process and its outcomes can be affected by future events. Occasionally, MBO's heavy reliance on measurable results and strict time frames can lead to an inflexible approach, which has detrimental effects in terms of adapting to necessary change.

Putting Planning into Perspective

Unless managers have a clear idea of their goals and have specified the means, resources, and activities that will be used to reach these goals, the chances of maintaining or improving performance are reduced.

KEY TERMS

Text page numbers where the terms are first defined are in parentheses.

plan (244)—a set of activities intended to achieve goals, whether for an entire organization, department, or an individual

mission (247)—a definition of an organization's fundamental purpose and its basic philosophy

mission statement (247)—a formal written declaration of the organization's mission; often includes the firm's philosophy, its primary products and markets, the intended geographic scope, and the nature of the relationships between the firm, its stakeholders, and society

goal (250)—the final result that a firm wishes to achieve

strategic goals (251)—goals set by upper managers that deal with such general topics as the firm's growth, new markets, or new goods and services

tactical goals (251)—the intermediate goals of the firm, which are designed to stimulate actions necessary for achieving the strategic goals

operational goals (253)—those short-term goals that address activities that must be performed before tactical goals can be fulfilled

strategic plans (258)—plans that are intended to achieve strategic goals

tactical plans (258)—plans that are designed to achieve tactical goals

operational plans (258)—plans that are intended to achieve operational goals

single-use plans (261)—plans that are used once and then discarded

program (261)—an intermediate plan that encompasses a wide set of activities with a common focus

project (261)—a subdivision of a program

budget (261)—a plan to allocate resources and expenses for a certain period of time

standing plans (261)—those plans that deal with recurring, as opposed to unique, situations

policy (261)—a broadly stated standing plan that provides general principles or guidelines for making decisions in many situations

rule (262)—a specific plan that either condones or prohibits certain kinds of behavior

procedures (262)—step-by-step descriptions that detail the action that firms or individuals undertake to carry out standing plans

contingency plans (263)—alternate courses of action to be undertaken if certain organizational or environmental conditions change

management by objectives (MBO) (263)—a management philosophy and systematic process through which managers of all levels communicate with subordinates in terms of goals and how specific activities of the subordinates can contribute to reaching these goals

REVIEW QUESTIONS

True/False

Indicate whether the following statements are true or false.

____ 1. Different levels or types of managers are concerned with the same time frames in the planning process.

____ 2. The last two steps in planning are implementation and evaluation.

____ 3. In general, organizations that cannot assume stability plans for shorter time periods and review and redesign plans more often than organizations that can assume stability.

____ 4. Common types of single-use plans include policies, rules, and procedures.

____ 5. The organizational mission must be the start of an organizationwide MBO planning effort.

Multiple Choice

Select the best answer for each question.

____ 6. The step in the planning process that involves determining the extent of the organization's resources and the firm's working relationship with its suppliers, financial backers, and consumers is:
   a. creating the mission statement
   b. assessing the current situation
   c. stating goals
   d. evaluating the gap between its current position and goals
   e. specifying assumptions about the future

____ 7. Which component is **not** necessary for a goal to be stated correctly?
   a. The attribute sought
   b. The target to be achieved
   c. Potential benefits from achieving goal
   d. An index to measure progress
   e. A time frame

____ 8. The step in the planning process that involves determining alternatives, evaluating alternatives, selecting an alternative, and specifying the steps is:
   a. evaluating the gap between the firm's current position and goals
   b. specifying assumptions about the future
   c. creating the plan
   d. implementing the plan
   e. evaluating the results of the plan

d 9. The step in the planning process where the organization goes from the "thinking" mode to the "doing" mode is:
   a. evaluating the gap between its current position and goals
   b. specifying assumptions about the future
   c. creating the plan
   d. implementing the plan
   e. evaluating the results of the plan

a 10. Which is **not** a characteristic of tactical plans?
   a. Can be classified by how many times they are used—single-use or standing
   b. Concerned with specific people, activities, and resources
   c. Most commonly associated with the various functional areas of a business, such as marketing, operations, finance, R&D, and human resources
   d. Normally designed for a relatively shorter time period than are strategic plans
   e. Usually designed and implemented by middle-level managers

Fill in the Blank

11. A/an Mission statement often includes the firm's philosophy; its primary products and markets; the intended geographic scope; and the nature of the relationships between the firm, its stakeholders, and society.
12. In 1993, Compaq Computer Corp. expressed the goal to increase market share enough by the first quarter of 1996 to replace IBM as the leading seller of personal computers.
13. Strategic goals deal with such general topics as the firm's growth, new markets, or new goods and services.
14. Alternate courses of action to be undertaken if certain organizational or environmental conditions change are called Contingency plans.
15. MBO was first fully described by management expert Peter Drucker.

Matching

Place the corresponding letter of the terms related to operational plans with each definition or description. Each answer can be used only once.

   a. program
   b. budget
   c. policy
   d. procedures
   e. rule

b 16. A plan to allocate resources and expenses for a certain period of time

d 17. Step-by-step descriptions that detail the action that firms or individuals undertake to carry out standing plans

e 18. A specific plan that either condones or prohibits certain kinds of behavior

a 19. An intermediate plan that encompasses a wide set of activities with a common focus

d 20. A broadly stated standing plan that provides general principles or guidelines for making decisions in many situations

Short Answer/Discussion Questions

21. List three benefits of planning.
22. According to Peter Drucker, what areas should managers consider when setting organizational goals?
23. Name the four difficulties inherent in goal setting.
24. Identify three approaches to planning that managers can use to improve the chances that the planning will be successful.
25. What does this quotation mean: "Failure to plan is planning to fail?"

ANSWERS TO REVIEW QUESTIONS

Text page numbers where the answers can be found are included in parentheses.

1. False (244)
2. True (247)
3. True (256)
4. False (261)
5. True (264)
6. b (249)
7. c (250)
8. c (256)
9. d (258)
10. a (259–260)
11. mission (247)
12. IBM (250)
13. strategic (251)
14. contingency (263)
15. Drucker (263)
16. b (261)
17. d (262)
18. e (262)
19. a (261)
20. c (261)
21. Planning can benefit organizations by forcing them to focus, helping to coordinate activities and people, and motivating employees and managers. (245)
22. market standing, innovation, productivity, physical or financial resources, profitability, manager performance and development, worker performance, and public responsibility. (250–251)
23. Different stakeholders' goals are often in conflict with one another; unpredictable changes can make the plans impossible to carry out; organizational reward structures can overemphasize short-term performance; and good planning requires courage and risk taking. (253–255)
24. (1) Sufficient information about all levels of planning should be conveyed to organizational members; (2) organizations create contingency plans that will allow them to react quickly to changes in environmental conditions; and (3) those involved in implementing the plan have input into developing the plans. (263)
25. Unless managers have a clear idea of their goals and have specified the means, resources, and activities that will be used to reach these goals, the chances of maintaining or improving performance are reduced. (265)

STUDENT EXERCISE

Understanding Your Attitude toward Goal Setting

The authors began this chapter by defining *plan,* which you may recall is "a set of activities intended to achieve goals, whether for an entire organization, department, or an individual." This exercise will allow you to understand your individual attitude toward goal setting.

Instructions

1. Complete the evaluation on page 105 by checking the box next to each statement that indicates the extent to which the following statements are true about you.
2. Determine your total points using the information provided on the last four lines of the chart.
3. See if you agree with the "Indications from Your Score" comments.

No.	*Statement*	*Very True*	*True*	*Somewhat True*	*Not True*	*Not True at All*
1	I feel that I have a more positive approach to life when I am reaching for a goal than when I am not.					
2	A day goes better for me when I start the day working towards achieving a goal.					
3	I think that it is a good idea to write out daily and weekly goals.					
4	I believe that each goal should have a reward attached to it.					
5	I feel better at the end of the day when I have accomplished something I set out to do as compared with days when I can point to nothing of substance being accomplished.					
6	I feel that goals are beneficial whether they are reached or not.					
7	My friends and family would identify me as a goal-oriented person.					
8	I believe that goal-oriented people are more positive than people who are not goal-oriented.					
9	Goal setting is the most important tool to help me live up to my potential.					
10	Goals are worth having, even if they might cause frustration and disappointment if not reached on time.					
	Total Number 4 in each column?					
	Multiply by:	4	3	2	1	0
	TOTAL POINTS FOR EACH COLUMN					
	GRAND TOTAL					

Indications from Your Score:

More than 30	You see goal setting as a major contributor to achieving your potential and are enthusiastic about using this skill.
15 to 30	You recognize the importance of goals and feel that they make a contribution to achieving your potential.
Less than 15	It appears that you prefer to live with few, if any, goals and achieve your potential in other ways.

4. Complete the following "Questions for You to Consider."

Questions for You to Consider:	***Yes***	***No***	***Unsure***
Are you satisfied with your attitude toward goals?			
Are you satisfied that you're using goal setting at the level where you should be?			
Do you believe that your goal-setting skills are developed enough to be able to use them effectively in leadership positions?			

Source: Corinne Livesay, *Strengthen Your Skills: A Skills Building Manual,* Austen Press, © 1995 Richard D. Irwin, Inc.

If you have not done so already, now is a good time to complete the "Strengthen Your Skills" exercise on pp. 269–271 of the text which will give you some practice at setting and achieving goals.

chapter ten

Strategic Management

LEARNING OBJECTIVES

- Define strategic management and strategy.
- Describe the steps involved in strategic management.
- Relate strategic management to the business environment.
- Differentiate among the major corporate strategies and tools that managers use to develop and implement strategies.
- Analyze several common business-level strategies.
- Evaluate the importance of strategy implementation.
- Assess a business's strategy and recommend alternative strategies.

CHAPTER OUTLINE

Introduction

Strategic Management
- Scope
- Resource Deployment
- Synergy
- Distinctive Competence

The Strategic Management Process
- Identifying Mission and Goals
- Analyzing Strengths, Weaknesses, Opportunities, and Threats
- Strategy Formulation
- Implementing and Evaluating the Strategic Plan
- Strategic Control

Levels of Strategy
- Societal
- Corporate
- Business
- Functional
- Integrating the Levels of Strategy

CHAPTER RECAP

Note: Boldface words are major chapter headings.

Introduction

Strategy can play a major role in the success or failure of a business. Strategic management in organizations focuses on how a company carries out its strategic plans.

Strategic Management

Central to strategic planning and strategic management is the development of a strategy, a course of action for implementing strategic plans and achieving strategic goals. To be complete, a strategy must have four components:

1. **Scope** refers to the number of markets in which a company intends to compete or the number of products it intends to sell.
2. **Resource deployment** indicates how an organization has chosen to invest its resources.
3. **Synergy** refers to how an organization's resources should be linked so that the combined performance of its subunits is greater than if those units were operating alone.
4. **Distinctive competence** is what a firm does well relative to its competitors.

The Strategic Management Process

The strategic management process includes the formulation and implementation activities listed below:

1. **Identifying mission and goals.**
2. **Analyzing strengths, weaknesses, opportunities, and threats**—An organization conducts a SWOT analysis when it evaluates the organization's internal strengths and weaknesses and the opportunities and threats associated with the business's external environment.
3. **Strategy formulation** happens when organizations determine how they will compete at the corporate, business unit, and functional level.
4. **Implementing and evaluating the strategic plan.**
5. **Strategic control** is the feedback mechanism in the strategic management process; it compares the firm's actual performance to its intended performance and makes appropriate adjustments.

Levels of Strategy

Societal. This level addresses the question, "What does society expect of the organization?"

Corporate. The basic question at this level is "What business or set of businesses should we be in?"

Business. This level of strategy attempts to answer the question, "Given our particular product/market, how do we best compete?"

Functional. At this level, organizations establish strategies for functional areas such as marketing, operations, research and development, finance, and human resource management, with the primary purpose of implementing selected aspects of the firm's strategic plan.

Integrating the levels of strategy is accomplished by distinguishing among the levels by (a) recognizing that each higher strategy level serves as a constraint on the activities of lower levels and (b) looking at the fraternal twins of business decisions—effectiveness and efficiency.

Corporate Strategy

Strategies for dealing with multibusiness organizations. A diversified company must develop a strategic plan for several businesses, each facing unique environmental circumstances. The three major strategic alternatives are diversification, joint ventures, and divestment.

Portfolio analysis allows managers to visualize their businesses as a set or portfolio using certain common criteria, such as profitability or growth potential. Using a matrix, such as the Boston Consulting Group Matrix or the GE Matrix, managers can position their SBUs, assess their relative attractiveness, and determine appropriate strategies for each.

Business-Level Strategy

A business-level strategy is the plan that identifies the specific actions an individual SBU should undertake to meet corporate strategy.

Types of business unit strategies include cost leadership, differentiation, and focus.

The product life cycle provides a useful framework for evaluating the changing phases of a product and for crafting business-level strategy.

Implementing Strategy

A firm will not achieve its mission and goals unless it effectively and expeditiously implements its strategies. The McKinsey 7-S framework provides an excellent visualization of the components of a business that managers must consider when implementing strategy. Those components are **strategy, structure, systems, skills, staffing, style,** and **shared values.**

Strategic Management: Pros and Cons

Despite some of the criticisms against it, strategic management, when properly utilized, offers several benefits by involving managers at all levels of the organization, lessening resistance to change, encouraging managers to study and understand the organization's environment and resources, securing a more unified organization, and requiring managers to be more proactive and less reactive.

KEY TERMS

Text page numbers where the terms are first defined are in parentheses.

strategic management (274)—all the processes an organization undertakes to develop and implement its strategic plan

strategy (274)—a course of action for implementing strategic plans and achieving strategic goals; a general statement of actions an organization intends to take or is taking that is based on the fit of the organization with its external environment

distinctive competence (276)—what a firm does well relative to its competitors

SWOT analysis (277)—the evaluation of the organization's internal strengths and weaknesses and the opportunities and threats associated with the business's external environment

corporate strategy (280)—the scope and resource deployment components of strategy for the enterprise as a whole

business-level strategy (282)—the area of responsibility usually assigned to the divisional-level managers

diversification (283)—a strategy of acquiring other businesses

related diversification (284)—a firm's acquisition of a business that has some connection with the company's existing businesses

unrelated diversification (284)—the action of diversifying into any business that is potentially profitable for the organization

conglomerates (284)—firms that pursue unrelated diversification strategies

divestment (284)—a strategy of selling off businesses that the company no longer wishes to maintain, either because they are failing or because the company has changed its corporate strategy and does not wish to be in those businesses any longer

turnaround strategy (285)—a strategy in which the firm attempts, through such measures as cost-cutting, quality enhancement, or the elimination of management positions, to restore economic strength to a declining business

liquidation strategy (285)—a strategy in which the firm dismantles an operation and/or sells off parts that may be more valuable as separate entities than as part of the business as a whole

strategic business unit (SBU) (285)—a separate division within a company that has its own mission, goals, strategy, and competitors

portfolio analysis (285)—a technique allowing managers to visualize their businesses as a set or portfolio using certain common criteria, such as profitability or growth potential

stars (286)—those businesses that have high market shares and operate in industries experiencing major growth

question marks (286)—those businesses that are viewed positively in the sense that they are located in attractive, fast-growing markets, but for which there is a question as to their ability to compete, given their low market share

cash cows (286)—those businesses that tend to generate excess cash over what is needed for their continued growth due to their high market share in a slow-growing market

dogs (286)—businesses that have only minimal profits or even losses due to their low market share in slow-growing markets

cost leadership (288)—a business-level strategy aimed at achieving the overall lowest cost structure in an industry

differentiation (288)—a business strategy in which the SBU offers a unique good or service to a customer at a premium price

focus (289)—a business strategy in which the business concentrates on one part or segment of the market and tries to meet the demands of that segment

product life cycle (289)—the cycle of birth, growth, and decline of a product

birth (290)—the initial stage when the product is introduced

growth (290)—the stage characterized by dramatic increases in the product's market share

maturity (290)—the stage when the product's market share either slows or has no growth

decline (290)—the stage marked by decreases in the product's market share

REVIEW QUESTIONS

True/False

Indicate whether the following statements are true or false.

___ 1. *Strategic planning* is a more encompassing term than *strategic management*.

___ 2. SWOT analysis is an implementation activity in the strategic management process.

___ 3. As a rule, a firm will formulate its strategy to capitalize on its greatest strengths and to keep its organizational weaknesses from being exploited by competitors and other factors in the environment.

___ 4. The two axes for the Boston Consulting Group matrix are market growth rate and relative market share.

___ 5. Businesses that fall in the three squares in the upper left-hand quarter of the GE Matrix model are the ones that the firm may wish either to continue or to earmark for increased investment levels.

Multiple Choice

Select the best answer for each question.

___ 6. Which component of strategy refers to the number of markets in which a company intends to compete or the number of products it intends to sell?
   a. scope
   b. resource deployment
   c. synergy
   d. distinctive competence
   e. strategic control

___ 7. If the company fails to attain its goals, which activity in the strategic management process allows the company to reevaluate the way the strategy was planned, formulated, and implemented?
   a. mission and goal identification
   b. SWOT analysis
   c. strategy formulation
   d. strategy implementation and evaluation
   e. strategic control

___ 8. Which level of strategy attempts to answer the question, "Given our particular product/market, how do we best compete?"
   a. societal
   b. corporate
   c. business
   d. functional
   e. product

___ 9. When an organization attempts to restore economic strength to a declining business, that organization has chosen which strategy?
   a. related diversification
   b. unrelated diversification
   c. joint venture
   d. turnaround strategy
   e. liquidation strategy

___10. Which is **not** one of the benefits of properly utilized strategic management?
   a. Strategic management involves managers at all levels of the organization.
   b. Strategic management lessens resistance to change.
   c. Strategic management encourages managers to study and understand the organization's environment and resources.
   d. Strategic management secures a more unified organization.
   e. Strategic management requires managers to be more reactive and less proactive.

Fill in the Blank

11. ______ refers to how an organization's resources should be linked so that the combined performance of its subunits is greater than if those units were operating alone.
12. Environmental ______ is the collection and analysis of important data concerning trends in the environment.
13. Westinghouse has chosen to pursue unrelated diversification strategies and is one of America's most prominent ______, with businesses in such diverse areas as electric utility equipment, financial services, broadcasting, and defense systems.
14. Those businesses that have high market shares and operate in industries experiencing major growth are called ______.
15. ______ is a business strategy in which the SBU offers a unique good or service to a customer at a premium price.

Matching

Listed below are five of the seven components of the McKinsey 7-S Framework. Place the corresponding letter of the business component with each definition or description. Each answer can be used only once.

a. structure
b. systems
c. skills
d. staffing
e. shared values

___16. The center of the McKinsey 7-S Framework model

___17. Employees' knowledge of the technical aspects of the business's goods or services and how to apply this knowledge

___18. Finding and placing employees in jobs for which they have the appropriate skills

___19. A firm's hierarchy or pattern of organization

___20. Procedures or guidelines that firms use in the course of doing business

Short Answer/Discussion Questions

21. What do the letters in SWOT stand for? Identify all four environmental factors as either internal or external.
22. Discuss effectiveness and efficiency as they relate to the three strategy levels—corporate, business, and functional.
23. Briefly describe the three business-level strategies of cost leadership, differentiation, and focus.
24. Relate the three strategies you identified in the preceding question with the product life cycle.
25. What is the key to the McKinsey 7-S Framework?

ANSWERS TO REVIEW QUESTIONS

Text page numbers where the answers can be found are included in parentheses.

1. False (274)
2. False (277)
3. True (278)
4. True (285)
5. True (287)
6. a (275)
7. e (278)
8. c (282)
9. d (285)
10. e (296)
11. synergy (275)
12. scanning (277)
13. conglomerates (284)
14. stars (286)
15. differentiation (288)
16. e (292)
17. c (293)
18. d (293)
19. a (293)
20. b (293)
21. Strengths and Weakness are internal; Opportunities and Threats are external.(277)
22. Effectiveness is "doing the right thing," and this is normally pursued at the corporate level and the business level. Efficiency is "doing things right" and tends to predominate activities at the functional level. (282)
23. **Cost leadership** is aimed at achieving the overall lowest cost structure in an industry. **Differentiation** is a business strategy in which the SBU offers a unique good or service to a customer at a premium price. **Focus** is a business strategy in which the business concentrates on one part or segment of the market and tries to meet the demands of that segment. (288–289)
24. If a product is in the **birth** or introduction stage, the appropriate strategy may be one of foçus, since at this point the price will be relatively high and the technology may be unsettled. While in the **growth** stage, firms can compete with just about any of the three strategies because of the potential for continued market share increases and because the exact number of competitors is unknown. The **maturity** stage normally favors a cost strategy because growth is sluggish and competitors will be competing primarily over price. (290–291)
25. All seven components must be managed during the implementation process. A change in any one component will result in the changing of the balance among the other six. (292)

STUDENT EXERCISE

Analyzing McDonald's Strategy

Many of the principles related to strategic management that you have read about in Chapter 10 are illustrated for you in the following statements taken from an article by Andrew E. Serwer entitled "McDonald's Conquers the World," *Fortune* (October 17, 1994), pp. 103–116.

After reading each selection, fill in the blank to identify the strategic management issue you think the statement best reflects.

1. It wasn't long ago that many predicted McDonald's was doomed to become a lumbering cash cow in a mature industry. As events have turned out, the company has remained the nation's most profitable major retailer over the past ten years, even as the competition has become nimbler. McDonald's profits have more than tripled to almost $1.1 billion on revenues of $7.4 billion and systemwide sales of over $23 billion from over 14,000 stores.

____

2. McDonald's opens three new stores each day—many of which are outside the United States. Chances are good that within a year's time, each of these stores will be grossing about $1.7 million a year and operating well in the black.

____

3. McDonald's is the largest fountain-sales customer of Coke, with all 14,500 or so of McDonald's stores serving Coke. The two companies focus on the future of the global marketplace, where both companies share much common ground. For example, together they opened up the Russian market earlier in this decade.

____

4. McDonald's is delivering world-standardized food, smiles, value, and cleanliness to every continent except Antarctica. The company sells its burgers in 73 countries and pulls in about 45 percent of its operating income from foreign operations. Compare these numbers from 1988 and 1994:

Year	*Number of Foreign Stores*	*Annual Overseas Revenue*
1988	2,600	$1.8 billion
1994	4,700	$3.4 billion

____

5. According to Tim Fenton, head of McDonald's Poland: "It's hard for Americans to understand, but McDonald's is almost heaven-sent to these people. It's some of the best food around. The service is quick, and people smile. You don't have to pay to use the bathroom. There's air conditioning. The place isn't filled with smoke. We tell you what's in the food. And we want you to bring kids."

____

6. What McDonald's really has to export around the globe is service by using simple strategies such as:
   - Putting your employees through arduous and repetitive management training.
   - Hiring locals whenever possible.
   - Forming paradigm-busting arrangements with suppliers.
   - Keeping pricing low to build market share. Profits will follow when economies of scale kick in.

   McDonald's slavish devotion to regimentation is also a key. According to Don Keough, a McDonald's board member and retired president of Coca-Cola: "Never have I seen a company more focused than McDonald's. The company is an army with one objective that has never strayed."

---

7. McDonald's has a $1.4 billion annual global advertising and promotion budget—making McDonald's the most advertised single brand in the world.

---

8. McCulture shows signs of becoming too rigid, too steeped in its own orthodoxy to cook up that all-important break-out-of-the-box, home run innovation. Most analysts believe a new hitwich on the order of the Big Mac or the Quarter Pounder will be required to solve McDonald's so-called "menu problem."

---

9. Burger King, Taco Bell, KFC, and Pizza Hut are fierce, moneyed competitors that have all won battles against McDonald's.

---

10. According to Jim Adamson, CEO of Burger King, "There are still so many new points of distribution out there—hospitals, sports arenas, and roadways. There's room for double-digit domestic growth in our business."

---

11. Supplying stores abroad is a constant challenge. Chicago-based meat supplier OSI Industries has joint ventures in 17 countries, where it works with local companies making McDonald's hamburgers.

---

12. One such joint-venture site in Bavaria cranks out some 2.5 million patties a day. Computers mix ground beef to ensure that fat content meets the McDonald's world standard, 20 percent or less. The specs and production demands are exacting, and with monthly evaluations, the pressure for quality is constant.

---

13. According to Dick Starmann, head of communications, McDonald's stopped using bleached white bags; three years ago. "Half the scientific community said nay on white bags, the other half said yea, but customers didn't want them, so we got rid of them." A pilot program in Holland that recycles 100 percent of the waste at each store may be expanded to other countries.

---

14. McDonald's puts a high priority on employee training, putting every employee—some 840,000 systemwide—through the paces for two to three days. McDonald's managers attend Hamburger University at company headquarters in Oak Brook, Illinois. Procter & Gamble, Amoco, and the Red Cross all have visited recently, looking for ways to improve their training. Fourteen times a year, 200 McDonald's managers with two to five years of experience arrive from 72 countries for the intensive two-week program. Simultaneous translation into 20 languages is provided for courses such as Building Market Share and Staffing and Retention II.

---

15. CEO Mike Quinlan states: "Want to know my definition of insanity? It's doing the same thing over and over again and expecting different results. If there's anything I try to impart to our people, it's to never be satisfied. That means coming up with new ideas."

ANSWERS TO STUDENT EXERCISE

Suggested answers for the student exercise are provided below—you may find other strategic management principles that also apply. The text page reference is provided in parentheses.

1. BCG Matrix—cash cows (286); product life cycle (290)
2. resource deployment (275)
3. synergy (275)
4. scope (275)
5. distinctive competence (276)
6. focus (289); cost leadership (288)
7. strength—SWOT analysis—internal strength (277)
8. weakness—internal (277)
9. threat—external (277)
10. opportunities—external (277)
11. joint ventures (284)
12. strategic control (278)
13. levels of strategy: societal (280)
14. McKinsey 7-S framework: staffing (293)
15. McKinsey 7-S framework: style (294)

chapter eleven

Making Decisions

LEARNING OBJECTIVES

- Define decision making and describe the types of decisions and conditions that may affect decision making.
- Specify the steps involved in decision making.
- Contrast the decision-making models.
- Examine the factors that may affect decision making.
- Summarize group decision techniques and the advantages and disadvantages of group decision making.
- Apply the decision-making models to a hypothetical situation.

CHAPTER OUTLINE

Introduction

The Essence of Decision Making
- Types of Decisions
- Conditions Affecting Decision Making

The Steps of Decision Making
- Identifying the Problem
- Generating Alternative Courses of Action
- Evaluating the Alternative
- Selecting the Best Alternative
- Implementing the Decision
- Evaluating the Decision

Decision-Making Models
- The Classical Model
- The Administrative Model
- Applying Decision-Making Models to the Real World

Factors that Affect Decision Making
- Intuition
- Emotion and Stress
- Framing
- Escalation of Commitment
- Confidence and Risk Propensity

Decision Making in Groups
- Group Decision Techniques
- Individual versus Group Decision Making
- Using Computers in Group Decision Making

CHAPTER RECAP

Note: Boldface words are major chapter headings.

Introduction

Making decisions is widely recognized as a key aspect of management, and many managers and academicians consider it to be the most crucial element of business management.

The Essence of Decision Making

Decision making is the process of choosing among alternative courses of action to resolve a problem.

Types of decisions include programmed (routine) and nonprogrammed (unique) decisions.

Conditions affecting decision making are (a) certainty—when decision makers are fully informed about a problem, its alternative solutions, and their respective outcomes; (b) risk—when decision makers must rely on incomplete, yet reliable information; and (c) uncertainty—when little or no factual information is available.

The Steps of Decision Making

1. **Identifying the problem** is probably the most critical part of the decision-making process, for it is what determines the direction that the decision-making process takes and, ultimately, the decision that is made.
2. **Generating alternative courses of action** involves identifying items or activities that could reduce or eliminate the difference between the actual situation and the desired situation.
3. **Evaluating the alternatives** occurs when the decision maker evaluates each alternative in terms of its feasibility, its effectiveness, and its consequences.
4. **Selecting the best alternatives** requires the decision maker to decide which alternative has the highest combined level of feasibility and effectiveness, coupled with the lowest costs to the organization.

5. **Implementing the decision** transforms the selected alternative from an abstract thought into reality and involves planning and executing the actions that must take place so that the selected alternative can actually solve the problem.
6. **Evaluating the decision** requires managers to gather information to determine the effectiveness of their decision.

Decision-Making Models

Management theory generally recognizes two major models of decision making:

1. **The classical model,** also called the rational model, outlines how managers should make decisions.
2. **The administrative model,** also called the organizational, neoclassical, or behavioral model, outlines how managers actually do make decisions. Two hallmarks of this model are bounded rationality and satisficing.

Applying decision-making models to the real world. The classical model illustrates how managers can strive to be more rational and logical in their decision making, while the administrative model illustrates how managers have limits to their rationality and how these limits affect their decision making. Both models help pave the way for managerial understanding and growth in the all-important management function of decision making.

Factors That Affect Decision Making

Factors that can get in the way of rational decision making include the following:

1. **Intuition** enables managers, based on years of practice and experience, to identify alternatives quickly without conducting a systematic analysis of alternatives and their consequences.
2. **Emotion and stress** can cause managers to make faulty—even damaging—decisions.
3. **Framing** occurs when managers are overly influenced by the manner in which something is presented.
4. **Escalation of commitment** is the tendency to commit to an apparently faulty decision for too long.
5. **Confidence and risk propensity** refer to the general idea that the higher your level of confidence in your decisions, the greater likelihood that you will take risks in decision making.

Decision Making in Groups

In today's organizations, more decisions are being made primarily by groups rather than individuals.

Group decision techniques include brainstorming, nominal group technique, and the Delphi group technique.

Individual versus group decision making. The advantages that group decision making has over individual decision making include: groups bring more information to the situation; they possess a broader perspective; they can generate more alternatives; they provide an opportunity for intellectual stimulation; and they allow participants who are affected by the decision to understand why the decision was made, thus increasing the likelihood that the decision will be accepted. Disadvantages include the extra time needed to reach a decision, the possibility of one or more group members dominating the group's discussion, the pressures to conform, settling for a less-than-optimal compromise to reduce time and conflict needed to reach a group decision, and ambiguity in who is responsible for the decision implementation and evaluation.

Using computers in group decision making. Today's managers have access to a wealth of computer information and technology that can aid and support their decision-making processes. (See Chapter 21 for an in-depth discussion.)

KEY TERMS

Text page numbers where the terms are first defined are in parentheses.

decision (302)—a choice made from alternative courses of action in order to deal with a problem

problem (302)—the difference between a desired situation and the actual situation

decision making (302)—the process of choosing among alternative courses of action to resolve a problem

programmed decisions (302)—decisions made in response to situations that are routine, somewhat structured, and fairly repetitive

nonprogrammed decisions (303)—decisions made in response to situations that are unique, relatively unstructured, undefined, and/or of major consequence to the organization

certainty (304)—the condition that exists when decision makers are fully informed about a problem, its alternative solutions, and their respective outcomes

risk (304)—the condition that exists when decision makers must rely on incomplete, yet reliable, information

uncertainty (304)— the condition that exists when little or no factual information is available about a problem, its alternative solutions, and their respective outcomes

classical model of decision making (309)—a prescriptive approach, asserting that managers are logical, rational individuals who make decisions that are in the best interests of the organization, that outlines how managers should make decisions; also known as the rational model

administrative model of decision making (309)—a descriptive approach, recognizing that people do not always make decisions with logic and rationality, that outlines how managers actually do make decisions; also known as the organizational, neoclassical, or behavioral model

bounded rationality (310)—the idea that people have limits, or boundaries, to their rationality

satisficing (310)—the decision maker's decision to choose the first alternative that appears to resolve the problem satisfactorily

intuition (311)—the immediate comprehension that something is the case, seemingly without the use of any reasoning process or conscious analysis

framing (313)—the tendency to view positively presented information favorably and negatively presented information unfavorably

escalation of commitment (314)—the tendency to persist with a failing course of action

confidence (315)—a person's faith that his or her decisions are reliable and good

risk propensity (315)—a person's willingness to take risks when making decisions

brainstorming (318)—a technique in which group members spontaneously suggest ideas to solve a problem

nominal group technique (319)—a process that involves the use of a highly structured meeting agenda and restricts discussion or interpersonal communication during the decision-making process

Delphi group technique (319)—a technique employing a written survey to gather expert opinions without holding a group meeting

groupthink (322)—a phenomenon occurring when cohesive "in-groups" let the desire for unanimity, or consensus, override sound judgment in generating and evaluating alternative courses of action

REVIEW QUESTIONS

True/False

Indicate whether the following statements are true or false.

___ 1. Managers all too often shortchange the step of generating alternative courses of action in the decision-making process because they are in search of a "quick fix."

___ 2. One of the great contributions of the administrative model of decision making is its recognition that people make decisions with logic and rationality.

___ 3. Confidence, in the language of decision making, is a manager's faith that his or her decisions are reliable and good.

___ 4. One of the reasons for the prevalence of group decision making in today's business world is that many decisions require more specialized knowledge than one person usually possesses.

___ 5. Of the various group decision-making techniques, the nominal group technique is unique because it never allows group members to have face-to-face contact.

Multiple Choice

Select the best answer for each question.

___ 6. Cost-benefit analysis and determining "pros and cons" are methods for which step of the decision-making process?
   a. identifying the problem
   b. generating alternative courses of action
   c. evaluating the alternatives
   d. selecting the best alternative
   e. implementing the decision

___ 7. Of the factors that affect decision making, which one is based on years of practice and experience that enables managers to identify alternatives quickly without conducting a systematic analysis of alternatives and their consequences?
   a. intuition
   b. emotion and stress
   c. framing
   d. escalation of commitment
   e. satisficing

e 8. Which of the following is one of the rules for brainstorming?
   a. Each member independently writes down his or her ideas for possible problem solutions.
   b. Results of the first questionnaire are compiled at a central location.
   c. In round-robin fashion, each member takes a turn presenting a single idea to the group.
   d. Each member individually and silently ranks the ideas in priority order on a secret written ballot.
   e. Criticism is not allowed.

b 9. Which is an **advantage** of group decision making?
   a. One or more group members may dominate the discussion.
   b. Less-experienced participants in group interaction learn a great deal about group dynamics by actually being involved in the group decision-making process.
   c. Groups take more time to reach a decision than would an individual.
   d. Groups may succumb to a phenomenon known as groupthink.
   e. Group participants can feel pressure to conform.

d 10. Which is a **disadvantage** of group decision making?
   a. Groups bring more information to the situation.
   b. Groups can generate more alternatives.
   c. Groups provide an opportunity for intellectual stimulation.
   d. There is no clear focus of decision responsibility.
   e. Groups allow participants who are affected by the decision to understand why the decision was made, and thus, are more likely to accept the decision.

Fill in the Blank

11. Non-programmed decisions are made in response to situations that are unique, relatively unstructured, undefined, and of major consequence to the organization.
12. The behavioral or administrative model of decision making is a descriptive approach that outlines how managers actually do make decisions.
13. The Classican model of decision making is based on economic assumptions and asserts that managers are logical, rational individuals who make decisions that are in the best interests of the organization.
14. The tendency of individuals and organizations to persist with failing courses of action is known as escalation of commitment.
15. Risk propensity refers to the extent to which a person is willing to take risks when making a decision.

Matching

Place the corresponding letter of the word or phrase with each definition or description. Each word or phrase can be used only once.

a. problem
b. risk
c. framing
d. nominal group technique
e. groupthink

d 16. A group decision technique that involves the use of a highly structured meeting agenda and restricts discussion and interpersonal communication during the decision-making process

c 17. Refers to the way in which information is phrased, presented, or labeled

a 18. The difference between a desired situation and an actual situation

e 19. The phenomenon that occurs when cohesive "in-groups" let the desire for unanimity, or consensus, override sound judgment when generating and evaluating alternative courses of action

b 20. The condition that exists when decision makers must rely on incomplete, yet reliable, information

Short Answer/Discussion Questions

21. List the six steps in the decision-making process.
22. If an implemented decision has not resolved the problem, what questions should a manager ask to determine why the decision-making process failed?
23. Name and describe the two hallmarks of the administrative model.
24. Which of the factors affecting decision making is blamed for the destruction of the world's largest real estate company?
25. List and briefly describe three common group decision techniques.

ANSWERS TO REVIEW QUESTIONS

Text page numbers where the answers can be found are included in parentheses.

1. True (306)
2. False (310)
3. True (315)
4. True (317)
5. False (319)
6. c (307)
7. a (311)
8. e (318)
9. b (320–321)
10. d (321–22)
11. nonprogrammed (303)
12. administrative (309)
13. classical (309)
14. escalation (314)
15. risk propensity (315)
16. d (319)
17. c (313)
18. a (302)
19. e (322)
20. b (304)
21. The six steps are: (1) identifying the problem, (2) generating alternative courses of action, (3) evaluating the alternatives, (4) selecting the best alternative, (5) implementing the decision, and (6) evaluating the decision. (306–309)
22. Was the wrong alternative selected? Was the correct alternative selected, but implemented improperly? Was the original problem identified incorrectly? Has management not given the implemented alternative enough time for it to be successful? (308–309)
23. bounded rationality (the idea that people have limits, or boundaries, to their rationality) and satisficing (the decision maker's decision to choose the first alternative that appears to resolve the problem satisfactorily. (309–310)
24. confidence and risk propensity. (316)
25. **Brainstorming** is a technique in which group members spontaneously suggest ideas to solve a problem. **Nominal group technique** is a process that involves the use of a highly structured meeting agenda and restricts discussion or interpersonal communication during the decision-making process. **Delphi group technique** is a technique employing a written survey to gather expert opinions without holding a group meeting. (318–319)

Leadership Style Indicator Checklist

- ❑ Is intellectual, and ingenious
- ❑ Wants control
- ❑ Has impersonal social orientation
- ❑ Is skilled in organizing facts and establishing controls
- ❑ Prefers limited control by others
- ❑ Completes tasks by applying rigorous analysis and preparing elaborate, detailed plans
- ❑ Is motivated by complex situations with variety and challenge
- ❑ Wants to be able to predict outcomes

- ❑ Is insightful and enthusiastic
- ❑ Has a very personal social orientation
- ❑ Shows concern for others' views
- ❑ Smooths over difficulties; is well liked
- ❑ Completes tasks by using intuition
- ❑ Seeks new ideas; is adaptive and flexible
- ❑ Is motivated by recognition from others
- ❑ Wants independence; enjoys achieving personal goals

- ❑ Is practical and authoritarian
- ❑ Has impersonal social orientation
- ❑ Needs power and status
- ❑ Is forceful
- ❑ Dislikes committees and group discussions
- ❑ Completes tasks quickly
- ❑ Is action and results oriented
- ❑ Is motivated by situations with measurable achievement potential and tangible rewards

- ❑ Is sociable
- ❑ Is friendly
- ❑ Is supportive
- ❑ Has interpersonal social orientation
- ❑ Has a talent for building teams and encouraging participation
- ❑ Is action oriented
- ❑ Holds meetings
- ❑ Is motivated to seek acceptance by peers and avoid conflict

CONCEPTUAL

ANALYTICAL

BEHAVIORAL

DIRECTIVE

STUDENT EXERCISE

Matching Your Decision Style with Your Leadership Style

Your textbook provides two features in Chapter 11 related to decision styles:

- The decision-style inventory in the "Strengthen Your Skills" exercise on pp. 326–329 gives you an opportunity to determine your preferred decision style (Directive, Analytical, Conceptual, or Behavioral). The table at the end of the exercise (p. 329) provides insight into understanding your style.
- The "Careers Corner" feature on p. 322 relates decision styles to organizational fit and the types of jobs individuals with each decision style gravitate toward.

Background

The exercise that follows provides you with a quick "two-minute" style indicator that will allow you to determine whether a match-up exists between your results on the decision-style inventory (p. 328) and this assessment that focuses on the leadership style characteristics of each of the decision styles.

Directions

1. Transfer from question 4 on p. 328 of your text the following results from completing the decision-styles inventory.

   Very dominant style(s) ______________________________

   Dominant style(s) ______________________________
2. As you read the information in each of the four quadrants on the Leadership Style Indicator Checklist on page 127 of the *Study Guide,* place checkmarks next to the characteristics[1] that best describe you. Select the quadrant that has the most checkmarks, and cut out that quadrant section (in case of a tie, cut out both quadrants). Turn the quadrant(s) over to see whether Directive, Analytical, Conceptual, or Behavioral describes your leadership style.
3. The results of this Leadership Style Indicator Checklist will most likely match your answers to number one above.

[1] Characteristics are categorized using information from Alan J. Rowe and Richard O. Mason, "Decision-Style Inventory" from *Managing with Style* (San Francisco: CA: Jossey Bass, 1987) © 1987 Alan J. Rowe.

chapter twelve

Organizing: Designing Jobs and Departments

LEARNING OBJECTIVES

- Discuss the concept of organizing and explain why it is important.
- Interpret an organizational chart.
- Explain why job specialization and division of labor are important for organizing.
- Assess the different approaches to grouping tasks into jobs and the advantages and disadvantages of each.
- Distinguish four different bases for grouping jobs into departments.
- Determine the relationships among authority, responsibility, and delegation.
- Describe decentralization and describe what strengths it has for employee development.
- Critique a company's new organizational structure.

CHAPTER OUTLINE

Introduction

The Nature of Organizing
- Reasons for Organizing
- Formal and Informal Relationships
- The Process of Organizing

Grouping Tasks into Jobs
- Classical Job Design
- The Behavioral Approach to Job Design

Grouping Jobs into Departments
- Functional Departmentalization
- Customer Departmentalization
- Product Departmentalization
- Geographic Departmentalization

Determining Authority Relationships
- Authority and Responsibility
- Authority Relationships
- Balancing Authority and Responsibility

CHAPTER RECAP

Note: Boldface words are major chapter headings.

Introduction

Organizing work is a major management activity, examples of which are dividing work into parts, assigning these parts to individuals, and coordinating the activities of these individuals.

The Nature of Organizing

Organizing can be defined as the activities involved in designing an appropriate organization structure, assigning employee duties, and developing working relationships among people and among tasks.

Reasons for organizing include permitting people to work together in order to achieve goals that would be difficult to achieve on their own, achieving synergy, avoiding duplication of resources, establishing lines of authority, and facilitating communication.

Formal and informal relationships. The organizational chart shows the structure of the formal organization, which is the arrangement of positions that dictates where work activities are completed, where decisions should be made, and the flow of information. The informal organization refers to the relationships among positions that are not connected by the organizational chart.

The process of organizing typically involves several activities: grouping tasks into jobs, grouping jobs into departments, and determining authority and channels of communication.

Grouping Tasks into Jobs

Job design is the process of grouping tasks into jobs. There are several schools of job design, two of which are discussed below:

Classical job design is based on the assumption that increasing job specialization and division of labor increases an organization's overall productivity.

The behavioral approach to job design is based on the view that workers are independent parts of the production process whose individual characteristics should be taken into account in forming jobs. Job enlargement, job rotation, and job enrichment are examples of the behavioral approach to job design.

Grouping Jobs into Departments

Once tasks have been grouped into jobs, the second major activity required in organizing is grouping jobs into departments. Departments are formed to group jobs that should be linked in order for the organization to more easily reach its objectives. Four basic types of departmentalization follow:

1. **Functional departmentalization** groups jobs that perform similar functional activities, such as finance, manufacturing, and human resources.
2. **Customer departmentalization** groups jobs so that the job holders interact with a specific customer group or clientele.
3. **Product departmentalization** groups jobs or activities around their principal goods and services.
4. **Geographic departmentalization** groups jobs according to physical geography.

Determining Authority Relationships

The third activity involved in organizing is determining authority relationships among employees.

Authority and responsibility. The structure of the organization indicates that some positions have authority over others, and subordinate positions must report to higher-level ones. Authority always carries with it the burden of responsibility, or being held accountable for attainment of the organization's goals.

Authority relationships are defined by the type of departmentalization the organization uses and are affected by the span of control (the actual number of subordinates over which a position has authority) and the chain of command (an organizing concept that ensures that all positions are directly linked in some way to top management). Two principles of chain of command are unity of command (a subordinate should report to only one immediate superior) and scaler chain (authority should flow through the organization from the top down, one level at a time).

Balancing authority and responsibility. Since the top manager cannot be directly involved in all decisions, delegation and decentralization are used to spread decision making and authority throughout the members of the organization. Delegation, or empowerment, is the assignment of work activities and authority to an employee or work group. Decentralization can be viewed as formalized delegation in the organization.

KEY TERMS

Text page numbers where the terms are first defined are included in parentheses.

organizational chart (334)—a pictorial display of the official lines of authority and communication within the organization

authority (334)—the right to give work orders to others in the organization; associated with a position within an organization, not with the individual occupying that position

formal organization (334)—the arrangement of positions, as shown on an organizational chart, that dictates where work activities are completed, where decisions should be made, and the flow of information

informal organization (335)—the relationships among positions that are not connected by the organizational chart

job specialization (338)—the division of work into smaller, distinct tasks

job design (338)—the process of grouping tasks into jobs

horizontal specialization (338)—the division of labor at the same level of the organization into simple, repetitive tasks

vertical specialization (338)—the division of labor at different levels of management into different tasks of planning, organizing, leading, and controlling

classical approach to job design (338)—the design of jobs based on the principles of division of labor and job specialization

behavioral approach to job design (340)—the design of jobs based on the view that workers are independent parts of the production process whose individual characteristics should be taken into account in forming jobs

job enlargement (340)—a behavioral approach to job design aimed at increasing the number of tasks that comprise a job

job rotation (341)—a behavioral approach to job design involving a deliberate plan to move workers to various jobs on a consistent, scheduled basis

job enrichment (341)—a behavioral approach in which jobs are designed to increase the number of similar tasks involved, especially tasks that require information processing and decision making

departmentalization (341)—the grouping of related jobs to form an administrative unit

functional departmentalization (343)—the grouping of jobs that perform similar functional activities, such as finance, manufacturing, and human resources

customer departmentalization (344)—the grouping of jobs so that the job holders interact with a specific customer group or clientele

product departmentalization (344)—the grouping of jobs or activities around a firm's principal goods and services

geographic departmentalization (346)—the grouping of jobs according to physical geography

responsibility (347)—the individual's burden of accountability for attainment of the organization's goals

span of control (348)—the actual number of subordinates over which a position has authority

chain of command (349)—an organizing concept that ensures that all positions are directly linked in some way to top management

unity of command (349)—the principle that a subordinate should report to only one immediate superior

scaler chain (349)—the principle of organizing whereby authority should flow through the organization from the top down, one level at a time

delegation (349)—the assignment of work activities and authority to a subordinate

centralization (351)—the pattern of concentrating authority in a relatively few, high-level positions

decentralization (351)—the pattern of dispersing authority to several positions at various levels in the organization

REVIEW QUESTIONS

True/False

Indicate whether the following statements are true or false.

___ 1. The behavioral approach to job design is based on the assumption that increasing job specialization and division of labor increases an organization's overall productivity.

___ 2. Job enlargement is aimed at increasing the number of tasks that comprise a job.

___ 3. One advantage of organizing by product is that it permits the firm to adjust quickly to changes in market needs.

___ 4. The third activity involved in organizing is grouping jobs into departments.

___ 5. No one in an organization can be expected to be responsible for something over which he or she has no authority.

Multiple Choice

Select the best answer for each question.

___ 6. Which is **not** among the reasons for organizing?
- a. achieving synergy
- b. paying for performance
- c. avoiding the duplication of resources
- d. establishing lines of authority
- e. facilitating communication

___ 7. Which of the following is a **disadvantage** of specialization?
- a. Workers can develop and utilize unique skills and knowledge.
- b. The available labor pool for any job is large because many people can perform simple jobs.
- c. Training costs are reduced.
- d. Performing the exact same task over and over becomes boring.
- e. Specialized equipment can be developed profitably.

___ 8. An advantage of this form of departmentalization is that it should give the firm some advantage in addressing the needs of clientele:
- a. functional departmentalization
- b. customer departmentalization
- c. supplier departmentalization
- d. product departmentalization
- e. geographic departmentalization

___ 9. Which form of departmentalization is often employed in smaller companies?
- a. functional departmentalization
- b. customer departmentalization
- c. supplier departmentalization
- d. product departmentalization
- e. geographic departmentalization

a 10. BellSouth Corporation has separate units for information systems, financial services, and mobile systems. BellSouth is organized using which form of departmentalization?
   a. functional departmentalization
   b. customer departmentalization
   c. supplier departmentalization
   d. product departmentalization
   e. geographic departmentalization

Fill in the Blank

11. Job specialization is the division of work into smaller, distinct tasks.
12. Job design is the process of grouping tasks into jobs.
13. The classical approach to job design is based on the principles of division of labor and job specialization.
14. Job enrichment is a behavioral approach in which jobs are designed to increase the number of similar tasks involved, especially tasks that require information processing and decision making.
15. Geographic departmentalization groups jobs according to physical geography.

Matching

Place the corresponding letter of the word or phrase with each definition or description. Each word or phrase can be used only once.

a. responsibility
b. span of control
c. chain of command
d. unity of command
e. scaler chain

d 16. The principle that a subordinate should report to only one immediate superior
a 17. The individual's burden of accountability for attainment of the organization's goals
e 18. The principle of organizing whereby authority should flow through the organization from the top down, one level at a time
b 19. The actual number of subordinates over which a position has authority
c 20. An organizing concept that ensures that all positions are directly linked in some way to top management

Short Answer/Discussion Questions

21. Why do informal relationships occur in an organization?
22. From top management's point of view, what negative effects can result from the informal organization?
23. List the activities typically involved in any organizing effort.
24. Which two basic principles of organization developed during the Industrial Revolution?
25. What problems are associated with product departmentalization?

ANSWERS TO REVIEW QUESTIONS

Text page numbers where the answers can be found are included in parentheses.

1. False (338)
2. True (340)
3. True (345)
4. False (346)
5. True (347)
6. b (333–334)
7. d (339)
8. b (344)
9. a (343)
10. ~~e (346)~~
11. specialization (338)
12. design (338)
13. classical (338)
14. enrichment (341)
15. geographic (346)
16. d (349)
17. a (347)
18. e (349)
19. b (348)
20. c (349)
21. Either, because the nature of the work forces the people occupying those positions to interact to complete the work more efficiently or because they have developed a friendship. (335)
22. Informal organizations are often the source of rumors, and occasionally the informal organization may not hold the same goals and values as the formal organization and may actually work at cross purposes. (336)
23. grouping tasks into jobs, grouping jobs into departments, and determining authority and channels of communication. (336)
24. job specialization and job design. (337–338)
25. an excessive amount of duplication in terms of functional efficiencies, costs, and effort; competition between the departments over organizational resources. (345)

STUDENT EXERCISE

Identifying the Type of Departmentalization

In this chapter, you studied four basic types of departmentalization: functional, customer, product, and geographic. This exercise will give you some practice at identifying these four forms of organizing.

Figure 12.1
Organizational Chart: An International Company

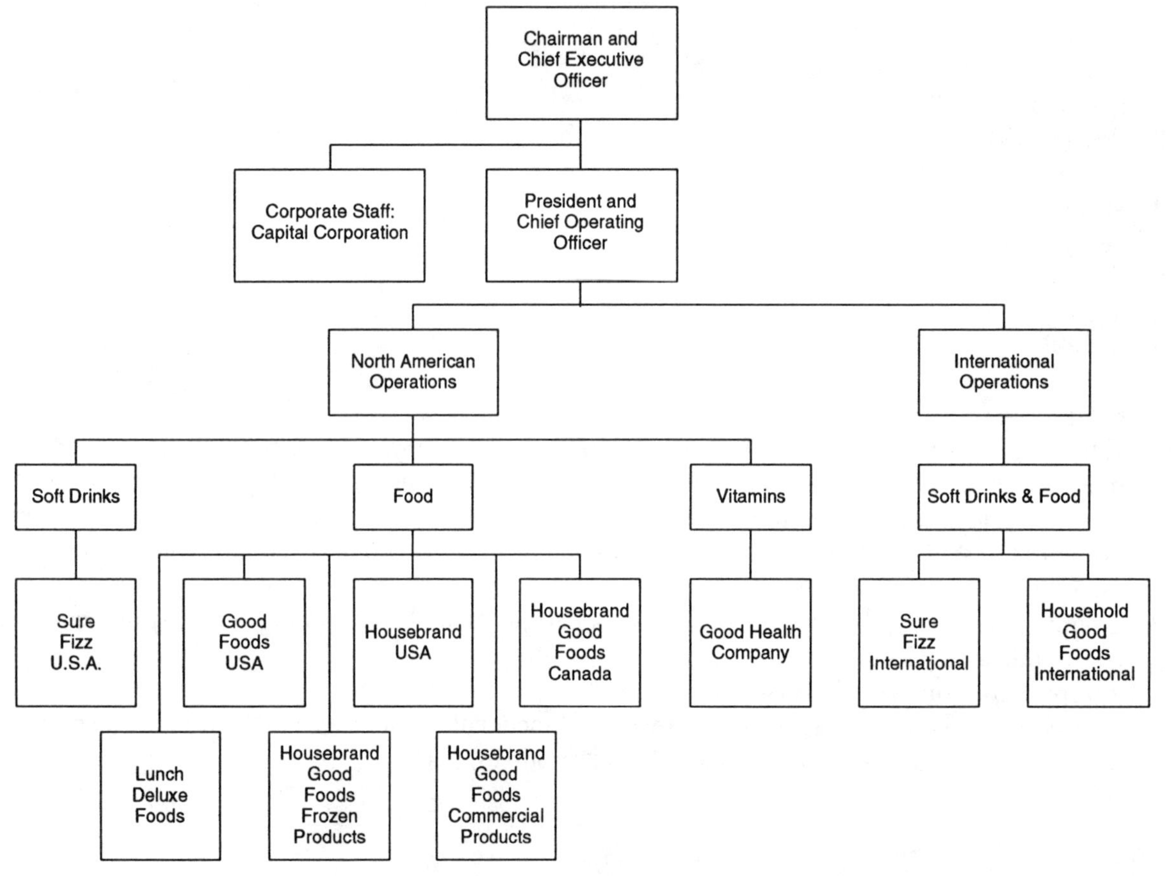

Source: Samuel C. Certo, *Supervision,* Austen Press, © 1993 Richard D. Irwin, Inc., p. 49.

1. What are the two types of departmentalization included in Figure 12.1?

Figure 12.2
Partial Organization Chart for Wiss, Janney, Elster Associates

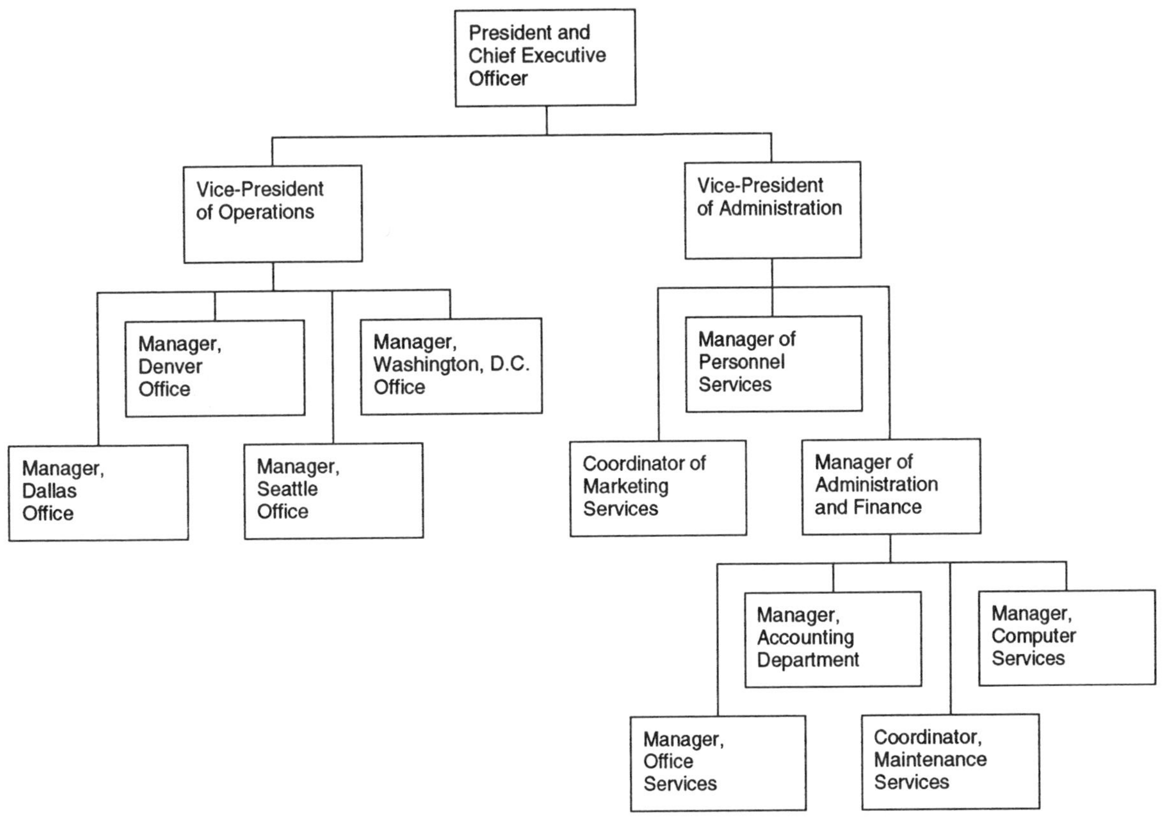

Source: Samuel C. Certo, *Supervision,* Austen Press, © 1993 Richard D. Irwin, Inc., p. 51.

2. What are the two types of departmentalization included in Figure 12.2?

Figure 12.3
Partial Organization Chart for Rosary College

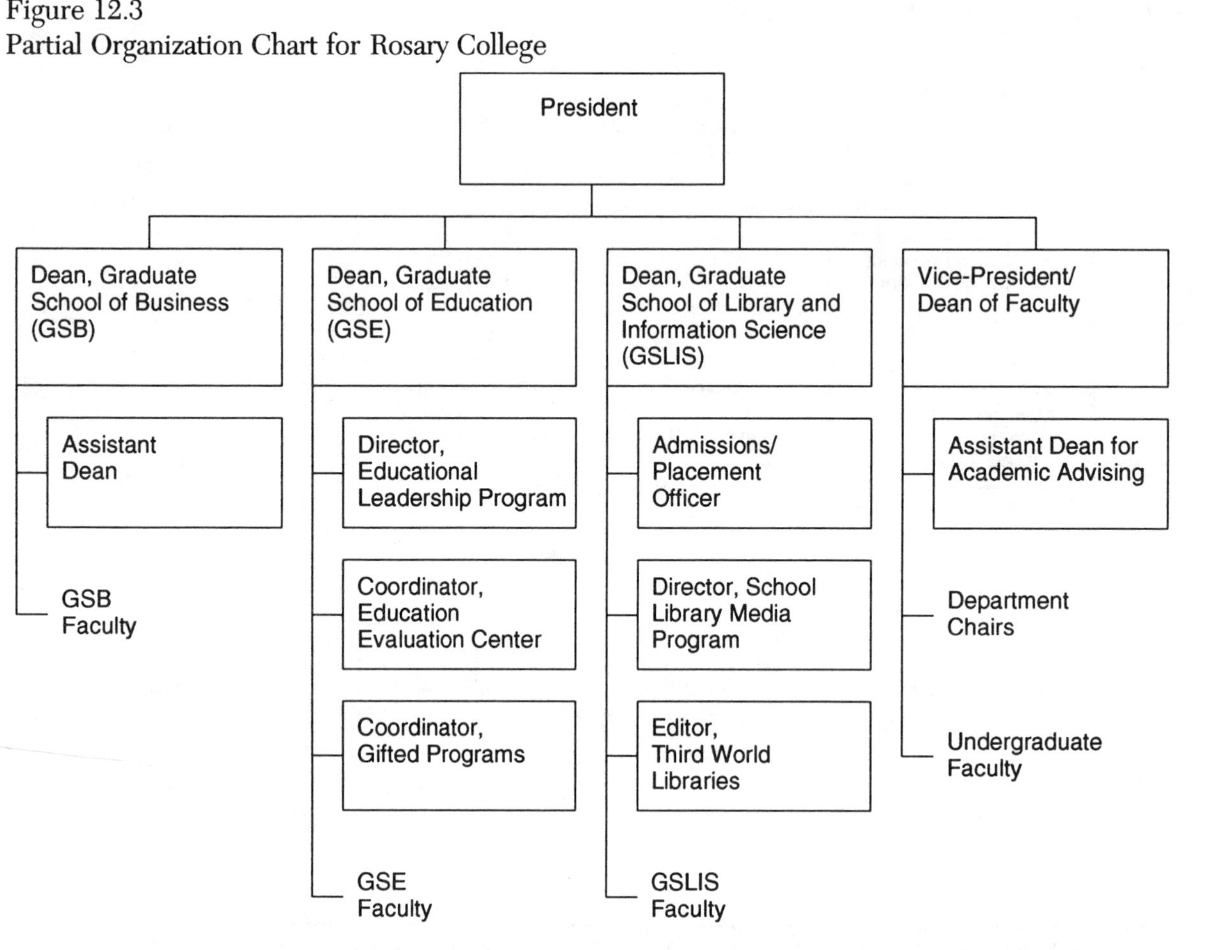

Source: Samuel C. Certo, *Supervision,* Austen Press, © 1993 Richard D. Irwin, Inc., p. 69.

3. What are the two types of departmentalization included in Figure 12.3?

ANSWERS TO STUDENT EXERCISE

1. **geographic** (North American and international operations) and **product** (soft drinks, food, and vitamins)
2. **functional** (personnel services, marketing services, administration and finance) and **geographic** (Denver; Washington, DC; Dallas; and Seattle)
3. **product** (an education and degree in a specific field) and **customer** (students who are interested in a specific product or field of study—four types of customers, graduate business students, graduate education students, graduate LIS students, and undergraduate students)

chapter thirteen

Organizing: Designing the Overall Organization

LEARNING OBJECTIVES

- Describe organizational structure.
- Detect four types of formal structures: functional, multidivisional, matrix, and networks/outsourcing.
- Specify three characteristics that define the latent structure of an organization.
- Summarize the contingency factors that influence the type of formal structure that is best for an organization.
- Describe the different types of coordinating mechanisms that can be used to support the organization structure.
- Distinguish among five organizational archetypes: simple structure, machine bureaucracy, professional bureaucracy, divisionalized form, and adhocracy.
- Assess an organization's structure.

CHAPTER OUTLINE

Coordinating Different Parts of the Organization
- Coordinating Mechanisms
- How Coordinating Mechanisms Work

Configurations of Structural Types
- Simple Structure
- Machine Bureaucracy
- Professional Bureaucracy
- Divisionalized Form
- Adhocracy
- How Best to Structure the Organization

CHAPTER RECAP

Note: Boldface words are major chapter headings.

Introduction

This chapter takes the discussion from Chapter 12 one step further by considering the variety of ways that organizations can be structured and the circumstances that will dictate the form that is most suitable for any given organization.

Structuring the Organization

In Chapter 12, you learned how managers group tasks into jobs and jobs into departments. The following paragraphs describe the different ways organizations can group departments into larger units, either divisions or projects:

1. **Functional structure**—grouping jobs according to similar economic activities, such as finance, production and operations, and marketing.
2. **Multidivisional structure**—organization of departments together into larger groups called divisions, based on the following methods of organizing (all defined under the Key Terms section): product division structure, geographic division structure, customer division structure, holding companies, and hybrid structure.
3. **Matrix structure**—a structure in which members of different functional departments are chosen to work together temporarily on a specific contract or project.
4. **Network organizations and outsourcing** have come into existence in recent years to meet the challenges of a world that is constantly changing. Network organizations do not make a good or provide a service but instead coordinate agreements and contracts with other organizations to produce, distribute, and sell products. Outsourcing is a strategy whereby the organization manufactures critical components, but contracts with other organizations to manufacture less important parts.

Latent Structures: What the Organization Is Really Like

The latent structure of an organization can be categorized according to the degree of centralization, complexity, and formalization.

Types of latent structures can be classified along a continuum where at one end are mechanistic—highly formal, highly complex, and highly centralized—organizations; and at the other end are organic—less formal, fairly simple, and decentralized—organizations.

Relating formal structures to latent structures. Any of the formal structures described at the beginning of the chapter can exhibit any combination of latent structures.

Factors Affecting Organizational Structure

Among the many factors that can affect the choice of appropriate structure for an organization are the following:

1. **Organization size.**
2. **Organization life cycle** (birth, growth, maturity, revival, and decline).
3. **Strategy.**
4. **Environment** (munificent, scarce, stable, and turbulent).
5. **Technology** (small-batch, mass, and continuous).

Putting it together. Organizations must consider the preceding five factors simultaneously when choosing an organizational structure. In some cases, the needs of one factor may contradict the needs of another.

Coordinating Different Parts of the Organization

Managers intending to design an organization have to coordinate many different aspects of the organization, both vertically and horizontally, to derive an effective and efficient organizational structure.

Coordinating mechanisms. The major agents of coordination are the organizational hierarchy, rules and procedures, committees, task forces, and liaison personnel.

How coordinating mechanisms work. Each of these coordinating mechanisms works by bringing together people from different parts and levels of the organization to solve a problem or accomplish a task that requires the cooperation of a diverse group.

Configurations of Structural Types

Researchers have found, by examining many successful organizations, that companies tend to organize using one of five general archetypes:

1. **Simple structure** is a structure with few departments, arranged by function, headed by an entrepreneur/owner, and with few technical support staff.
2. **Machine bureaucracy** is a highly structured, formal organization that emphasizes procedures and rules, has a functional formal structure, and contains a latent structure emphasizing complexity, formalization, and centralization.
3. **Professional bureaucracy** is an organization that has a functional structure, is medium sized, and works best in stable environments, but has primarily professional employees and a decentralized latent structure.

4. **Divisionalized form** is a multidivisional structure or hybrid; typically, a very large corporation that has organized its departments into divisions.
5. **Adhocracy** is a centralized, informal, but complex organization that tries to maintain flexibility in the face of rapid environmental changes by using a matrix or network formal structure.

How Best to Structure the Organization

While organizations tend to fall into one of these five archetypes, there are no two companies that share exactly the same structure. Furthermore, organizational structures change almost continually, always evolving to meet the needs of changing strategies, technologies, environments, and phases of the life cycle.

KEY TERMS

Text page numbers where terms are first defined are in parentheses.

organizational structure (360)—the way managers group jobs into departments and departments into divisions

functional structure (360)—the grouping of jobs according to similar economic activities, such as finance, production and operations, and marketing

multidivisional structure (361)—the organization of departments together into larger groups called divisions

product division structure (361)—the organization of divisions by product

geographic division structure (362)—the organization of divisions by geographic region

customer division structure (363)—the organization of divisions by customer

holding company (364)—an organization composed of several very different kinds of businesses, each of which is permitted to operate largely autonomously

hybrid structure (364)—a combination of several different structures; the most common form of organizational structure

matrix structure (366)—a structure in which members of different functional departments are chosen to work together temporarily on a specific contract or project

network organization (367)—a structure, primarily a command unit, that does not make a good or provide a service but instead coordinates agreements and contracts with other organizations to produce, distribute, and sell products

complexity (370)—the level of differentiation among structural units, including the specialization of jobs, geographical dispersion, and height of the firm

formalization (370)—the degree to which the organization's procedures, rules, and personnel requirements are written down and enforced

mechanistic organization (371)—structures that are highly formal, complex, and centralized

organic organization (371)—structures that are less formal, fairly simple, and decentralized

munificent environment (376)—an environment in which the organization has a large market for its product and has funds needed to continue operations readily available, and other stakeholder groups are satisfied or pleased with the organization's performance

scarce environment (376)—an environment wherein money is tight, the market is stagnant or declining, or stakeholder groups are making conflicting or difficult demands

stable environment (377)—an environment in which stakeholder demands, and specifically customer desires, are well understood and relatively stable over time

turbulent environment (377)—an environment wherein customer or other stakeholder demands are continuously changing or the primary technology of the firm is constantly being improved and updated

small-batch technology (379)—the production of small numbers of goods in response to a specific customer request

mass technology (379)—the production of large numbers of the same product

continuous technology (379)—a method of production in which raw materials flow continuously through a system that transforms them into finished products

coordination (381)—the linking of jobs, departments, and divisions so that all parts of the organization work together to achieve goals

vertical coordination (381)—the integration of succeeding levels of the organization

horizontal coordination (381)—the linking of subunits on the same level

simple structure (383)—a structure with few departments, arranged by function, headed by an entrepreneur/owner, and with few technical support staff

machine bureaucracy (383)—a highly structured, formal organization that emphasizes procedures and rules, has a functional formal structure, and contains a latent structure emphasizing complexity, formalization, and centralization

professional bureaucracy (383)—an organization that has a functional structure, is medium sized, and works best in stable environments, but has primarily professional employees and a decentralized latent structure

divisionalized form (384)—a multidivisional structure or hybrid; typically a very large corporation that has organized its departments into divisions

adhocracy (384)—a centralized, informal, but complex organization that tries to maintain flexibility in the face of rapid environmental changes by using a matrix or network formal structure

REVIEW QUESTIONS

True/False

Indicate whether the following statements are true or false.

___ 1. The matrix structure is an attempt to capture the benefits of both the functional and multidivisional forms while eliminating the disadvantages.

___ 2. As an organization grows in size, the structure tends to become less complicated.

___ 3. An organization in the revival stage of the organization life cycle typically undergoes significant changes in its organization structure.

___ 4. All organizations proceed sequentially through all five phases of the organization life cycle.

___ 5. If an organization's environmental characteristics can be described as munificent and stable, the organization is likely to use a multidivisional or hybrid (mechanistic) structure.

Multiple Choice

Select the best answer for each question.

___ 6. Because it is involved in only one industry, convenience stores, Southland Corporation makes use of which organizational structure?
a. functional
b. multidivisional
c. matrix
d. network organization
e. outsourcing

___ 7. Which organizational structure can be formed based on product, geography, customer, or a combination (hybrid)?
a. functional
b. multidivisional
c. matrix
d. network organization
e. outsourcing

___ 8. Which of the following is a **disadvantage** of multidivisional structure?
a. It permits delegation of decision-making authority.
b. It permits those closest to the action to make the decisions that will affect them.
c. It tends to promote loyalty and commitment among those making the decisions.
d. Work tends to be more innovative and creative.
e. It creates work duplication.

___ 9. Which organizational structure is a variation on the idea of network structures?
   a. functional
   b. multidivisional
   c. matrix
   d. network organization
   e. outsourcing

___10. Which environment is one in which the organization has a large market for its product and has the funds needed to continue operations readily available, and other stakeholder groups are satisfied or pleased with the organization's performance?
   a. steady environment
   b. scarce environment
   c. stable environment
   d. munificent environment
   e. turbulent environment

Fill in the Blank

11. A/an ______________ company describes an organization composed of several very different kinds of businesses, each of which is permitted to operate largely autonomously.
12. A/an ____________ organization is primarily a command unit and does not make a good or provide a service but instead coordinates agreements and contracts with other organizations to produce, distribute, and sell products.
13. ____________ structures describe what an organization is really like and can be categorized according to degree of centralization, complexity, and formalization.
14. _________ technology is the production of large numbers of the same product.
15. ____________ coordination is the linking of subunits on the same level.

Matching

Place the corresponding letter of the word or phrase with each definition or description. Each word or phrase can be used only once.

   a. simple structure
   b. machine bureaucracy
   c. professional bureaucracy
   d. divisionalized form
   e. adhocracy

___16. An organization that has a functional structure, is medium sized, and works best in stable environments, but has primarily professional employees and a decentralized latent structure

___17. A structure with few departments, arranged by function, headed by an entrepreneur/owner, and with few technical support staff

___18. A centralized, informal, but complex organization that tries to maintain flexibility in the face of rapid environmental changes by using a matrix or network formal structure

___19. A multidivisional structure or hybrid; typically a very large corporation that has organized its departments into divisions

___20. A highly structured, formal organization that emphasizes procedures and rules, has a functional formal structure, and contains a latent structure emphasizing complexity, formalization, and centralization

Short Answer/Discussion Questions

21. Contrast mechanistic organizations with organic organizations.
22. Discuss the significance of the organization life cycle as it relates to organizational structure.
23. What are the three basic levels of technology that influence an organization's structure?
24. Contrast committees with task forces.
25. How accurate are the five archetypes of structure in describing individual organizations?

ANSWERS TO REVIEW QUESTIONS

Text page numbers where the answers can be found are included in parentheses.

1. True (366)
2. False (372)
3. True (373)
4. False (374)
5. True (378)
6. a (360)
7. b (361–364)
8. e (365)
9. e (368)
10. d (376)
11. holding (364)
12. network (367)
13. latent (370)
14. mass (379)
15. horizontal (381)
16. c (383)
17. a (383)
18. e (384)
19. d (384)
20. b (383)
21. Mechanistic organizations are highly formal, highly complex, and highly centralized organizations; therefore, they tend to make decisions slowly and are easily bogged down in rules and procedures. Some employees prefer such environments because the rules are well known and well understood. At the other end of the continuum are organic organizations, which are less formal, fairly simple, and decentralized organizations. Organic organizations tend to make decisions quickly, experience rapid change, and can be uncomfortable places at which to work because the rules are not clearly known or understood. (371)
22. A company may try to change its position in the life cycle (birth, growth, maturity, revival, and decline) by changing its structure. A firm in the decline phase may try to spark a revival by changing to a different kind of multidivisional structure, such as going from a geographic divisional structure to a product divisional structure or even to something more dramatic, such as a network structure. (374)
23. small-batch technology, mass technology, and continuous technology. (379)
24. While committees are formal, permanent groups of people brought together to monitor and keep track of ongoing situations, task forces are temporary groups of employees responsible for bringing about a particular change. (382)
25. Because there are so many factors that a company must account for and so many alternate methods it may use in order to facilitate its becoming more efficient and effective, no two companies ever share exactly the same structure. Also, organizational structures change almost continually, always evolving to meet the needs of changing strategies, technologies, environments, and phases of the life cycle. (384)

STUDENT EXERCISE

Rendering Your Decision

This exercise is designed to increase your understanding of the continuum presented in Figure 13.9, Mechanistic/Organic Continuum, on page 371 of the text. Understanding the differences that characterize mechanistic and organic organizations will help you grasp an important concept related to organizational structure.

Background

The case you will be rendering your decision on is *Mechanistic Latent Structure v. Organic Latent Structure*, Case No. 96-10788-9 in the Superior Court of Corporate America. Because the option for trial by jury was waived by the parties, you, acting as judge, will determine the outcome of the case.

Your Task

At the conclusion of closing arguments, the attorney representing the plaintiff and the attorney representing the defendant approach the bench and hand you a document, asking you to base your decision, contrary to the normal procedure, on your personal preferences. You look at the piece of paper in your hand and realize it is an assessment for you to complete and score. The attorneys request that the results of this assessment be used to determine the outcome of the case. You will present your decision to the parties involved using a legal document called the *summary judgment*.

What Type of Organization Do You Prefer?

Directions: Describe the characteristics you prefer to experience in an organization. Use your personal beliefs and values as a guide to score each of the 12 characteristics on a 5-point scale, where 5 means "strongly agree" with the statement and 1 means "strongly disagree." Circle your preference.

		Agree				Disagree
1.	People should know where they fit in a well-defined hierarchy of explicit authority-status relationships.	5	4	3	2	1
2.	Supervision, decisions, and controls should be exercised through a chain of command of clearly understood roles.	5	4	3	2	1
3.	Codified systems of formal rules, policies, and procedures should simplify the handling of routine activities.	5	4	3	2	1
4.	Division of labor should be refined through job specialization.	5	4	3	2	1
5.	Technical competence and seniority should be the basis for job staffing.	5	4	3	2	1
6.	Promotions and pay should be based on individual performance merit.	5	4	3	2	1
7.	Roles should be fluid, changing with new goals and needs.	5	4	3	2	1
8.	Planning should take place throughout the organization; plans should not simply be handed down from the top.	5	4	3	2	1
9.	High involvement in challenging, complex tasks should be a greater source of motivation than management style or formal rewards.	5	4	3	2	1
10.	Teams rather than individuals should be the primary source of output.	5	4	3	2	1
11.	Primary work tasks should occur more in a horizontal work flow than within specialized functional departments with vertical responsibilities.	5	4	3	2	1
12.	Performance should be measured more by external results (customer satisfaction) than by internal statistics (costs per hour).	5	4	3	2	1

Scoring and Interpretation:

Enter the sum of your scores to questions 1-6 here: ______ M
Enter the sum of your scores to questions 7-12 here: _______ O

Subtract the smaller score from the larger. If M is larger, on balance you prefer more mechanistic or bureaucratic organizations. If O is larger, your preference is for organic or flexible organizations.

Source: Robert E. Coffey, Curtis W. Cook, Phillip L. Hunsaker, *Management and Organizational Behavior* (Homewood, IL: Austen Press, 1994), p. 427.

Rendering your decision

The summary judgment (which you may assign the writing of to one of your able paralegals—in other words, it's not part of this exercise) will favor either the plaintiff, Mechanistic Latent Structure, or the defendant, Organic Latent Structure, depending on the difference between your M and O scores. If the difference is 17 or greater, your preference is quite strong. If the difference between your scores is 9 to 16, a moderate preference is indicated; if 1 to 8, your preference is slight. Obviously, a zero is neutral, which will result in a "hung" judge; and the case will have to be retried before a different judge.

chapter fourteen

Managing Human Resources

LEARNING OBJECTIVES

- Discuss the term *human resource management* and its activities.
- Summarize how managers may plan for human resource needs.
- Specify how organizations recruit new employees.
- Explain how companies use application forms, interviews, and tests in selecting new employees.
- Formulate the information used in designing effective training programs.
- Describe the types of performance appraisal.
- Explain the purposes of compensation systems and the basic steps in setting up these systems.
- Summarize some of the major laws that affect employment decisions.
- Assess an organization's attempts to select, train, and appraise its employees with an improved human resource management program.

CHAPTER OUTLINE

Introduction

The Nature of Human Resource Management
- The Importance of Human Resource Management
- Information Needed for Human Resource Management

Human Resource Planning
- Forecasting Demand for Employees
- Forecasting Supply of Employees
- Planning Programs

Recruiting
- The Purposes of Recruiting
- Fulfilling Recruiting Purposes

Selecting Employees
- The Application
- The Interview
- Tests
- Reference Checks

Orientation and Training
- Orientation
- Training

Appraising Performance
- Objective Measures
- Subjective Measures

Compensating Employees
- Determining Compensation
- Benefits

Promoting, Transferring, and Terminating Employees
- Promotions and Transfers
- Termination
- Legal Aspects of Termination

The Legal Environment of Human Resource Management

CHAPTER RECAP

Note: Boldface words are major chapter headings.

Introduction

Because the main purpose of human resource management is to make sure the organization has employees who have the appropriate skills for their jobs, effective human resource management is critical to an organization's success.

The Nature of Human Resource Management

Human resource management includes all activities that forecast the number and type of employees an organization will need and then find and develop employees with necessary skills.

The importance of human resource management (HRM). HRM addresses issues related to increasing the skill levels of employees in order to compete more effectively in our global economy, rewarding employees for high performance, complying with the increased numbers of federal and state laws affecting employer-employee relations, finding employees that have the skills necessary to use new technology in business operations, and also developing technology skills in current employees.

Information needed for human resource management. HR managers need three types of information in making job-related decisions about individuals. The first two types—job characteristics and worker qualifications—are gathered using job analysis. Job analysis identifies the tasks that make up a job; the worker knowledge, skills, and abilities (KSAs) needed on the job; the information, equipment, and materials used; and the working conditions. The third type of information—job performance information—is acquired through the performance appraisal process.

Human Resource Planning

Human resource planning is the forecasting of an organization's future demand for employees and the future supply of employees within the organization and the designing of programs to correct the discrepancy between the two.

Forecasting demand for employees involves predicting how many employees the firm will need in specific jobs in the future.

Forecasting supply of employees involves predicting (1) how many employees there would be in the organization in specific jobs if the HR programs currently in place continue; and (2) how many individuals in the external labor market would have the necessary skills for employment in the organization at a specific time in the future.

Planning programs are based on the demand and supply forecasts. If they are similar, the HR planners may choose to continue current HRM programs. If there is a discrepancy between the two forecasts, then managers must redesign HRM programs either to reduce or increase the supply of employees to meet future demand.

Recruiting

Recruiting is the process of attracting potential new employees to the organization.

The purposes of recruiting are threefold: (1) provide enough applicants from which to select future employees; (2) attract at least minimally qualified applicants; (3) attract a demographically and culturally diverse applicant pool.

Fulfilling recruiting purposes is achieved by the company controlling (1) the sources through which potential applicants are contacted, (2) the information given to applicants, and (3) the contacts between the applicants and the company.

Selecting Employees

Selection is the process of collecting systematic information about applicants and using that information to decide which applicants to hire. When collecting information using the four devices of selection listed below, remember that the questions should reflect the activities of the job to be filled:

1. **The application.**
2. **The interview.**
3. **Tests** (ability tests, performance or work-sample tests, assessment center tests, integrity tests, personality inventories, and physical examinations).
4. **Reference checks.**

Orientation and Training

New hires must be oriented to the organization and trained to do their jobs.

Orientation is the process of familiarizing newly hired employees with fellow workers, company procedures, and the physical properties of the organization.

Training involves a three-step process: (1) identify what the training needs are; (2) develop a training program to meet those needs—on-the-job training, off-job educational program, computer instruction, etc.; and (3) evaluate the results of the training to see if the training was successful.

Appraising Performance

Performance appraisal is a formal measurement of the quantity and quality of an employee's work within a specific period of time.

Objective measures. Objective performance measures count tangible products of work performance. These could be measures of quantity or quality.

Subjective measures. Subjective measures are judgments—made about either workers' traits or workers' behaviors—about how an employee is performing.

Compensating Employees

A compensation system is the basis on which an organization gives money, goods, or services to its employees in exchange for their work.

Determining compensation. To set up a compensation system, a company must determine (1) through wage and salary surveys, what comparable organizations pay some specific jobs, and (2) by using a job evaluation method, the worth of each job to the organization itself. These two factors, in addition to how well or how long individual employees have done that job, determine how individual employees are paid.

Benefits. The major benefits categories are mandatory protection programs (Social Security, unemployment compensation, and workers' compensation), pay for time not worked, optional protection programs, and private retirement plans.

Promoting, Transferring, and Terminating Employees

A major HRM concern is the movement of employees after they have been selected and trained to perform their initial job with the organization.

Promotions and transfers. Promotion is the advancement of a current employee to a higher-level job within the organization, while a transfer is the reassignment of a current employee to another job at the same level as the original job.

Termination. There are two major types of termination: for-cause terminations and layoffs.

Legal aspects of termination. There are a number of factors that limit employment-at-will: Equal employment laws provide protection for a number of demographic groups against disproportionate termination, union contracts give some protection to union members, and wrongful discharge identifies four exceptions to employment-at-will.

The Legal Environment of Human Resource Management

Three main categories of laws affecting human resource management include: (1) equal employment opportunity laws—designed to protect individuals from unfair discrimination in employment decisions; (2) health and safety laws; and (3) labor-management laws.

KEY TERMS

Text page numbers where terms are first defined are in parentheses.

human resource management (HRM) (394)—all activities that forecast the number and type of employees an organization will need and then find and develop employees with necessary skills

job analysis (395)—the systematic process of gathering information about important work-related aspects of a job

human resource planning (395)—the forecasting of an organization's future demand for employees and the future supply of employees within the organization and the designing of programs to correct the discrepancy between the two

recruiting (398)—the process of attracting potential new employees to the organization

selection (400)—the process of collecting systematic information about applicants and using that information to decide which applicants to hire

training and experience form (401)—an application device that presents a small number of the important tasks of a job and asks the applicants whether they have ever performed or been trained in each of the activities

ability tests (402)—paper-and-pencil quizzes, usually multiple choice, that measure an applicant's knowledge of specific work content or cognitive ability

performance or work-sample tests (402)—examinations that verify an applicant's ability to perform actual job behaviors identified from a job analysis

assessment center tests (402)—programs that typically simulate managerial tasks

integrity tests (402)—tests that measure an applicant's attitudes and opinions about dysfunctional behaviors such as theft, sabotage, physical abuse, and substance abuse

personality inventories (402)—programs that measure the thoughts, feelings, and behaviors that define an individual and determine that person's pattern of interaction with the environment

physical examinations (403)—tests that qualify an individual's placement in manually and physically demanding jobs

orientation (404)—the process of familiarizing newly hired employees with fellow workers, company procedures, and the physical properties of the organization

training (404)—the process of instructing employees in their job tasks and socializing them into the organization's values, attitudes, and other aspects of its culture

on-the-job training (405)—a technique in which the employee learns the job tasks while actually performing the job

performance appraisal (407)—a formal measurement of the quantity and quality of an employee's work within a specific period of time

trait appraisal (408)—a subjective evaluation of an employee's personal characteristics such as attitude, motivation, cooperation, and dependability

behavior-based appraisal (408)—a subjective evaluation of the way an employee performs job tasks

compensation system (410)—the basis on which an organization gives money, goods, or services to its employees in exchange for their work

wage and salary survey (411)—a study that tells the company how much compensation is paid by comparable firms for specific jobs the firms have in common

job evaluation methods (411)—techniques that determine the value of an organization's jobs and arrange these jobs in order of pay according to their value

promotion (413)—the advancement of a current employee to a higher-level job within the organization

transfer (413)—the reassignment of a current employee to another job at the same level as the original job

termination (413)—the separation of an employee from the organization

REVIEW QUESTIONS

True/False

Indicate whether the following statements are true or false.

___ 1. The starting point of human resource planning is the organization's strategic plan and goals.

___ 2. Checking references has substantial evidence to support its use in the selection process.

___ 3. On-the-job training, off-job educational programs, and computer instruction are all examples of training methods.

___ 4. Objective performance measures include trait appraisals and behavior-based appraisals.

___ 5. Mandatory benefits include Social Security, unemployment compensation, and health insurance.

Multiple Choice

Select the best answer for each question.

___ 6. Which of the following selection devices is perhaps the most often used?
- a. the application
- b. the interview
- c. tests
- d. physical examinations
- e. reference checks

___ 7. Which test used during the selection process verifies an applicant's ability to perform actual job behaviors identified from a job analysis?
- a. ability tests
- b. performance or work-sample tests
- c. assessment center tests
- d. integrity tests
- e. personality inventories

___ 8. Which of the following training methods used primarily for training managers requires managers to demonstrate how they would carry out a specific activity?
- a. coaching
- b. committee assignments
- c. job rotation
- d. role playing
- e. case study

___ 9. Which performance judgment error do supervisors make when they rate all employees very highly?
- a. leniency error
- b. horn error
- c. severity error
- d. central tendency error
- e. halo error

___10. When an organization stops recruiting and selecting new employees and allows retirements, voluntary resignations, and individual termination to reduce the number of employees, this is called:

a. attrition
b. early retirement programs
c. job sharing
d. reduced work hours
e. group dismissal

Fill in the Blank

11. __________ ______________ is the systematic process of gathering information about important work-related aspects of a job.
12. The three letters in KSAs stand for worker ______________, skills, and ________________.
13. An application device that presents a small number of the important tasks of a job and asks the applicants whether they have ever performed or been trained in each of the activities is called a training and ______________ ___________.
14. __________________ is the process of familiarizing newly hired employees with fellow workers, company procedures, and the physical properties of the organization.
15. ______________ measures are judgments about how an employee is performing.

Matching

Place the corresponding letter of the law with each description. Each answer can be used only once.

a. Title VII of Civil Rights Act of 1964 & Civil Rights Act of 1991
b. Occupational Safety and Health Act of 1970
c. Workers' Compensation
d. Labor Management Relations Act of 1947
e. Fair Labor Standards Act of 1938

___16. Establishes safety standards, inspections of workplaces, and citations for violations of standards

___17. Establishes a minimum wage, requires overtime pay, and provides standards for child labor

___18. Prohibits discrimination based on race, color, religion, sex, and national origin

___19. Provides for payments to workers due to injury or illness, regardless of fault

___20. Establishes that certain union actions are unfair labor practices and permits state right-to-work laws that make union membership nonmandatory

Short Answer/Discussion Questions

21. Cite three reasons for the importance of human resource management.
22. Name the two methods used to forecast demand for employees.
23. Name three purposes of the recruiting function of HR.
24. List the three ways in which organizations move employees after they have been selected and trained to perform their initial job with the organization.
25. Describe the legal aspects of termination.

ANSWERS TO REVIEW QUESTIONS

Text page numbers where the answers can be found are included in parentheses.

1. True (396)
2. False (403)
3. True (405)
4. False (408)
5. False (412)
6. b (401)
7. b (402)
8. d (406)
9. a (409)
10. a (414)
11. job analysis (395)
12. knowledge, abilities (395)
13. experience form (401)
14. orientation (404)
15. subjective (408)
16. b (416)
17. e (416)
18. a (416)
19. c (416)
20. d (416)
21. (a) Organizations use HRM programs to make work-related decisions about employees, which are important in trying to increase the skill levels of employees in order to compete more effectively in our global economy; (b) HR specialists help organizations to comply with the many federal and state laws affecting employer-employee relations and to meet their needs for an effective work force; and (c) with the increasing use of new technology in business operations, HR managers play a key role in helping organizations find employees that have the necessary skills. They also help develop necessary skills in current employees. (394–395)
22. quantitative forecasting methods and qualitative forecasting methods. (396)
23. (1) provide enough applicants from which to select future employees; (2) attract at least minimally qualified applicants; (3) attract a demographically and culturally diverse applicant pool. (398)
24. promotion, transfer, and termination. (413)
25. When terminating employees, be sure to be in compliance with the equal employment laws in that the terminations are not affecting larger percentages of the protected demographic groups than others. Also, if the terminations are taking place in a unionized organization, follow the contract language regarding terminations. Finally, be aware of the wrongful discharge guidelines that identify four instances that are exceptions to the employment-at-will principle. (415)

STUDENT EXERCISE

Effective Human Resources Management Can Reduce Workplace Stress

To further appreciate the importance of human resource management to organizational success, you will complete a stress test that identifies factors related to job stress. As you complete the test, you will note that many of the 46 assessment factors include areas related to the human resource management function.

Background

Northwestern National Life developed The NWNL Workplace Stress Test in 1991 to help employers identify factors that either produce or reduce job stress. In 1992, NWNL refined the test to a cross-section of U.S. private-sector companies. The revised version of the test presented here allows employers to compare their score to other companies on a scale showing low, medium, and high levels for various categories.

Directions

1. Based on the conditions at your current place of employment, place a check mark in the column that represents your level of agreement/disagreement with each statement below. If you are not currently working, you may wish to ask the questions of a friend or family member regarding his or her place of employment.

A. EMPLOYEE SUPPORT AND TRAINING	Disagree Strongly	Disagree Somewhat	Neutral or Don't Know	Agree Somewhat	Agree Strongly
1. Management is supportive of employees' efforts.					
2. Management encourages work and personal support groups.					
3. Management and employees talk openly.					
4. Employees receive training when assigned new tasks.					
5. Employees are recognized and rewarded for their contributions.					
6. Work rules are published and are the same for everyone.					
7. Employees have current and understandable job descriptions.					
8. Management appreciates humor in the workplace.					
9. Employees and management are trained in how to resolve conflicts.					
10. Employees are free to talk with one another.					

B. WORKING CONDITIONS	Disagree Strongly	Disagree Somewhat	Neutral or Don't Know	Agree Somewhat	Agree Strongly
11. Workloads vary greatly for individuals or between individuals.					
12. Employees have work spaces that are not crowded.					
13. Employees have access to the technology they need.					
14. Few opportunities for advancement are available.					
15. Employees are given little control in how they do their work.					
16. Employees generally are physically isolated.					
17. Mandatory overtime is frequently required.					
18. Employees have little or no privacy.					
19. Performance of work units generally is below average.					
20. Personal conflicts on the job are common.					
21. Consequences of making a mistake on the job are severe.					

C. ORGANIZATIONAL CHANGE	Disagree Strongly	Disagree Somewhat	Neutral or Don't Know	Agree Somewhat	Agree Strongly
22. Employees expect that the organization will be sold or relocated.					
23. There has been a major reorganization in the past 12 months.					

D. EMPLOYEE BENEFITS	Disagree Strongly	Disagree Somewhat	Neutral or Don't Know	Agree Somewhat	Agree Strongly
24. Meal breaks are unpredictable.					
25. Medical and mental health benefits are provided by the employer.					
26. Employees are given information regularly on how to cope with stress.					
27. Sick and vacation benefits are below that of similar organizations.					
28. Employee benefits were significantly cut in the past 12 months.					
29. An employee assistance program (EAP) is offered.					
30. Pay is below the going rate.					
31. Employees can work flexible hours.					
32. Employees have a place and time to relax during the workday.					
33. The employer has a formal employee communications program.					

E. PROGRESSIVE PROGRAMS	Disagree Strongly	Disagree Somewhat	Neutral or Don't Know	Agree Somewhat	Agree Strongly
34. Child care programs of referral services are available.					
35. Referral programs or day care for elderly relatives offered.					
36. Special privileges are granted fairly, based on an employee's level.					
37. New machines or ways of working were introduced in the past year.					
38. The employer offers exercise or other stress-reduction programs.					

F. JOB DESIGN AND PHYSICAL ENVIRONMENT	Disagree Strongly	Disagree Somewhat	Neutral or Don't Know	Agree Somewhat	Agree Strongly
39. Work is primarily sedentary or physically exhausting.					
40. Most work is machine-paced or fast-paced.					
41. Staffing or expense budgets are inadequate.					
42. Noise or vibration is high, or temperatures are extreme or fluctuating.					
43. Employees deal with a lot of red tape to get things done.					
44. Downsizing or layoffs have occurred in the past 12 months.					
45. Employees can put up personal items in their work area.					
46. Employees must react quickly and accurately to rapidly changing conditions.					

2. Circle the numbers in the boxes below that correspond with your responses. For example, if you checked "Agree Somewhat" with the first statement, you would circle the "1" in the "Agree Somewhat" column in the first line.

A. EMPLOYEE SUPPORT AND TRAINING

	Disagree Strongly	Disagree Somewhat	Neutral or Don't Know	Agree Somewhat	Agree Strongly
1.	4	3	2	1	0
2.	4	3	2	1	0
3.	4	3	2	1	0
4.	4	3	2	1	0
5.	4	3	2	1	0
6.	4	3	2	1	0
7.	4	3	2	1	0
8.	4	3	2	1	0
9.	4	3	2	1	0
10.	4	3	2	1	0

B. WORK CONDITONS

	Disagree Strongly	Disagree Somewhat	Neutral or Don't Know	Agree Somewhat	Agree Strongly
11.	0	1	2	3	4
12.	4	3	2	1	0
13.	4	3	2	1	0
14.	0	1	2	3	4
15.	0	1	2	3	4
16.	0	1	2	3	4
17.	0	1	2	3	4
18.	0	1	2	3	4
19.	0	1	2	3	4
20.	0	1	2	3	4
21.	0	1	2	3	4

Total for all circled numbers in 1–10: _______

Total for all circled numbers in 11–21: _______

C. ORGANIZATIONAL CHANGE

	Disagree Strongly	Disagree Somewhat	Neutral or Don't Know	Agree Somewhat	Agree Strongly
22.	0	1	2	3	4
23.	0	1	2	3	4

D. EMPLOYEE BENEFITS

	Disagree Strongly	Disagree Somewhat	Neutral or Don't Know	Agree Somewhat	Agree Strongly
24.	0	1	2	3	4
25.	4	3	2	1	0
26.	4	3	2	1	0
27.	0	1	2	3	4
28.	0	1	2	3	4
29.	4	3	2	1	0
30.	0	1	2	3	4
31.	4	3	2	1	0
32.	4	3	2	1	0
33.	4	3	2	1	0

Total for all circled numbers in 22–23: _______

Total for all circled numbers in 24–33: _______

E. PROGRESSIVE PROGRAMS

	Disagree Strongly	Disagree Somewhat	Neutral or Don't Know	Agree Somewhat	Agree Strongly
34.	4	3	2	1	0
35.	4	3	2	1	0
36.	4	3	2	1	0
37.	4	3	2	1	0
38.	4	3	2	1	0

F. JOB DESIGN AND PHYSICAL ENVIRONMENT

	Disagree Strongly	Disagree Somewhat	Neutral or Don't Know	Agree Somewhat	Agree Strongly
39.	0	1	2	3	4
40.	0	1	2	3	4
41.	0	1	2	3	4
42.	0	1	2	3	4
43.	0	1	2	3	4
44.	0	1	2	3	4
45.	4	3	2	1	0
46.	0	1	2	3	4

Total for all circled numbers in 34–38: _______

Total for all circled numbers in 39–46: _______

GRAND SCORE for 1–46: ______

3. Compare your scores with the Scoring Guide below.

Scoring Guide: Work sites that record low stress scores are less likely to suffer the costs associated with high turnover and frequent stress-related illnesses among employees. Scores within ranges were determined by research.

A. EMPLOYEE SUPPORT AND TRAINING

This scale is composed of 10 measures of how well management communicates with employees and encourages a nonthreatening, comfortable work atmosphere. The scale also reflects the adequacy of training, clearness of direction, and fairness of management. A low score on the scale indicates the organization is characterized by behaviors that reduce workplace stress.

Low		Medium		High	
0	14.1	14.2	19.6	19.7	40

B. WORK CONDITIONS

This scale is composed of 11 items measuring how effectively workloads and employees are managed. A low score indicates that management reduces stress by empowering employees, handling personnel issues, ensuring that adequate resources are available, and allocating work effectively and equitably.

Low		Medium		High	
0	17.8	17.9	22.2	22.3	44

C. ORGANIZATION CHANGE

This scale comprises two changes that significantly affect workplace stress: a major reorganization and the expectation that the company will be sold or relocated. A low score indicates fewer stressors related to change.

Low		Medium		High	
0	2.3	2.4	4.6	4.7	8

D. EMPLOYEE BENEFITS

This scale is composed of 10 items describing the employee benefits and workplace amenities that are offered by an organization. Employers who provide a wide range of benefits and competitive compensation will record a lower score and lower organizational stress level.

Low		Medium		High	
0	18.3	18.4	22.1	22.2	40

E. PROGRESSIVE PROGRAMS

This scale is composed of five advanced programs or activities that help employees cope with job stress. A low score indicates lower workplace stress.

Low		Medium		High	
0	12.9	13.0	14.2	14.3	20

F. JOB DESIGN AND PHYSICAL ENVIRONMENT

This scale uses eight characteristics of the organization's working environment that affect stress. The scale reflects type of work, staffing levels, and physical conditions.

Low		Medium		High	
0	15.9	16.0	18.8	18.9	32

GRAND SCORE 0 to 184

This score reflects the overall risk that the organization will suffer from the negative effects of job stress.

Low		Medium		High	
0	81.1	81.2	101.5	101.6	184

4. List the specific areas where your organization is doing an effective job in reducing stress factors—those categories where scoring fell within the low range.

____

____

5. List the areas where your organization's score fell within the high range.

____

____

If given the opportunity, what recommendations would you make to management regarding how they could reduce the stress factors related to those areas that indicate that improvements are necessary (categories falling into the high range)?

____

____

____

6. Is the overall risk for whether your organization will suffer from the negative effects of job stress in the low, medium, or high range (based on your grand score total)? ______________

Source: Reprinted with permission from Northwestern National Life Insurance Company, "Employee Burnout: Causes and Cures," 1992.

chapter fifteen

Building Successful Groups and Teams in Organizations

LEARNING OBJECTIVES

- Distinguish between the terms *group* and *team.*
- Summarize a general model of group effectiveness, including its primary components.
- Describe the types of groups that exist in organizations.
- Specify five stages of group development.
- Discuss how group size, norms, cohesiveness, and trust affect group performance.
- Determine different roles that members can play in a group.
- Relate some of the problems associated with group functioning.
- Analyze a business's use of teams.

CHAPTER OUTLINE

CHAPTER RECAP

Note: Boldface words are major chapter headings.

Introduction

In this chapter, you will learn about group behavior in organizations, with an emphasis on understanding how work groups develop and function, the potential pitfalls they face, and how managers can make groups function more like teams.

The Nature of Groups and Teams

Some experts see the concepts of groups and teams as different, with groups being the more general of the two. In other words, all teams are groups, but not all groups are teams.

Groups versus teams. One major difference between groups and teams revolves around how work gets done. Work groups emphasize individual work products, individual accountability, and even individual-centered leadership. In contrast, work teams share leadership roles, have both individual and mutual accountability, and create collective work products.

Benefits of teams. Teams contribute to the bottom line in the following ways: (1) teams help motivate workers; (2) teams can be a major part of the quality effort; (3) teams help companies be innovative; (4) teams enhance productivity and cut costs; and (5) teams can enhance worker involvement, information sharing, and perceived task/job significance.

A Model of Work Group Effectiveness

Figure 15.1 on page 429 of the text shows that organizational context and group structure and processes interact to influence the effectiveness of work groups and are influenced, in turn, by the groups' results through feedback.

Structural Influences on Group Effectiveness

The following factors influence group effectiveness:

Types of groups. A number of variables can be used in classifying groups. Among these variables are the level of empowerment; whether they are formal or informal groups; whether they are functional or cross-functional groups; and whether their purpose is to recommend things, make or do things, or run things. Specific kinds of groups and teams are task forces, committees, project teams, quality-assurance teams, and self-directed work teams.

Size of groups. Early research suggested that the ideal group size is about seven. Recently, more flexibility is being seen in group size, with as many as 12 members being viewed as a desirable number for most types of teams discussed thus far. In fact, for groups trying to function as teams, 20 may be about as many members as the team can use effectively.

Composition of groups. No group can be successful without the right mix of skills and abilities. Also, the more heterogeneous a group, the more likely it is to be able to solve problems.

Process Influences on Group Effectiveness

Group success depends on how the group develops, the norms that evolve in the group, the roles that members perform, and how well the members perform a number of important group processes.

Stages of group development. Groups have a life cycle that can be described using the following stages: forming, storming, norming, performing, and adjourning.

Group norms. Group norms are important because they prescribe appropriate behavior of group members that help reduce the disruption and chaos that would ensue if group members didn't know how to act. Norms tend to be of three levels: pivotal, relevant, and peripheral (defined in the Key Terms section that follows). Norms are developed over time based on (1) explicit statements of group leaders, (2) some critical event in a group's history, (3) the first behavior patterns that emerge in a group, and(4) a carryover from past experiences.

Group roles. The kinds of roles that emerge in groups include task-specialist roles, maintenance roles, antigroup roles, and boundary-spanning roles (all defined in the Key Terms section that follows).

Group cohesiveness. Cohesiveness refers to the tendency of group members to unite in their pursuit of group goals and to be attracted to the group and each other.

Additional interpersonal processes. A number of interpersonal processes influence the effectiveness of groups. Among them are conflict resolution, trust, and group facilitation.

Contextual Influences on Group Effectiveness

Factors within the overall organization and environment that have a major impact on how groups function include culture, task design/technology, mission clarity, autonomy, feedback mechanisms, reward and recognition systems, training and consultation, and physical environments.

Problems in Groups

Among the problems groups experience are role ambiguity and role conflict; difficulties in establishing positive group norms consistent with the organizational culture; getting the right mix of skills, abilities, and traits; free-riding; and various antigroup behaviors. Two additional problems that may occur in group interaction follow.

Conformity and agreement. Two cases of group conformity are groupthink (a condition in which poor decision making occurs because the desire to maintain group cohesiveness precludes the critical evaluation of alternative courses of action) and Abilene Paradox (a situation that occurs when members of a group publicly agree on a course of action even though there is an underlying consensus agreement that an alternative course is preferred).

Politics. Political maneuvering is considered negative because it consumes valuable time better spent on productive matters, often subverts organizational goals, diverts human energy, and can result in the loss of valuable employees who cannot or do not wish to "play the game." Among the ways managers can minimize the effects of politics are establishing a trusting and honest communication climate, promoting team goals and rewards, discouraging competition for limited outcomes, and rewarding those who help others instead of competing with them.

KEY TERMS

Text page numbers where terms are first defined are included in parentheses.

group (426)—two or more individuals who communicate with one another, share a collective identity, and have a common goal

team (426)—a small number of people with complementary skills who are committed to a common purpose, set of performance goals, and approach for which they hold themselves mutually accountable

empowerment (430)—the extent of a group's authority and ability to make and implement work decisions

formal groups (430)—groups created by the organization that generally have their own formal structure

informal groups (430)—groups that arise naturally from social interaction and relationships and are usually very loosely organized

functional groups (430)—groups that perform specific organizational functions, with members from several vertical levels of the hierarchy

cross-functional groups (430)—groups that cut across the firm's hierarchy and are composed of people from different functional areas and possibly different levels

task force (430)—a temporary group of employees responsible for bringing about a particular change

committee (430)—a permanent formal group that does some specific task; may be either a functional or cross-functional group

project teams (431)—groups similar to task forces, but usually responsible for running an operation and in control of a specific work project

product-development teams (431)—a special type of project team formed to devise, design, and implement a new product

quality-assurance teams (431)—generally small groups formed to recommend changes that will positively affect the quality of the organization's products

self-directed work team (SDWT) (431)—an intact group of employees who are responsible for a *whole* work process or segment that delivers a product or service to an internal or external customer

free-riding (433)—the tendency of some individuals to perform at less than their optimum in groups, relying instead on others to carry their share of the workload

forming stage (435)—the stage when group members meet for the first time or two, become acquainted, and familiarize themselves with the group's task

storming stage (435)—the stage when conflict usually occurs and in which group members begin to assert their roles, jockey for leadership positions, and make known their feelings about a task

norming stage (435)—the stage when conflicts are largely resolved and harmony ensues

performing stage (435)—the stage in which members have reached a level of maturity that facilitates total task involvement

adjourning stage (436)—the stage in which task forces, project teams, or committees complete their task and disband

norms (436)—prescriptions for appropriate behavior of group members that help reduce the disruption and chaos that would ensue if group members didn't know how to act

pivotal norms (437)—standards that are critical for group success

relevant norms (437)—norms that are important, but not as critical as the pivotal norms

peripheral norms (437)—norms that are accepted by some, but are not important for organizational success

socialization (438)—the process by which an individual learns the norms, values, goals, and expectations of the organization

role (439)—a description of the behaviors expected of a specific group member

task-specialist roles (440)—behaviors oriented toward generating information and resolving problems

group-maintenance roles (440)—behaviors that help the group engage in constructive interpersonal relationships and help members fulfill personal needs and derive satisfaction from group participation

antigroup roles (440)—behaviors that disrupt the group, draw attention to individual rather than group functioning, and detract from positive interactions

boundary-spanning roles (441)—group behaviors involving interaction with members in other units of the organization or outside the organization

cohesiveness (441)—the tendency of group members to unite in their pursuit of group goals and to be attracted to the group and each other

competing style (443)—a management style involving a stance of high assertiveness with low cooperation

avoiding style (443)—a style displaying low assertiveness and low cooperation

accommodating style (444)—a style exhibiting low assertiveness and high cooperation

compromising style (444)—a style that reflects a moderate concern for both your goals and the other person's goals

collaborating style (444)—a style displaying both high assertiveness and high competition

facilitators (445)—leaders who help the group overcome internal obstacles or difficulties so that it may achieve desired outcomes

conformity (449)—adherence to the group's norms, values, and goals

Abilene Paradox (450)—a situation occurring when members of a group publicly agree on a course of action even though there is an underlying consensus agreement that an alternative course is preferred

politics (452)—the maneuvering by an individual to try to gain an advantage in the distribution of organizational rewards or resources

REVIEW QUESTIONS

True/False

Indicate whether the following statements are true or false.

___ 1. According to the Model of Work Group Effectiveness, the factors that influence the effectiveness of work groups most directly are those found within the group or team itself: structure and process.

___ 2. Free-riding tends to increase as group size decreases.

___ 3. Regardless of the type or size of a group, none will be successful without the right mix of skills and abilities.

___ 4. The four methods through which norms develop over time include explicit statements, critical events, past experiences, and first behaviors.

___ 5. When a group member exhibits low assertiveness and high cooperation, he or she is using a collaborating style for dealing with conflict.

Multiple Choice

Select the best answer for each question.

___ 6. Which stage of group development is characterized by group members asserting their roles, jockeying for leadership positions, and making known their feelings about a task?
   a. forming
   b. storming
   c. norming
   d. performing
   e. adjourning

___ 7. When group members exhibit such behaviors as setting group standards, encouraging, and gatekeeping, they are performing which group role?
   a. task-specialist role
   b. group-maintenance role
   c. antigroup role
   d. boundary-spanning role
   e. cohesiveness role

___ 8. Which of the following is **not** a contextual influence on group effectiveness?
   a. level of autonomy
   b. feedback mechanisms
   c. reward and recognition systems
   d. physical environments
   e. number of meetings

___ 9. Which problem in groups is characterized by an individual maneuvering to try to gain an advantage in the distribution of organizational rewards or resources?
   a. politics
   b. Abilene Paradox
   c. conformity
   d. role ambiguity
   e. free-riding

___10. What is one way managers can minimize the effects of politics?
   a. keeping important information to themselves
   b. generating destructive competition
   c. promoting team goals and rewards
   d. showing favoritism
   e. encouraging competition for limited outcomes

Fill in the Blank

11. ________________ is the extent of a group's authority and ability to make and implement work decisions.
12. Group __________ are important because they prescribe appropriate behavior for group members and help reduce the disruption and chaos that would ensue if group members didn't know how to act.
13. The process of learning the norms, values, goals, and expectations of an organization is called ________________.
14. The leaders who help the group overcome internal obstacles or difficulties so that it may achieve desired outcomes are called ________________.
15. A special case of groupthink called the ____________ ____________ occurs when members of a group publicly agree on a course of action even though there is an underlying consensus agreement that an alternative course is preferred.

Matching

Place the corresponding letter of the word or phrase with each definition or description. Each word or phrase can be used only once.

   a. task force
   b. committee
   c. project teams
   d. product-development teams
   e. quality-assurance teams

___16. A temporary group of employees responsible for bringing about a particular change

___17. Groups similar to task forces, but usually responsible for running an operation and in control of a specific work project

___18. Generally small groups formed to recommend changes that will positively affect the quality of the organization's products

___19. A special type of project team formed to devise, design, and implement a new product

___20. A permanent formal group that does some specific task; may be either a functional or cross-functional group

Short Answer/Discussion Questions

21. Contrast groups with teams.
22. List five benefits of teams.
23. Of the three levels of norms, which is the most critical for success within a group?
24. When considering the model of the effect of group cohesiveness and norms on performance (Figure 15.5), which combination of cohesiveness and norms may provide the most severe challenge for a manager? Why?
25. List four of the eight symptoms of groupthink.

ANSWERS TO REVIEW QUESTIONS

Text page numbers where the answers can be found are included in parentheses.

1. True (429)
2. False (433)
3. True (433)
4. True (437)
5. False (444)
6. b (435)
7. b (440)
8. e (446)
9. a (452)
10. c (453)
11. empowerment (430)
12. norms (436)
13. socialization (438)
14. facilitators (445)
15. Abilene Paradox (450)
16. a (430)
17. c (431)
18. e (431)
19. d (431)
20. b (430)
21. Groups are more general than teams, meaning all teams are groups, but not all groups are teams. One major difference between groups and teams revolves around how work gets done. Work groups emphasize individual work products, individual accountability, and even individual-centered leadership. In contrast, work teams share leadership roles, have both individual and mutual accountability, and create collective work products. (426–427)
22. Teams contribute to the bottom line in the following ways: (1) teams help motivate workers; (2) teams can be a major part of the quality effort; (3) teams help companies be innovative; (4) teams enhance productivity and cut costs; and (5) teams can enhance worker involvement, information sharing, and perceived task/job significance. (427–428)
23. pivotal norms.(437)
24. groups with low performance norms and high cohesiveness because they have set low standards and members are strongly in agreement on the production level due to their cohesiveness. (442)
25. All eight symptoms are as follows: (1) illusion of invulnerability, (2) illusion of morality, (3) illusion of unanimity, (4) collective rationalization, (5) mindguarding, (6) shared stereotypes, (7) self-censorship, and (8) direct pressure. (450)

STUDENT EXERCISE

Building a Really Great Team

Revisit Figure 15.1 in your text (page 429). The authors stated about this "Model of Work Group Effectiveness" that the "factors that influence the effectiveness of work groups most directly are those found within the group or team itself: structure and process." Let's test that statement by having you answer some questions about your personal experiences in being involved with groups and teams.

1. Think about all the different kinds of groups and teams you've been a member of or involved with. Here's a checklist to help you remember them—with "Other" spaces to fill in ones not listed. Check all that apply.

   School Groups/Teams

   - ❑ Sports teams
   - ❑ Cheerleading squad
   - ❑ Musical groups
   - ❑ Hobby clubs
   - ❑ Language clubs
   - ❑ Study groups
   - ❑ Parent-teacher groups
   - ❑ School committees
   - ❑ Other _______________

   Community and Church Groups/Teams

   - ❑ Fund-raising groups
   - ❑ Church committees
   - ❑ Church groups
   - ❑ Sports teams
   - ❑ Chamber of commerce
   - ❑ Fraternal orders
   - ❑ Political groups
   - ❑ Boy/Girl Scout troops
   - ❑ Volunteer organizations
   - ❑ Special-interest groups
   - ❑ Other _______________

Employment Groups/Teams

- ❑ Management teams
- ❑ Cross-functional teams
- ❑ Problem-solving teams
- ❑ Quality circles
- ❑ Boards of directors
- ❑ Work committees
- ❑ Work-unit teams
- ❑ Project teams
- ❑ Employee committees
- ❑ Labor union groups
- ❑ Work crew
- ❑ Other _______________

2. Go back over all the checked ones and circle those that you would define—any way you like—as a "really great team."
3. Think about the "really great ones" and see if you can capture on paper what was different about these teams that you couldn't say about the teams you didn't choose to circle. What was it that made you feel truly special about being on that "really great" team?

____

____

____

____

____

4. Examine the following table[1] and circle those characteristics from columns two and three that were represented in your "really great" team experiences.

Indicator	***Good Team Experience***	***Not-So-Good Team Experience***
Do members arrive on time?	Members are prompt because they know others will be.	Members drift in sporadically, and some leave early.
Are members prepared?	Members are prepared and know what to expect.	Members are unclear what the agenda is.
Is the meeting organized?	Members follow a planned agenda.	The agenda is tossed aside, and freewheeling discussion ensues.
Do the members contribute equally?	Members give each other a chance to speak; quiet members are encouraged.	Some members always dominate the discussion; some are reluctant to speak their minds.
Do discussions help members make decisions?	Members learn from others' points of view, new facts are discussed, creative ideas evolve, and alternatives emerge.	Members reinforce their belief in their own points of view, or their decisions were made long before the meeting.

[1] Michael D. Maginn, *Effective Teamwork* (Burr Ridge, IL: Business One Irwin/Mirror Press, 1994), p. 10. © 1994 Richard D. Irwin, Inc.

Indicator	***Good Team Experience***	***Not-So-Good Team Experience***
Is there any disagreement?	Members follow a conflict-resolution process established as part of the team's policies.	Conflict turns to argument, angry words, emotion, and blaming.
Is there more cooperation or more conflict?	Cooperation is clearly an important ingredient.	Conflict flares openly, as well as simmering below the surface.
Is there commitment to decisions?	Members reach a consensus before leaving.	Compromise is the best outcome possible; some members don't care about the result.
What are members' feeling after a team decision.	Members are satisfied and valued for their ideas.	Members are glad it's over, but not sure of results or outcome.
Do members support the decision afterward?	Members are committed to implementation.	Some members second-guess or undermine the team's decision.

5. What can you take with you from your positive team experiences and apply to a work-related group or team situation in which you might be involved?

____

____

____

____

____

ANSWERS TO STUDENT EXERCISE

1. After working your way through this question, you may have been involved with more teams than you realized.
2. Typically, most people categorize very few of the teams they've been involved with as "really great."
3. Some responses might include:
   - We all had to pull together.
   - There was a high level of excitement about what we were doing.
   - We believed in what we were doing.
   - We all seemed to have a lot of passion for achieving our goals.
   - We felt like we owned it.
   - There was a clear challenge.
   - We all felt like we could make a difference.
   - People took individual responsibility for doing their best.
   - We looked out for each other and cared about each other as individuals.
4. You should have had most, if not all, of your circled characteristics fall under column two.
5. Answers will vary; however, some ideas include: have a clearly defined and clearly communicated vision or goal for the team that everybody on the team can take ownership of, and establish some guidelines among the team members that include adopting the characteristics of a "Good Team Experience" from the chart.

chapter ■ *sixteen*

Motivating People

LEARNING OBJECTIVES

- Define motivation and explain its importance to managers.
- Compare and contrast the content theories of Abraham Maslow, Frederick Herzberg, and David McClelland.
- Analyze the various process theories relating to how managers can motivate employees, including equity theory, expectancy theory, and the Porter-Lawler expectancy model.
- Determine how managers may use reinforcement theory to motivate employees to behave as expected.
- Explain how goal-setting theory can be used to enhance employee motivation.
- Specify how managers may design jobs or apply strategies to motivate employees.
- Evaluate a company's efforts to motivate its sales team.

CHAPTER OUTLINE

Introduction

What Is Motivation?

- The Importance of Motivation
- Historical Perspectives on Motivation

Content Theories of Motivation

- Maslow's Hierarchy of Needs
- Herzberg's Two-Factor Theory
- McClelland's Achievement Motivation Theory

Process Theories of Motivation

- Equity Theory
- Expectancy Theory
- The Porter-Lawler Expectancy Model

Reinforcement Theory

- Types of Reinforcement
- Schedules of Reinforcement
- Applying Reinforcement Theory

Goal-Setting Theory

Motivation and Job Design
- Hackman and Oldham's Job Characteristics Model
- Flexible-Scheduling Strategies in Work Design
- Paying for Performance

Integration of Motivation Theories

CHAPTER RECAP

Note: Boldface words are major chapter headings.

Introduction

Managers who understand how to motivate their employees can help them be more productive and thus contribute to the achievement of organizational goals.

What Is Motivation?

Because motivation is an inner drive that directs behavior toward goals, it explains why we do what we do. Likewise, a lack of motivation explains why we avoid doing what we should do.

The importance of motivation. Motivation is more than a tool that managers can use to foster employee loyalty and boost productivity. It is a process that affects all the relationships within an organization and influences many areas such as pay, promotion, job design, training opportunities, and reporting relationships. Efforts to motivate employees should consider organizational and individual needs to be successful.

Historical perspectives on motivation. Our current understanding of motivation comes from three distinctive historical approaches: (1) the traditional approach (based on the principle of hedonism, which maintains that people are motivated to seek pleasure and avoid pain); (2) the human relations approach (based on the idea that giving employees feedback and some level of self-esteem and appreciating their performance would best motivate them); and (3) the human resource approach (encompasses, yet goes beyond, the traditional and human relations approaches by viewing workers as complex entities who are valuable resources to the organization as well as important in their own right).

Content Theories of Motivation

Content theories assume that workers are motivated by the desire to satisfy needs; therefore, these theories try to determine "what" motivates employees and seek to identify what their needs are. Three common content theories include the following:

1. **Maslow's hierarchy of needs** theorizes the order in which people strive to satisfy the five basic needs—physiological, security, social, esteem, and self-actualization.
2. **Herzberg's two-factor theory** identifies two categories of job factors: *maintenance factors*—those aspects of a job that relate to the work setting, including adequate wages, comfortable working conditions, fair company policies, and job security—and *motivational factors*—those aspects of

a job that relate to the content of the work, including achievement, recognition, the work itself, involvement, responsibility, and advancement.

3. **McClelland's achievement motivation theory** identifies the needs of achievement, affiliation, and power.

Process Theories of Motivation

Process theories try to determine "how" and "why" employees are motivated to perform. A summary of three process theories follow:

Equity theory states that the extent to which people are willing to contribute to an organization depends on their assessment of the fairness of the rewards they will receive in exchange.

Expectancy theory states that motivation depends not only on how much a person wants something but also on the person's perception of how likely he or she is to get it.

The Porter-Lawler expectancy model, an extension of the expectancy theory, states that satisfaction is the result rather than the cause of performance and that different levels of performance lead to different rewards, which, in turn, produce different levels of job satisfaction.

Reinforcement Theory

Reinforcement theory is a process theory that assumes behavior may be reinforced by relating it to its consequences.

Types of reinforcement include positive reinforcement, negative reinforcement or avoidance, punishment, and extinction—all of which are defined in the Key Terms section that follows.

Schedules of reinforcement are important to reinforcement theory because the timing of reinforcement is just as important as the kind of reinforcement used. Schedules of reinforcement are fixed-interval schedule, variable-interval schedule, fixed-ratio schedule, and variable-ratio schedule—all of which are defined in the Key Terms section that follows.

When **applying reinforcement theory,** managers who want to motivate employees to behave appropriately should carefully consider the long-term effects of punishment and reward before selecting a policy. Research suggests that punishment can be used in the workplace without undesirable side effects. In the long run, however, rewarding appropriate behavior will generally be more effective in modifying behavior.

Goal-Setting Theory

Goal-setting theory recognizes the importance of goals in improving employee performance because goals direct attention and action, mobilize effort, create patterns of persistent behavior, and develop strategies for goal attainment.

Motivation and Job Design

Managers have several strategies that apply various motivation theories to the structuring of jobs in order to increase productivity and morale. Among these strategies are the following:

1. **Hackman and Oldham's job characteristics model** shows how the influence of the five job characteristics (skill variety, task identify, task significance, autonomy, and feedback) on employees'

psychological states (experienced meaningfulness, experienced responsibility, and knowledge of results) results in high work motivation, high work performance, high satisfaction, and low absenteeism and turnover. The model includes a factor called employee growth-need strength, which focuses attention on the fact that managers need to identify employees' needs and design jobs accordingly.

2. **Flexible-scheduling strategies in work design** include flextime, compressed work week, and job sharing—all of which are defined in the Key Terms section that follows.
3. **Paying for performance** is a motivational strategy used by many companies today.

Integration of Motivation Theories

In seeking to understand motivation, it is best to relate the various theories—and the similarities from model to model—to create a synergy. The integrated model provides insights identifying key areas to address in increasing employee motivation.

KEY TERMS

Text page numbers where terms are first defined are in parentheses.

motivation (460)—an inner drive that directs behavior toward goals

morale (460)—the sum total of employees' attitudes toward their jobs, employer, and colleagues

content theories (465)—a group of theories that assume that workers are motivated by the desire to satisfy needs and that seek to identify what their needs are

Maslow's hierarchy of needs (465)—the order in which people strive to satisfy the five basic needs as theorized by Maslow—physiological, security, social, esteem, and self-actualization

maintenance factors (467)—those aspects of a job that relate to the work setting, including adequate wages, comfortable working conditions, fair company policies, and job security

motivational factors (468)—those aspects of a job that relate to the content of the work, including achievement, recognition, the work itself, involvement, responsibility, and advancement

process theories (469)—a set of theories that try to determine "how" and "why" employees are motivated to perform

equity theory (469)—a theory stating that the extent to which people are willing to contribute to an organization depends on their assessment of the fairness of the rewards they will receive in exchange

expectancy theory (470)—a theory stating that motivation depends not only on how much a person wants something but also on the person's perception of how likely he or she is to get it

expectancy (471)—a person's expectation that effort will lead to high performance

instrumentality (471)—a person's expectation that performing a task will lead to a desired outcome

valence (471)—the importance of each potential outcome to the individual

Porter-Lawler expectancy model (472)—an extension of the expectancy theory stating that satisfaction is the result rather than the cause of performance and that different levels of performance lead to different rewards, which, in turn, produce different levels of job satisfaction

reinforcement theory (474)—a process theory that assumes that behavior may be reinforced by relating it to its consequences

behavior modification (474)—an application of reinforcement theory, which involves changing behavior and encouraging appropriate actions by relating the consequences of behavior to the behavior itself

positive reinforcement (474)—the act of strengthening a desired behavior by rewarding it or providing other positive outcomes

avoidance (474)—the act of strengthening a desired behavior by allowing individuals to avoid negative consequences by performing the behavior

punishment (474)—the act of weakening or eliminating an undesired behavior by providing negative consequences

extinction (474)—weakening an undesired behavior by not providing positive consequences

fixed-interval schedule (475)—a pattern of reinforcement at specified periods of time, regardless of behavior

variable-interval schedule (475)—a pattern whereby the period of reinforcement varies between one reinforcement and the next

fixed-ratio schedule (475)—a pattern offering reinforcement after a specified number of desired performance behaviors, regardless of the time elapsed between them

variable-ratio schedule (475)—a pattern whereby the number of behaviors required for reinforcement is varied

goal-setting theory (476)—a theory that recognizes the importance of goals in improving employee performance

flextime (479)—a work schedule that allows employees to choose their starting and ending times as long as they are at work during a specified time period

compressed work week (479)—a four-day (or shorter) period in which an employee works 40 hours

job sharing (479)—a working arrangement whereby two employees do one job

REVIEW QUESTIONS

True/False

Indicate whether the following statements are true or false.

___ 1. Elton Mayo's approach to motivation was based on the principle of hedonism: that people are motivated to seek pleasure and avoid pain.

___ 2. In Herzberg's two-factor theory, the satisfaction of maintenance factors will motivate an individual to excel.

___ 3. In expectancy theory, three basic variables are considered that influence employee motivation: expectancy, instrumentality, and valence.

___ 4. In reinforcement theory, the timing of reinforcement is more important than what kind of reinforcement is used.

___ 5. One of the contributions of Oldham and Hackman to motivational theory is their recognition that different individuals bring different needs to the workplace.

Multiple Choice

Select the best answer for each question.

___ 6. Which historical approach to understanding motivation maintains that the maximum utility for both the company and the workers lies in using as much of the employee's skill and ability as possible to accomplish organizational goals?
a. behavioral approach
b. contingency approach
c. human relations approach
d. human resources approach
e. traditional approach

___ 7. Which of the following is a motivational factor according to the two-factor theory?
a. recognition
b. adequate wages
c. job security
d. comfortable working conditions
e. fair company policies

___ 8. Which of the following is a **false** statement regarding the Porter-Lawler Expectancy Model?
a. Different levels of performance lead to different rewards.
b. Different rewards produce different levels of job satisfaction.
c. Satisfaction is the cause rather than the result of performance.
d. Performance results in both internal and external rewards.
e. Employees can be motivated by the intrinsic satisfaction that comes from performing a task.

___ 9. Which of the following is a job characteristic in Hackman and Oldham's job characteristics model?
a. employee growth-need strength
b. knowledge of the results of the work
c. high-quality performance
d. autonomy
e. experienced meaningfulness of the work

___10. A working arrangement whereby two employees do one job is called:
a. flextime
b. a work-at-home program
c. a compressed work week
d. part-time employment
e. job sharing

Fill in the Blank

11. The sum total of employees' attitudes toward their jobs, employer, and colleagues is called ___________________.
12. Fundamentally, employees are motivated by the nature of the satisfying relationships they have with their supervisors, by the nature of their jobs, and by characteristics of the ___________________.

13. Maslow's hierarchy of needs includes five basic needs—physiological, security, social, ____________, and self-actualization.
14. Hierarchy of needs, two-factor theory, and achievement motivation theory are all classified as ______________ theories of motivation.
15. Fixed-__________ schedule is a pattern offering reinforcement after a specified number of desired performance behaviors, regardless of the time elapsed between them.

Matching

Place the corresponding letter of the theory with the person associated with that theory. Each answer can be used only once.

a. J. Stacy Adams
b. David McClelland
c. Victor Vroom
d. Frederick Herzberg
e. B. F. Skinner

___16. Expectancy theory

___17. Two-factor theory

___18. Reinforcement theory

___19. Equity theory

___20. Achievement motivation theory

Short Answer/Discussion Questions

21. Why has Maslow's hierarchy not found widespread support from management researchers?
22. Contrast content theories with process theories.
23. Use a ratio format to describe the equity theory.
24. What does recent research suggest about applying the reinforcement theory?
25. Name some examples of noncash incentives associated with pay for performance.

ANSWERS TO REVIEW QUESTIONS

Text page numbers where the answers can be found are included in parentheses.

1. False (464)
2. True (468)
3. True (471)
4. False (475)
5. True (479)
6. d (464–465)
7. a (468)
8. c (472)
9. d (478)
10. e (479)
11. morale (460)
12. organization (461)
13. esteem (465)
14. content (465)
15. ratio (475)
16. c (470)
17. d (467)
18. e (474)
19. a (469)
20. b (468)
21. Beyond the first two basic needs, people vary in their need emphasis. The steps in Maslow's hierarchy are not necessarily experienced in a sequential manner: people can have more than one need at the same time. Because of the overly simplified nature of Maslow's model, it provides little to help managers motivate employees. Instead, it functions best in enhancing managers' awareness of individuals' needs and the complex and broad nature of these needs. (467)
22. Whereas content theories try to determine "what" motivates employees, the process theories try to determine "how" and "why" employees are motivated to perform. (469)
23. $\frac{\text{Inputs (Self)}}{\text{Outcomes (Self)}} = \frac{\text{Inputs (Other)}}{\text{Outcomes (Other)}}$ (469)
24. Punishment can be used in the workplace without undesirable side effects. In the long run, however, rewarding appropriate behavior will generally be more effective in modifying behavior. (476)
25. merchandise, travel, recognition, and status. (482)

STUDENT EXERCISE

Playing Hard at Work

In this exercise, you will examine the traditional ways you view work and then you will try viewing work from a nontraditional perspective. This nontraditional perspective of work should provide you with some insights for taking a more motivated approach to job performance.

Directions

Please answer the questions that follow. Discussing your answers with others may provide a broader perspective to the issues raised in this exercise.

1. What is your favorite recreation activity you enjoy during your leisure time? Maybe you have a passion for playing tennis, hiking in the mountains, water skiing, golfing, or bicycling. ________________________

2. What is it about yourself that is different when you're "at play," doing whatever activity it is you enjoy doing, and when you're "on the job," performing a task?

   ____
   ____
   ____
   ____
   ____
   ____

3. What characteristics does "play" possess that "work" often does not that can make "play" more appealing than "work"?

   ____
   ____
   ____
   ____
   ____
   ____

4. Now look at the table that follows. You will note several characteristics of "play" in column one. If some of the ideas you listed in answering question 3 do not appear in the table, fill those ideas in the blank spaces provided at the end of the list.

5. Fill in column two, "Management Application to WORK," by selecting 7–10 characteristics of play from the list and thinking about how managers could make "work" more like "play." For example, night-shift crews and day-shift crews can compete for prizes; or top performers can be named "Employees of the Month."

Characteristics of PLAY	Management Application to WORK
1. Alternatives are available.	
2. New games can be played on different days.	
3. It provides contact with equals, friends, and peers.	
4. It has the flexibility of choosing teammates.	
5. It has a flexible duration of play.	
6. There is a flexible time of when to play.	
7. There is opportunity to be/express oneself.	
8. The opportunity exists to use one's talents.	
9. Skillful play brings applause, praise, and recognition from spectators.	
10. Healthy competition, rivalry, and challenge exist.	
11. The opportunity for social interaction is available.	
12. The opportunity exists for on-going teams to develop.	
13. Mechanisms for scoring one's performance are available (feedback).	
14. Rules assure basic fairness and justice.	
15. Playing involves experiences of achievement, thrill of winning, handling losing with grace, etc.	
16.	
17.	
18.	
19.	
20.	

6. What prevents managers from making work more like play?

___

___

___

7. Are these forces real or imagined?

___

___

___

8. What would be the likely (positive and negative) results of making work more like play?

___

___

___

9. Could others in the organization accept such creative behaviors?

___

___

___

Source: Adapted from Edward E. Scannell and John W. Newstrom, *Still More Games Trainers Play* (New York: McGraw-Hill, Inc., 1991), pp. 265–267. © 1991. Reprinted with permission of McGraw-Hill, Inc.

ANSWERS TO STUDENT EXERCISE

Here are some suggested answers to the questions in this exercise. There are, of course, other possible answers.

1. Answers will vary.
2. Because I have chosen when to play, what to play, and where to play, there are no pressures, deadlines, or requirements imposed on me by others. The freedom that comes from play often does not exist when I'm "on the job," so my approach to both tends to be totally different.
3. Answers in the table after question 5 provide many of the responses for this question.
4. There is no question to answer for question 4—just directions to follow.
5. Many other options apply to this section; here are a few:

    a. Provide employees with a chance to create and express themselves in their work; use job enrichment and job enlargement.

    b. Use job rotation.

    c. Use self-directed work teams; develop group incentive plans.

    d. When there's a job opening in a work group, let the remaining group members be involved in the process of hiring a replacement.

    e. Allow job sharing.

    f. Allow flextime.

    g. Implement appropriate employee suggestions.

    h. Use career paths, educational opportunities, and the assignment of challenging projects.

    i. Give employee of the month awards and other recognition and reward systems that allow for regular recognition; use press releases and employee newsletter announcements.

    j. Have production goals for various teams with competition to see which team does better—the winning team gets an all-expenses paid weekend to some vacation destination.

    k. Organize employee softball or bowling teams.

    l. Provide training opportunities; encourage participation.

    m. Use profit sharing and peer performance appraisals.

    n. Use tactful and consistent discipline.

    o. Have recognition ceremonies where awards are given with a degree of fanfare.

6. Many managers believe that people can't be enjoying themselves *and* be getting work done at the same time. Work, to them, is serious business. Therefore, they tend not to encourage many of the applications outlined in question 5. Many of these options also cause some managers to feel as though they have lost control over employees' behavior because the environment is too loose or because employees have so much say about how, where, and when the work gets done.
7. For the most part, these forces are imagined because research supports there is increased productivity in environments that allow creativity, humor, and other less restrictive behaviors to take place. Obviously, it is possible for everybody to be focused on having fun to the neglect of getting the job done. As with everything in life, balance is necessary.
8. Likely positive results are increased synergy, more creative approaches to solving problems, increased feelings of ownership for what's going on, greater job satisfaction, and increased productivity. Likely

without the right kind of leadership, these systems can be misdirected; and not all employees are suited to many of these approaches.

9. It depends on how they perceive the behaviors. Most likely, however, if others in the organization see tangible results coming out of work groups characterized by such creative behaviors, they will be more inclined to accept the behaviors.

chapter seventeen

Getting Results through Effective Leadership

LEARNING OBJECTIVES

- Differentiate leadership from the process of management.
- List the sources of power leaders use to influence others' behavior.
- Distinguish successful leaders from less-successful leaders and nonleaders, according to their traits.
- Compare and contrast the major dimensions of leadership behavior used in the behavioral theories.
- Summarize the contingency factors covered in Fiedler's contingency theory, Blanchard's situational leadership theory, and path-goal theory.
- Determine what may neutralize, or substitute for, leadership behavior.
- Specify the leadership practices that can contribute to successful transformational leadership and that distinguish it from transactional leadership.
- Evaluate a leader's efforts to manage a crisis situation.

CHAPTER OUTLINE

Introduction

The Nature of Leadership
- Leadership versus Management
- The Sources of Power
- The Use of Power

Trait Approach to Leadership

Behavioral Models of Leadership
- The Ohio State Studies
- The University of Michigan Studies
- The Leadership Grid

Contingency Theories of Leadership
- Situational Leadership Theory
- Fiedler's Contingency Theory
- Path-Goal Theory
- Vroom-Yetton-Jago Participation Model

Current Trends in the Study and Practice of Leadership
- Leadership Substitutes Theory
- Leader-Member Exchange Theory
- Charismatic Leadership
- Transactional versus Transformational Leadership
- The Leadership Challenge

CHAPTER RECAP

Note: Boldface words are major chapter headings.

Introduction

Leadership is one of the most fascinating and discussed aspects of management. This chapter will distinguish leadership from management, examine different sources of leadership power, explore several theories that attempt to determine what makes an effective leader, and will conclude by discussing some of the newer approaches in the study and practice of leadership.

The Nature of Leadership

Leadership is the process of influencing the activities of an individual or group toward the achievement of a goal.

Leadership versus management. Management is a broad concept that encompasses activities such as planning, organizing, staffing, controlling, and leading. Leadership, on the other hand, focuses almost exclusively on the "people" aspects of getting a job done—inspiring, motivating, directing, and gaining commitment to organizational activities and goals.

The sources of power. Leaders, in their efforts to influence the behavior and attitudes of others, have eight major sources of power (all of which are defined in the Key Terms section that follows): legitimate power, reward power, coercive power, expert power, referent power, charisma, information power, and affiliative power.

The use of power. Managers and leaders exercise power to gain an appropriate response from others. Responses from subordinates fall into three major categories: commitment, compliance, or resistance. Commitment is a likely response when leaders use personal sources of power as the primary means of influencing their employees' behavior. Organizational power sources, particularly legitimate and coercive, should be used selectively.

Trait Approach to Leadership

Early research on leadership focused not on the process of influencing others, but on the personal characteristics of the leaders themselves. Experts now recognize that certain traits increase the likelihood that a person will be an effective leader, but they do not guarantee effectiveness, and the relative importance of different traits depends on the nature of the leadership situation. The following list condenses the important primary leadership traits into six core-trait categories: (1) drive, (2) motivation, (3) honesty and integrity, (4) self-confidence, (5) cognitive ability, and (6) business knowledge.

Behavioral Models of Leadership

The Ohio State studies concluded that leadership behavior consists of the two dimensions, called consideration behaviors and initiating-structure behaviors (both defined in the Key Terms section that follows).

The University of Michigan studies, as summarized by Rensis Likert, identified that the most effective managers are called employee-centered leaders, and they engage in both dimensions of leadership behavior (task-oriented and relationship-oriented behaviors). Less-effective managers are mostly directive in their approaches and are called job-centered leaders. All four terms related to this model are defined in the Key Terms section that follows.

The leadership grid, developed originally as a managerial grid by Robert Blake and Jane Mouton, builds on the Ohio State and Michigan studies and depicts a leader's style as a position in or on a 9 x 9 grid. Differing levels of leadership behavior as indicated on the model's two continuums, concern for people and concern for production, combine to form five major styles: impoverished management (1,1), country club management (1,9), authority-compliance management (9,1), middle-of-the-road management (5,5), and team management (9,9).

Contingency Theories of Leadership

Situational leadership theory states that a leader's style should be contingent on subordinates' competence and commitment.

Fiedler's contingency theory suggests that successful leadership requires matching leaders with primarily stable leadership styles to the demands of the situation. Leadership style is measured by the least preferred coworker (LPC) scale. Situational contingencies include: leader-member relations, task structure, and position power.

Path-goal theory is concerned with how a leader affects employees' perceptions of their personal and work goals and the paths to goal attainment. Leader behaviors include directive leadership, supportive leadership, participative leadership, and achievement-oriented leadership. Situational factors that affect what leadership behaviors are appropriate include employees' personal characteristics and environmental pressures and demands with which the employee must cope to accomplish the goal.

The Vroom-Yetton-Jago participation model provides a set of rules for employee participation in decision making. First, analyze the situation according to eight important variables, and then apply the best of five different levels of participation.

Current Trends in the Study and Practice of Leadership

Leadership substitutes theory identifies three situational aspects: leadership substitutes and leadership neutralizers can severely limit the leaders' ability to influence outcomes; while leadership enhancers have a positive impact on the leader behaviors.

Leader-member exchange (LMX) theory provides a description of how leaders develop "unique" working relationships with each of their employees, based on the nature of their social exchanges.

Charismatic leadership, as exhibited in the business world, is characterized by leaders who tend to promote causes that deviate greatly from the status quo; take personal risks that often appear heroic; assess the environment realistically and implement innovative strategies when the environment appears favorable; engage in self-promotion to inspire employees by presenting the status quo as negative and their vision and themselves as the solution; and maintain intensely personal relationships with their followers, based on emotional rather than rational grounds.

Transactional versus transformational leadership highlights the contrast between two major leadership styles currently being discussed by leadership experts: transactional leadership (a more traditional approach in which managers engage in both task- and consideration-oriented behaviors in an exchange manner) and transformational leadership (a style that goes beyond mere exchange relationships by inspiring employees to look beyond their own self-interests and by generating awareness and acceptance of the group's purposes and mission). Characteristics that seem to distinguish transformational leaders from the more traditional transactional leaders are charisma, inspiration, intellectual stimulation and empowerment, individual consideration, change facilitation, and integrity.

The leadership challenge, a book by James Kouzes and Barry Posner, lists five major leadership practices that the authors found present in successful leaders: challenging the process, inspiring a shared vision, enabling others to act, modeling the way, and encouraging the heart.

KEY TERMS

Text page numbers where terms are first defined are in parentheses.

leadership (492)—the process of influencing the activities of an individual or group toward the achievement of a goal

power (493)—a person's capacity to influence the behavior and attitudes of others

organizational power (493)—a person's ability to satisfy or deny satisfaction of anothers' need, based on a formal contractual relationship between an organization and the individual

personal power (493)—a person's ability to satisfy or deny satisfaction of anothers' need, based on an interpersonal relationship between individuals or on his or her personal characteristics

legitimate power (493)—the influence that comes from a person's formal position in an organization and the authority that accompanies that position

reward power (494)—organizational power that stems from a person's ability to bestow rewards

coercive power (494)—an organizationally based source of power derived from a leader's control over punishments or the capacity to deny rewards

expert power (494)—power or influence derived from a person's special knowledge or expertise in a particular area

referent power (495)—personal power that results when one person identifies with and admires another

charisma (495)—the ability to inspire admiration, respect, loyalty, and a desire to emulate, based on some intangible set of personality traits; a personal source of power

information power (495)—power that is a result of having access to important information that is not common knowledge, or of having the ability to control the flow of information to and from others

affiliative power (496)—power that is derived by virtue of a person's association with someone else who has some source of power

consideration behaviors (498)—patterns of being friendly and supportive by listening to employees' problems, supporting their actions, "going to bat" for them, and getting their input on a variety of issues

initiating-structure behaviors (498)—defining and structuring leader-employee roles through activities such as scheduling, defining work tasks, setting deadlines, criticizing poor work, getting employees to accept work standards, and resolving problems

task-oriented behaviors (499)—behaviors—such as planning and scheduling work, coordinating employee activities, and providing necessary supplies, equipment, and technical assistance—designed primarily and specifically to get tasks completed

relationship-oriented behaviors (499)—behaviors such as being considerate, supportive, and helpful to employees by showing trust and confidence, listening to employees' problems and suggestions, showing appreciation for contributions, and supporting employees' concerns

employee-centered leaders (499)—the most effective managers, who engage in both dimensions of leadership behaviors by getting employees involved in the operation of their departments or divisions in a positive and constructive manner, setting general goals, providing fairly loose supervision, and recognizing employees' contributions

job-centered leaders (500)—less-effective managers, who are mostly directive in their approaches and more concerned with closely supervising employees, explaining work procedures, and monitoring progress in task accomplishment

situational leadership theory (501)—a leadership model whose premise is that a leader's style should be contingent on subordinates' competence and commitment

contracting for leadership style (503)—a process whereby employees may not initially agree with a manager's assessment of their developmental level, thus requiring a leader's skill in arriving at an assessment consensus and an agreed-upon leadership style

contingency theory (503)—the suggestion that successful leadership requires matching leaders with primarily stable leadership styles to the demands of the situation

least preferred coworker (LPC) scale (503)—a measurement of a leader's style consisting of a series of adjective continuums

path-goal theory (504)—a model concerned with how a leader affects employees' perceptions of their personal and work goals and the paths to goal attainment

Vroom-Yetton-Jago (VYJ) participation model (507)—a model that provides a set of rules for employee participation in decision making

leadership substitutes (510)—aspects of the task, subordinates, or organization that act in place of leader behavior and thus render it unnecessary

leadership neutralizers (510)—aspects of the task, subordinates, or organization that have the effect of paralyzing, destroying, or counteracting the effect of a leadership behavior

leadership enhancers (510)—aspects of the task, subordinates, or organization that amplify a leader's impact on employees

leader-member exchange (LMX) theory (511)—a description of how leaders develop "unique" working relationships with each of their employees, based on the nature of their social exchanges

transactional leadership (513)—a more traditional approach in which managers engage in both task- and consideration-oriented behaviors in an exchange manner

transformational leadership (513)—a style that goes beyond mere exchange relationships by inspiring employees to look beyond their own self-interests and by generating awareness and acceptance of the group's purposes and mission

REVIEW QUESTIONS

True/False

Indicate whether the following statements are true or false.

___ 1. Legitimate power, reward power, and coercive power are all organizationally based sources of power.

___ 2. The earliest approaches to the study of leadership focused on the process of influencing others.

___ 3. One of the strengths of Fred Fiedler's contingency theory is the strong research-based support that substantiates the use of his LPC scale to measure leadership style.

___ 4. The path-goal theory of leadership states that two categories of situational factors determine appropriate leadership behaviors: (1) employees' personal characteristics and (2) environmental pressures and demands on employees.

___ 5. Charismatic leadership behaviors cannot be learned.

Multiple Choice

Select the best answer for each question.

___ 6. Leaders and managers are said to differ in a number of ways. Which of the following describes leaders more so than managers?
a. They develop stability in response to the complexity of large chaotic organizations.
b. They organize and staff human systems to plan and structure jobs.
c. They set a direction by developing a vision of the future and strategies for change.
d. They execute plans through control and problem solving.
e. They establish a culture of stability with predictable results and moderate, incremental improvements.

___ 7. Which of the following sources of a manager's power is least likely to get commitment from a subordinate?
a. referent power
b. expert power
c. legitimate power
d. charisma power
e. coercive power

___ 8. Researchers at Ohio State University discussed what two major categories of leadership behavior?
a. referent and expert behaviors
b. autocratic and participative behaviors
c. consideration and initiating structure behaviors
d. passive and active behaviors
e. employee-centered and job-centered behaviors

___ 9. Identify the management style Blake and Mouton describe in their leadership grid as emphasizing employee satisfaction often to the detriment of work goal accomplishment.
   a. impoverished management (1,1)
   b. team management (9,9)
   c. authority-compliance management (9,1)
   d. country club management (1,9)
   e. middle-of-the-road management (5,5)

___10. Which of the following is **not** one of the leadership styles used in Hersey and Blanchard's situational leadership theory?
   a. analyzing
   b. directing
   c. coaching
   d. supporting
   e. delegating

Fill in the Blank

11. Leader-member relations, task structure, and position power are all ____________________ contingencies in Fiedler's contingency theory.
12. Four major types of behavior of the ________________ theory are directive, supportive, participative, and achievement-oriented leadership.
13. Leadership ________________ are aspects of the task, subordinates, or organization that have the effect of paralyzing, destroying, or counteracting the effect of a leadership behavior .
14. The ____________________________ ______________ theory describes how leaders develop "unique" working relationships with each of their employees, based on the nature of their social exchanges.
15. The characteristics that seem to distinguish transformational leaders from the more traditional transactional leaders are charisma, inspiration, intellectual stimulation and empowerment, individual consideration, change facilitation, and ____________________.

Matching

Place the corresponding letter of the sources of power with each definition. Each answer can be used only once.

a. legitimate
b. expert
c. referent
d. information
e. affiliative

___16. Power that is derived by virtue of a person's association with someone else who has some source of power

___17. Personal power that results when one person identifies with and admires another

___18. Power or influence derived from a person's special knowledge or expertise in a particular area

___19. Power that is a result of having access to important information that is not common knowledge, or of having the ability to control the flow of information to and from others

___20. The influence that comes from a person's formal position in an organization and the authority that accompanies that position

Short Answer/Discussion Questions

21. List the six core-trait categories that represent the important primary leadership traits.
22. How did Rensis Likert summarize the findings of the University of Michigan studies?
23. Describe the Vroom-Yetton-Jago (VYJ) participation model.
24. Compare transactional leadership with transformational leadership.
25. Compare the five major leadership practices espoused by Kouzes and Posner with the characteristics of transformational leadership.

ANSWERS TO REVIEW QUESTIONS

Text page numbers where the answers can be found are included in parentheses.

1. True (493–494)
2. False (497)
3. False (504)
4. True (506)
5. False (513)
6. c (493)
7. e (496)
8. c (498)
9. d (500)
10. a (502)
11. situational (504)
12. path-goal (505)
13. neutralizers (510)
14. leader-member exchange (511)
15. integrity (514)
16. e (496)
17. c (495)
18. b (494)
19. d (495)
20. a (493)
21. drive, motivation, honesty and integrity, self-confidence, cognitive ability, and business knowledge. (497–498)
22. The most effective managers are employee-centered leaders, who engage in both dimensions of leadership behavior by getting employees involved in the operation of their departments or divisions in a positive and constructive manner, setting general goals, providing fairly loose supervision, and recognizing their contributions. Less-effective managers—job-centered leaders—are mostly directive in their approaches and more concerned with closely directing employees, explaining work procedures, and monitoring progress in task accomplishment. (499–500)
23. The VYJ model provides a set of rules for employee participation in decision making. First, analyze the situation according to eight important variables related to the problem itself or the problem's impact on subordinates. Second, apply the best of five different levels of participation—two autocratic styles (AI and AII), two consultative styles (CI and CII), and one group style (GII). (507–509)
24. Transactional leadership is a more traditional approach in which managers engage in both task- and consideration-oriented behaviors in an exchange manner, while transformational leadership is a style that goes beyond mere exchange relationships by inspiring employees to look beyond their own self-interests and by generating awareness and acceptance of the group's purposes and mission. (513–514)

25. One way to compare the two is by taking the six characteristics that distinguish transformational leaders from the more traditional transactional leaders (left column) and matching them up with the five leadership practices espoused by Kouzes and Posner (right column). There is no direct match-up for the fourth characteristic in the left column; however, individual consideration is inherent in many of the characteristics in the right column.

Characteristics of Transformational Leadership	Kouzes and Posner's Five Major Leadership Practices
• Charisma	• Inspiring a shared vision
• Inspiration	• Encouraging the heart
• Intellectual stimulation and empowerment	• Enabling others to act
• Individual considerations	• (Inherent in several practices)
• Change facilitation	• Challenging the process
• Integrity	• Modeling the way

(514–516)

STUDENT EXERCISE

A Stewardship Leadership Case Study

The authors conclude the chapter by discussing issues related to transformational leadership. The following case study is taken from Peter Block's book entitled *Stewardship: Choosing Service over Self-Interest.* It will provide you with a chance to apply transformational leadership characteristics to solve the problems you identify in the case. After reading the case facts, you will be asked to answer two questions: "What is the problem?" and "What is the solution?"

A CASE STUDY: Sometime Later in the Week

The Need

February 11—My requirements seem simple enough. All winter I have been staring at two telephone poles and their wires winding up the center of my front yard. I finally call the power company to request that the power line to my house be put underground. They tell me that a field technician would have to make a site visit to determine feasibility and cost. I will have to call the field technician between 7:00 and 9:00 in the morning or 3:00 and 4:00 in the afternoon. The field technicians cannot call me; they have too many requests and are presently in the field.

The Players

February 12—I call the field technician. He is busy. I say it is urgent; he comes to the phone. I ask when he can come to the house. He says that this week is booked and he will not schedule next week until Thursday. Besides, the phone company needs to be there at the same time because it is their pole. I ask who coordinates with the phone company. The customer, he says.

February 25—Arthur, the field technician, walks the property. The phone company is in attendance. I ask, "Can we put this power line underground?" Arthur replies, "Don't see why not, but it is not the field technician's call." I ask, "What will it cost?" Arthur says, "It is hard to tell; depends on the length of the distance from the street." Patiently, I ask, "Can you measure the distance?" Arthur measures and, says it is 400 feet from the street. The power company covers the first 150 feet; the rest requires a customer contribution. I ask, "When can it be done?" Arthur doesn't know. He has to go back to the office and calculate the cost and requirements and have the line foreman look at it. He agrees to send me the customer contribution letter. When I pay the money, he can see about scheduling the work. That's fine.

The Squeeze

Four weeks pass. No letter. No word from Arthur. The electrician, contractor, phone company, and cable company all agree this is typical. Hassling does not help. I call Arthur; he is busy. I say it is urgent; he comes to the phone. "Arthur, where is my customer contribution letter? Has the foreman been to the site? When can we schedule the work?" Arthur says he has been busy locating lines. The letter takes about ten minutes to write, but he has been busy locating lines. I ask what I can do to make this a priority. Arthur suggests I call his boss, Mr. Phillips. He is the one having Arthur locate all those lines. He says he will try to get to my job soon.

I call again in four days; he says the letter is going out that very day, even as we speak. I ask what the process is once I pay and return the letter. He says I need the meter moved, hooked up to the panel in the basement, and inspected by the town building inspector. Next, I need to get the phone company to put in a new pole and then contact Arthur, who will have the line foreman schedule the work.

April 5—I get the customer contribution letter. It is called a "customer contribution" to emphasize the point that my payment only covers part of the cost of the job. I make my contribution.

April 8—The meter is approved. The new pole is in place. The contractor who is doing other work on my house says they have been trying to get Arthur going with no success. I call Arthur. He is not available. I say it is urgent; Arthur comes to the phone. I ask what is now needed to get my line in. He says I need to dig the trench, and the foreman has to inspect it. Then, beginning on Thursday, the foreman schedules the work for the following week. Arthur says if I dig the trench by Thursday, the foreman will inspect it on Friday and the crew will be there on Monday to lay the line, rebuild the pole, and remove the old transformer. I agree to have the trench dug by Thursday. I ask what else is required; he says the phone company and cable company have to be there to put their lines in the trench before we can cover it up. All need to be there on Monday at 8:30 a.m. I ask Arthur if he will coordinate with them, since he is doing this with them all the time. No, Arthur says the power company does not get involved in scheduling with other utilities, that is the customer's responsibility. So I contact them all and get them ready to go on Monday.

April 15—The trench was dug by Thursday. Monday morning, on-site are the contractor, the electrician, the cable company, the telephone company, the backhoe operator, and a worker to refill the trench. Six people, organizing their schedules around the power company, are ready to go at 8:30 a.m. The power company does not show. I call Arthur, he is in the field locating lines. At 1:00 p.m., my gang of six gives up waiting. They say this is typical. The phone company and cable company lay their lines, even though we have not gotten the official OK from the power line foreman. At 3:00 p.m., one of the carpenters working on the job sees the yellow truck of the power company. He goes out to see what is happening, and the truck takes off. No contact.

The Crisis

April 16—At 7:00 a.m., I call Arthur. He is tied up. I say it is urgent. Arthur comes to the phone. I ask, "What happened?" He doesn't know; he was out locating lines. I ask when he could find out. He puts me on hold and contacts the line foreman. Arthur comes back and says the line foreman inspected the job on Monday and the trench is fine. I say that the work was scheduled for Monday morning. What happened? He had promised that the inspection would be done the prior Friday. Arthur says he never said that; he claims he had said the inspection would be done Friday or Monday. If I had scheduled all those people there Monday morning, it was my mistake. I ask, "When can we get this scheduled?" Arthur puts me on hold, comes back, and says the foreman will try to schedule the job "sometime later in the week." I lose it. I tell Arthur that I cannot ask six people to be available "sometime later in the week." He says the foreman told him that four of his linemen are in commercial driver's training class this week, so he is shorthanded. Sometime later in the week, they would try to get to the job. I shout to Arthur, "I am a customer, Arthur. Is there anyone in your company who will treat me like a customer?" Arthur thinks for a moment. I can tell it is a difficult question. He says, "If that is what you want, maybe you should try Mr. Graham, supervisor of line foremen." I call Mr. Graham, who does, in fact, treat me like a customer. In an hour, he has called me back and scheduled the job for Thursday, April 18, at 8:30 a.m. Thursday comes and so do the power company, the electrician, the contractor, the tractor operator, and worker; and the job gets done.

WHAT IS THE PROBLEM?

Multiple choice: Circle the number that best answers the question, "What is the problem?"

1. Arthur is an unmotivated worker. He brings his body to work and leaves his mind and his heart at home.
2. Arthur lacks training in customer relations and empowerment.
3. The power company lacks teamwork and coordination among departments. The customer is left to navigate between the silos in the company.
4. The problem is a lack of clear goals. Arthur's boss, Mr. Phillips, has not made it clear to Arthur how to balance locating lines versus satisfying residential customers.
5. Mr. Phillips lacks supervisory skills. Arthur's time is too tightly controlled and Arthur is given no real freedom or responsibility to satisfy customers.
6. The appraisal process does not give adequate emphasis to timeliness or customer service.
7. The power company does not have a strong corporate culture. Arthur has not been enrolled in top management's vision and values, which are to satisfy customers requests.
8. The power company has not made the commitment to total quality. Their "Quality through Excellence" program has somehow missed Arthur.
9. Being a public utility and a virtual monopoly, there is no real economic incentive for Arthur to complete this job.
10. Where is the problem? The job got done. The customer got what he wanted. Why is everybody in such a hurry?
11. All of the above. Therefore, none of the above.
12. Other

WHAT IS THE SOLUTION?

Now that the problem is defined, we need an action plan. Your solution will grow out of your assessment of the problem. Here are some general categories of solutions:

Training

Most companies are investing heavily in training to change Arthur's behavior. Arthur gets trained; Mr. Phillips gets trained. The training can be on total quality, customer focus, team development, and/or dealing with difficult subordinates.

Sign here if you think training is the answer. ______________________________

Communication

Many places have efforts to communicate heavily with Arthur and Mr. Phillips. Meetings are held about the new era of competition, the importance of the customer, the new values, and the change in culture that is required. Videotapes of top management are made for emphasis and for those who cannot attend.

Sign here if you think better communication is the answer. ______________________________

Clear Standards and Rewards

Expectations of both Arthur and Mr. Phillips could be made clearer. Minimum response times could be set for Arthur. The power company's performance appraisal process could focus more on customer service. The customer could be sent surveys on satisfaction, and these could be used in Mr. Phillips' and Arthur's evaluations. In addition, pay and rewards would then be geared to customer outcomes and the new values.

Sign here if you think the answer is better standards and rewards. ______________________

Work Redesign and Self-Management

Another bundle of solutions involves changing practices and redesigning work. Arthur's unit could be organized around the customer, providing one-stop shopping for the customer. Arthur would be part of a team where each member would have the capability to locate a line, price a job, remove a transformer, inspect a trench, schedule an installation, and communicate with other utilities.

Sign here if you think restructuring work is the answer. ______________________

ANSWERS TO STUDENT EXERCISE

All of these actions will help. Their impact will be limited, though, unless the more fundamental beliefs about governance are examined. The power company now operates on the belief that to achieve high performance they need:

- Each department doing one thing and doing it well.
- Clear boundaries between what the power company does and what the customer is responsible for.
- All customers treated the same.
- Sharply defined jobs so Arthur knows exactly what to do.
- Sophisticated ways of measuring costs and pinpointing accountability. Arthur is measured on lines located.
- Bosses that plan and workers that do.
- Training done in a cost-efficient way.
- Employees informed about other operations on a need-to-know basis.
- Job security for employees.

Although these all sound reasonable, a belief in this way of operating is why it takes two months and fourteen phone calls to get a power line placed in a trench. Initiating training, communicating, and creating new rules and new structures, without changing the beliefs about control and consistency, are incomplete solutions. They will yield temporary benefits. They are useful, but not enough to capture a marketplace or make the power company as competitive as it will soon need to be.

"So what's the real answer?" you ask. There is no one solution; but if there were, it would focus on the elements of stewardship, some of which are outlined below:

1. Renegotiate the contract with Mr. Phillips and Arthur about the kind of response time, responsibility, and attention to customers that is now required. They should invite customers to talk to them about what is not working. The new contract includes the fact that changes are needed to move toward the idea of partnership, internally and externally.
2. Arthur and Mr. Phillips have to agree to be accountable for the new expectations and commit to delivering results. No promise, no process. In the long run, no promise, no job.
3. Hold meetings to explain how the whole system works. Employees focus will be on customers, not functions.
4. Eliminate the boundaries of the functional organization. Move from separate units of field technicians, construction, installation, and scheduling toward units organized around customers. Each new unit would expect all members to learn all jobs.
5. Change Arthur's role. Give Arthur the ability to inspect, schedule, price, and coordinate with other utilities, as well as locate lines. Give Arthur a cellular phone so he can talk to customers. Arthur gets his performance reviews from customers and his peers.
6. Have the bosses work for their subordinates. Mr. Phillips becomes accountable to Arthur and also receives his performance review from Arthur. He can coach Arthur for six months, then will most likely become a peer of Arthur with no cut in pay. The goal is to give Arthur the capability of responding the way Mr. Graham did in the story.

7. Promote Mr. Graham to president, and have him and his shrinking executive team be accountable to support Arthur and his team. Since Arthur's team is one of their customers, they need a conversation about how they can help the team. Start inviting Arthur and some of his team to the top group's meetings so Arthur gets a feel for the larger picture.
8. Have Arthur and his team work on what practices and procedures they need to make this work.
9. Have the staff bill their services directly to Arthur's team. Whatever support his team does not think they need from groups like finance, personnel, and systems, should no longer be offered.
10. The team defines what they will be measured on and how they will be tracked The measures have to contain dimensions that are important to customers and address costs, revenue, and the most efficient use of resources.
11. Have the team decide what additional skills they require, and give them a menu of job-related training options to choose from, requiring that they take 80 percent of the training as a team and stay within a certain budget.
12. After a year, change the pay system for Arthur so it reflects whatever system is in place for the top two levels. Arthur is paid on how his department and the power company performs. Keep the option open of rewarding Arthur for exceptional contribution.

Source: Reprinted with permission of the publisher from *Stewardship: Choosing Service over Self-Interest* 1993, pp. 55–61, 218–220, by Peter Block. © 1993 by Peter Block, Berrett-Koehler Publishers, San Francisco, CA.

chapter eighteen

Communicating in Organizations

LEARNING OBJECTIVES

- Define communication and explain its importance to managers.
- Describe the communication process and the factors that affect it.
- Compare and contrast the various communication forms and channels and the "richness" of each.
- Distinguish between formal and informal communication in an organization.
- Determine how groups and teams communicate.
- Detect the barriers to effective communication and specify potential ways to overcome them.
- Critique an organization's communication efforts.

CHAPTER OUTLINE

Introduction

What Is Communication?
- The Importance of Communication
- The Communication Process

Forms of Communication
- Verbal Communication
- Written Communication
- Nonverbal Communication
- Communication Channels

Perception and Distortion

Communicating in Organizations
- Formal Communication Channels
- Informal Communication Channels
- Communication in Groups and Teams

Barriers to Effective Communication

Personal Barriers

Organizational Barriers

Environmental Barriers

Overcoming Communication Barriers

CHAPTER RECAP

Note: Boldface words are major chapter headings.

Introduction

Because managers spend over 75 percent of their time communicating in some way, management and communication go hand in hand.

What Is Communication?

Communication is the process through which information and meaning are transferred from one person to another.

The importance of communication. Managers use communication skills in carrying out the planning, organizing, leading, and controlling functions. Research shows that both organizational and individual performance improve when managerial communication is effective. Likewise, communication competency is a fundamental aspect of job performance and managerial effectiveness.

The communication process. The definite and identifiable components of the communication process are: the sender, encoding, channel, the receiver, decoding, feedback, and noise, all of which are defined in the Key Terms section that follows.

Forms of Communication

In this section, we will examine the three forms of communication (verbal, written, and nonverbal) and conclude with a discussion of the communication channels:

1. **Verbal communication.** Research has found that managers spend as much as 90 percent of their total communication time involved in oral communication. Verbal communication can take place through various channels (such as face to face or over the telephone) and can take place on different levels (individually or in a group).
2. **Written communication.** Written communication, such as memos, reports, and electronic mail, tends to be more accurate than verbal communication because senders take more time to collect, organize, and send the information.
3. **Nonverbal communication.** Nonverbal communication plays a critical role in shared understanding and meaning because it influences messages sent and received. (See the Student Exercise for this chapter for further insights on nonverbal communication.)

Communication channels. Choosing the appropriate channel is an important consideration when communicating information. Routine messages can be effectively communicated through less rich channels, such as written memos. Nonroutine communications are characterized by ambiguity, time, pressure, and surprise, resulting in a high potential for misunderstanding. Therefore, richer channels, such as face to face or telephone, should be used because they encourage immediate feedback and allow for the handling of more cues simultaneously.

Perception and Distortion

Perception is the process through which we receive, filter, organize, interpret, and attach meaning to information taken in from the environment. Distortion is a deviation between the sent message and the received message. Perceptual selection (the choosing of stimuli from the environment for further processing, also known as filtering or screening); perceptual organization (the natural and essential process of organizing, interpreting, and attaching value to the selected stimuli); and stereotyping (a type of perceptual organization in which we categorize people into groups based on certain characteristics, such as race, sex, or education level, and then make generalizations about them according to their group) can impact how meaning is transferred from one person to another.

Communicating in Organizations

Following are three perspectives from which to examine communicating in organizations:

1. **Formal communication channels** are intentionally defined and designed by the organization. They represent the four directions that communication flows within the formal organizational structure: *upward communication* (communication flowing from lower to higher levels of the organization, such as progress reports, suggestions, inquiries, and grievances); *downward communication* (the traditional flow of information from upper organizational levels to lower levels, such as job directions, assignment of tasks, performance feedback, and information concerning the organization's goals); *horizontal communication* (the exchange of information among individuals on the same organizational level, either across or within departments); and *diagonal communication* (the flow of information, often in matrix structures, between individuals from different units and organizational levels).
2. **Informal communication channels** do not abide by the formal organizational hierarchy or chain of command. Two types of informal communication channels are the grapevine and management by walking around (MBWA).
3. **Communication in groups and teams** follows one of three basic communication patterns: the highly centralized wheel pattern, the less centralized Y pattern, and the most decentralized network pattern.

Barriers to Effective Communication

Communication barriers occur at three levels:

1. **Personal barriers** are often the result of differing individual characteristics, semantics, channel selection, consistency of signals, credibility problems, and incrimination.
2. **Organizational barriers** include power and status problems, goal and priority differences, and organizational structure.
3. **Environmental barriers** include noise, information overload, and physical barriers within the environment.

Overcoming communication barriers. You can use several techniques for improving the chances that effective communication will occur. These include listening, providing feedback, being aware of cultural diversity, choosing an appropriate channel, structuring the organization appropriately, and improving interpersonal relationships.

KEY TERMS

Text page numbers where terms are first defined are in parentheses.

communication (526)—the process through which information and meaning are transferred from one person to another

sender (527)—the person who wishes to relay or share particular information and meaning, and initiates the communication process

encoding (528)—the process of transforming information into understandable symbols, typically spoken or written words or gestures

channel (528)—the medium or method used to transmit the intended information and meaning, such as by phone or in person

receiver (528)—the person to whom the information and meaning are sent

decoding (528)—the process of interpreting and attaching personal meaning to the message

feedback (528)—the receiver's response to the sender's communication

noise (528)—anything acting as an information filter, such as knowledge, attitudes, and other factors, that interferes with the message being communicated effectively

verbal or oral communication (529)—words spoken through various channels to convey information and meaning

written communication (530)—information and meaning transferred as recorded words, such as memos, reports, and electronic mail

nonverbal communication (530)—information conveyed by actions and behaviors rather than by spoken or written words

body language (530)—the broad range of body motions and behaviors, from facial expressions to the distance one person stands from another, that send messages to a receiver

channel richness (531)—a channel's ability to transmit information, including the ability to handle multiple cues simultaneously, encourage feedback, and focus personally on the receiver

perception (533)—the process through which we receive, filter, organize, interpret, and attach meaning to information taken in from the environment

distortion (533)—a deviation between the sent message and the received message

perceptual selection (533)—the choosing of stimuli from the environment for further processing; also known as filtering or screening

perceptual organization (533)—the natural and essential process of organizing, interpreting, and attaching value to the selected stimuli

stereotyping (533)—a type of perceptual organization in which we categorize people into groups based on certain characteristics such as race, sex, or education level, and then make generalizations about them according to their group

upward communication (534)—communication flowing from lower to higher levels of the organization, such as progress reports, suggestions, inquiries, and grievances

downward communication (534)—the traditional flow of information from upper organizational levels to lower levels, such as job directions, assignment of tasks, performance feedback, and information concerning the organization's goals

horizontal communication (534)—the exchange of information among individuals on the same organizational level, either across or within departments

diagonal communication (535)—the flow of information, often in matrix structures, between individuals from different units and organizational levels

grapevine (536)—informal communication channels, found in virtually all organizations

gossip chain (536)—the spreading of information by one person to many others

cluster chain (536)—an exchange in which one person or a selected few share information with only a few others

semantics (541)—the different uses and meanings of words, often influencing the effectiveness of a message

information overload (543)—the condition of having too much information to process

REVIEW QUESTIONS

True/False

Indicate whether the following statements are true or false.

___ 1. Research has found that managers spend over 75 percent of their time communicating in some way.

___ 2. If verbal and nonverbal communication contradicts one another, the receiver is likely to give more weight to the verbal communication.

___ 3. The most decentralized group communication pattern is the wheel pattern.

___ 4. Goal and priority differences among organizational functions, departments, or divisions have virtually no impact on how effectively a message will be sent and/or received.

___ 5. The success of the entire organization hinges on effective communication, both internally and externally.

Multiple Choice

Select the best answer for each question.

___ 6. What is the name for the flow of information, often in matrix structures, between individuals from different units and organizational levels?
a. upward communication
b. forward communication
c. horizontal communication
d. diagonal communication
e. downward communication

___ 7. Individual characteristics that can be personal barriers to effective communication include all but which of the following?
a. mood
b. personality
c. power and status
d. basic beliefs
e. social background

___ 8. When a receiver does not consider the sender trustworthy or knowledgeable about the subject being communicated, he or she will most likely be reluctant even to listen to the message. This is an example of which personal barrier to effective communication?
a. semantics
b. channel selection
c. consistency
d. credibility
e. incrimination

___ 9. At what level of listening does the receiver encourage the sender (either verbally or nonverbally) to continue with his or her message?
   a. unrelated listening
   b. tangential listening
   c. active listening
   d. furthering listening
   e. feeling listening

___10. Which of the following is a characteristic of effective feedback?
   a. It focuses on behavior, not personality.
   b. It addresses behavior that the receiver can do nothing about or has no control over.
   c. It is imposed.
   d. It involves making demands.
   e. It is concerned with *why* something happened as opposed to *what* actually happened.

Fill in the Blank

11. ____________________ ____________________, also known as filtering or screening, is the choosing of stimuli from the environment for further processing.
12. While the gossip chain is the spreading of information by one person to many others, the ______________ chain is an exchange in which one person or a selected few share information with only a few others.
13. A form of communication whereby managers informally interact and exchange information with employees by simply circulating around the office or plant on a regular basis is called management by ______________ ______________.
14. ________________ is the different uses and meanings of words, often influencing the effectiveness of a message.
15. When people are apprehensive and, therefore, reluctant to transmit a message because they fear it might anger a boss or make the transmitter look bad, the communication barrier is called ______________________.

Matching

Match the communication channels (16–20) with the corresponding letter representing its correct position on the model of the continuum of channel richness. Each answer can be used only once.

low channel richness	a.	b.	c.	d.	e.	high channel richness

___16. Telephone

___17. Memos, letters

___18. Formal report

___19. Face-to-face verbal

___20. Electronic mail

Short Answer/Discussion Questions

21. Briefly list and describe the key components of the communication process.
22. Discuss how managers can best deal with their organization's grapevine.
23. Name three environmental barriers that can disrupt the communication process.
24. List five steps that can help you be an active listener.
25. What can an organization do to overcome structural communication barriers?

ANSWERS TO REVIEW QUESTIONS

Text page numbers where the answers can be found are included in parentheses.

1. True (526)
2. False (530)
3. False (537)
4. False (542)
5. True (547)
6. d (535)
7. c (539–540)
8. d (541)
9. d (544)
10. a (545)
11. perceptual selection (533)
12. cluster (536)
13. walking around (537)
14. semantics (541)
15. incrimination (542)
16. d (531)
17. b (531)
18. a (531)
19. e (531)
20. c (531)
21. The seven key components of the communication process are (1) sender—the person who wishes to relay or share particular information and meaning and initiates the communication process; (2) encoding—the process of transforming information into understandable symbols, typically spoken or written words or gestures; (3) channel—the medium or method used to transmit the intended information and meaning, such as by phone or in person; (4) receiver—the person to whom the information and meaning are sent; (5) decoding—the process of interpreting and attaching personal meaning to the message; (6) feedback—the receiver's response to the sender's communication; and (7) noise—anything acting as an information filter, such as knowledge, attitudes, and other factors, that interferes with the message being communicated effectively. (527–528)
22. Accept it and control it where and when possible. For example, maintaining open communication channels throughout the organization can help determine what is being said on the grapevine, as well as the information's accuracy. Managers can also use the grapevine to their advantage—as a "sounding device" for possible new policies, for example. (536)
23. Noise, information overload, and physical barriers within the environment. (543)
24. (a) maintain frequent eye contact; (b) be sensitive to nonverbal messages (body language); (c) know yourself (your perceptions and biases); (d) eliminate both physical and mental noise; and (e) remain open-minded and sensitive. (544)
25. Provide employees with proper communication training; foster a climate of trust and openness; ensure that formal communication channels are available in all directions (upward, downward, horizontal, diagonal); encourage the use of multiple channels, including both formal and informal communications. (546)

STUDENT EXERCISE

Being Sensitive to Nonverbal Cues

The authors state on page 531:

> Because nonverbal communication has such a dramatic influence, managers should pay close attention to their nonverbal actions and behaviors when communicating. In particular, they should ensure that their nonverbal messages agree with their verbal or written messages. Managers should also pay attention to the nonverbal messages sent by others; research suggests that the more effective managers tend to be those who are sensitive to nonverbal cues.

This exercise will give you more insight into nonverbal cues so that you can be more sensitive to them.

Directions

1. Study the chart that follows:

Nonverbal Communication Channels

Channel	Explanation	Example(s)
Actions	Body language or kinesics	Facial expressions, eye movements, posture, and gestures
Symbols	Pictures or characteristics that represent meaning	Corporate logos (Prudential's "piece of the rock" or the Rolex crown), computer software icons (clicking the picture of the printer, for example, sends your document to the printer to be printed), road signs and signals (red, yellow, and green lights communicate the same thing no matter what country you're in), and status symbols (what kind of house you live in or the kinds of clothes or jewelry you wear)
Tactile	The use of touch to impart meaning	Patting someone on the back while congratulating them
Vocal	How things are said	Pitch, rate, rhythm, clarity, and changes in loudness all produce different meanings
Use of time	Because time is a continuous and irreversible scarce resource, whom we spend it with and how much we give communicate our feelings about who and what are important to us	Responding quickly to a written communication conveys such meanings as respect, interest, a sense of urgency, or efficiency

Nonverbal Communication Channels *(continued)*

Channel	Explanation	Example(s)
Use of image	People do judge a book by its cover; through clothing and other dimensions of physical appearance, we communicate our values and expectations	This nonverbal communication channel also impacts written communications. Here are some contrasting examples to illustrate: Laser jet vs. dot matrix output Four-color glossy brochure vs. black and white Résumé printed on high-quality, expensive bond paper vs. 3¢ Kinkos copy
Use of space	Also known as proxemics; the way we use physical space to communicate things about us	• Territory—some people sit in the same area of the classroom in every class. When they can't sit in their favorite territory, they feel uncomfortable. In an organizational context, consider a top-floor office with a view versus a basement office with no window—who's more important to the company based on territory assigned? • Things—office arrangement; do people have to talk to each other with barriers between them, such as a big desk, or are the chairs arranged to convey a more open communication environment? • Personal space zones—few people are allowed in our intimate distance, which in the U.S. is 0 to 18 inches. If someone tries to get into our intimate zone who doesn't belong, we find ourselves backing away.

2. Use the 12 questions that follow to practice interpreting nonverbal cues.
3. Read the items in column one labeled "Observed Nonverbal Communication Cue."
4. In column two, fill in which one of the seven nonverbal communication channels (actions, symbols, tactile, vocal, time, image, space) is represented by the cue.
5. In the last column, determine the most likely interpretation you would make from the cue from the "Likely Interpretation Choices" listing that is provided.
6. Because some interpretations may vary from culture to culture, your answers should be based on the U.S. culture.

Likely Interpretation Choices:

a. amazement or doubt
b. embarrassed, nervous, or hiding something
c. excited or angry
d. status and importance
e. honesty, interest, openness, and confidence
f. support, liking, or intimacy
g. agreement
h. does not care
i. frustration
j. evaluation
k. careless
l. owns a Nissan Infiniti

	Observed Nonverbal Communication Cue		**Channel***		**Likely Interpretation**
1.	avoids eye contact with you	1.	____________	1.	____________
2.	large office	2.	____________	2.	____________
3.	direct eye contact	3.	____________	3.	____________
4.	unpolished shoes with worn-down heels	4.	____________	4.	____________
5.	hand rubbing back of neck	5.	____________	5.	____________
6.	a smile and a nod	6.	____________	6.	____________
7.	holding a ring of keys containing emblem	7.	____________	7.	____________
8.	raised eyebrows	8.	____________	8.	____________
9.	gentle touching, like a hand on an arm or a hug	9.	____________	9.	____________
10.	peering over glasses	10.	____________	10.	____________
11.	raising one's voice	11.	____________	11.	____________
12.	frequently late to department meetings	12.	____________	12.	____________

*Select from actions, symbols, tactile, vocal, time, image, and space.

Source: Corinne R. Livesay, *Strengthen Your Skills: A Skills-Building Manual* (Homewood, IL: Austen Press, 1995), pp. 31–33. © 1995 Richard D. Irwin, Inc.

ANSWERS TO STUDENT EXERCISE

Channel		Likely Interpretation	
1.	Actions	1.	b
2.	Use of space	2.	d
3.	Actions	3.	e
4.	Image	4.	k
5.	Actions	5.	i
6.	Actions	6.	g
7.	Symbols	7.	l
8.	Actions	8.	a
9.	Tactile	9.	f
10.	Actions	10.	j
11.	Vocal	11.	c
12.	Use of time	12.	h

chapter nineteen

Organizational Change and Development

LEARNING OBJECTIVES

- Define organizational change and explain the dimensions and types of change.
- Interpret three models of change, particularly the steps involved in the comprehensive model of change.
- Determine the major causes of resistance to change and recommend how managers can deal with change resistance.
- Explain organization development (OD) and summarize the major OD interventions.
- Assess an organization's change program.

CHAPTER OUTLINE

Introduction

The Nature of Organizational Change

- Forces Causing Organizational Change
- Dimensions of Organizational Change
- Types of Organizational Change

Models of Planned Change

- Lewin's Model of Change
- Congruence Model of Change

Comprehensive Model of Planned Change

- Recognizing the Need for Change
- Creating Readiness for Change
- Overcoming Resistance to Change
- Creating a Vision
- Developing Political Support
- Managing the Transition
- Sustaining the Momentum of the Change

Organizational Development

- The Nature of Organizational Development
- OD Interventions

CHAPTER RECAP

Note: Boldface words are major chapter headings.

Introduction

In addressing the process of organizational change, this chapter will teach you about the major forces influencing organization change, the steps and techniques managers may use to deal with the process of planned change, and the people-oriented approaches to planned change, called organizational development.

The Nature of Organizational Change

Organizational change is any modification in the behaviors or ideas of an organization or its units. The following three points will provide more insight about the nature of organizational change:

1. **Forces causing organizational change** include external forces such as technological, economic, sociocultural, political-legal, and international influences, as well as customers, suppliers, competitors, substitutes, and potential new entrants to the industry. These forces were discussed in Chapter 3. The major internal forces for change are owners, top management, and employees, primarily through internal feedback mechanisms. Tremendous impetus for change can occur when the internal forces respond to what is happening in the external environment.
2. **Dimensions of organizational change** include the degree of planning (along a continuum where at one end is reactive change and at the other end is planned change), the degree of planned change (ranging from incremental change to quantum change), the degree of organizational members' involvement in learning how to change, the target of change, and the amount of organization being emphasized.
3. **Types of organizational change** include changes in strategy, organizational structure or design, technology, and human processes and culture—none of which are mutually exclusive.

Models of Planned Change

1. **Lewin's model of change** grew out of the force field analysis technique that depicts the driving forces, which are pushing for change in behavior, and restraining forces, those striving to maintain the status quo, that keep a situation stable. Lewin's model of change has three phases: (a) unfreezing—the disruption of forces maintaining the existing state (state A) or level of behavior; (b) moving—the transition period (state B) during which the behaviors of the organization or department are shifted to a new level (desired state C); and (c) refreezing—the phase in which the organization is stabilized at a new state of behavioral equilibrium (state C).
2. **Congruence model of change,** an outgrowth of the systems approach to organizational theory, emphasizes the interrelationships among the various parts of an organization and how change in one part will cause reactive changes in other parts.

Comprehensive Model of Planned Change

Here is a step-by-step plan for implementing major change that encompasses all of the facets of change discussed thus far and more:

1. **Recognizing the need for change.** The change process begins with someone recognizing a need for change after scanning the organization's environment.
2. **Creating readiness for change.** Preparing people for change requires direct and forceful feedback about the negatives of the present situation, as compared to the desired future state, and sensitizing people to the forces of change that exist in their environment.
3. **Overcoming resistance to change.** Because there will almost always be resistance when change occurs, understanding why resistance occurs can give managers some insight into how to deal with it. Some of the most common reasons for resisting change include uncertainty and insecurity, reaction against the way change is presented, threats to vested interests, cynicism and lack of trust, perceptual differences, and lack of understanding. Strategies managers may apply to deal with resistance to change include education and communication, participation and involvement, facilitation and support, negotiation and agreement, manipulation and co-optation, and coercion.
4. **Creating a vision.** Managers can facilitate change by clearly defining and communicating their vision of where their firms are headed.
5. **Developing political support.** For change to be successful, leaders of change must identify key stakeholders and then develop support within the key political groups.
6. **Managing the transition.** Three major activities are required during the transition period during which the organization learns the behaviors needed to reach the desired future state: activity planning (designing the road map and noting specific events and activities that must be timed and integrated to produce the change); commitment planning (identifying key political powers in the organization and getting them involved in the transition activities in order to gain their support); and management structures (those who help run things during the transition, plan the direction of the changes, and keep ongoing operations running smoothly as the change occurs).
7. **Sustaining the momentum of the change.** Managers can help sustain the momentum of the change by providing resources, developing new competencies and skills, reinforcing new behaviors, and building a support system for those initiating the change.

Organizational Development

Organizational development is an approach to planned change that focuses primarily on people processes as the target of change.

The nature of organizational development. OD can be defined as a systemwide application of behavioral science knowledge to the planned development and reinforcement of organizational strategies, structures, and processes for improving an organization's effectiveness. Six features of OD are (1) it deals with whole systems; (2) it uses behavioral science knowledge; (3) it involves planned change that is characterized by an adaptive, flexible, and ongoing process of diagnosing and solving people-related problems; (4) it involves the creation and reinforcement of change; (5) it can encompass strategy, structure, and process changes; and (6) it focuses on improving organizational effectiveness, in terms of both productivity and quality of work life.

OD interventions. Following are some examples of OD interventions that serve to illustrate the varied nature of the OD approach to change, as well as the different levels at which change might be targeted:

- Survey feedback—the gathering of data through questionnaires and/or personal interviews and the return of that data to employees in a structured form to facilitate discussion and problem solving
- Process consultation—a technique in which a consultant focuses on the dynamic task-related processes and assists the client organization in diagnosing how to enhance these kinds of processes
- Team building—the use of structured group experiences to help ongoing work teams function more effectively through better decision making, goal setting, and intragroup communications
- Intergroup team building—a set of activities designed to facilitate functioning between two or more groups by helping the groups understand and deal with areas of conflict
- Role negotiation—the structuring of interactions between interdependent persons or groups to clarify and negotiate role behaviors and expectations
- Life and career planning—the use of structured counseling and group discussions to assist employees in planning career paths and integrating life and career goals
- Third-party peacemaking—a process in which a consultant facilitates conflict resolution between two individuals
- Techno-structural redesign—a large-scale intervention that involves redesigning the organizational structure to better address environmental contingencies and better utilize information and process technologies
- Job redesign—changing the nature of how tasks are performed
- Grid OD—a six-phase organization intervention that comprehensively and systematically attempts to enhance personal management style, team functioning, intergroup organizational functioning, and the organization's ability to improve its method for solving problems, resolving conflicts, and making decisions

The success of OD interventions depends on matching the correct intervention to the organizational need, the skill of the OD practitioner at implementing the program, and the readiness of the client organization to accept the intervention.

KEY TERMS

Text page numbers where terms are first defined are in parentheses.

organizational change (554)—any modification in the behaviors or ideas of an organization or its units

performance gap (556)—the difference between an organization's desired and actual performance levels

reactive change (557)—a situation in which organizational members react spontaneously to external and internal forces but do little to modify these forces or their behaviors

planned change (557)—the deliberate structuring of operations and behaviors, often in anticipation of environmental forces

incremental change (558)—a relatively small change in processes and behaviors within just one or a few systems or levels of the organization

quantum change (558)—a large-scale planned change in how the firm operates

unfreezing (561)—the disruption of forces maintaining the existing state (state A) or level of behavior

moving (561)—the transition period (state B) during which the behaviors of the organization or department are shifted to a new level (desired state C)

refreezing (562)—the phase in which the organization is stabilized at a new state of behavioral equilibrium (state C)

congruence model of change (563)—an approach that emphasizes the interrelationships between the various parts of an organization and how change in one part will cause reactive change in other parts

comprehensive model of planned change (564)—a step-by-step plan for implementing major change

transition state (570)—the period during which the organization learns the behaviors needed to reach the desired future state

organizational development (OD) (573)—a systemwide application of behavioral science knowledge to the planned development and reinforcement of organizational strategies, structures, and processes for improving an organization's effectiveness

action research (574)—an approach to change that involves an ongoing process of joint (with clients) problem discovery, diagnosis, action planning, action implementation, and evaluation

process consultation (576)—a technique in which a consultant focuses on the dynamic task-related processes and assists the client organization in diagnosing how to enhance these kinds of processes

team building (576)—the use of structured group experiences to help ongoing work teams function more effectively through better decision making, goal setting, and intragroup communications

intergroup team building (577)—a set of activities designed to facilitate functioning between two or more groups by helping the groups understand and deal with areas of conflict

role negotiation (577)—the structuring of interactions between interdependent persons or groups to clarify and negotiate role behaviors and expectations

life and career planning (577)—the use of structured counseling and group discussions to assist employees in planning career paths and integrating life and career goals

third-party peacemaking (577)—a process in which a consultant facilitates conflict resolution between two individuals

techno-structural redesign (577)—a large-scale intervention that involves redesigning the organizational structure to better address environmental contingencies and better utilize information and process technologies

grid OD (577)—a six-phase organization intervention that comprehensively and systematically attempts to enhance personal management style, team functioning, intergroup organizational functioning, and the organization's ability to improve its method for solving problems, resolving conflicts, and making decisions

REVIEW QUESTIONS

True/False

Indicate whether the following statements are true or false.

___ 1. Kurt Lewin devised the "force field analysis" technique, which describes change as consisting of three phases (unfreezing, moving, and refreezing).

___ 2. Lewin's model of change suggests that managers should find ways to unfreeze the existing equilibrium before any change will occur.

___ 3. The change process begins by preparing people for change.

___ 4. In the long run, getting employee participation in change decisions and increased involvement in all aspects of the change may be the single best method to overcome resistance.

___ 5. For change to be successful, leaders of change must identify key stakeholders and then develop support within the key political groups.

Multiple Choice

Select the best answer for each question.

___ 6. Among the internal forces causing organizational change are:
a. owners
b. competitors
c. suppliers
d. customers
e. substitutes

___ 7. Which of the following is **not** an example of types of organizational change:
a. changing strategy
b. changing structure and design
c. changing stakeholders
d. changing technology
e. changing people processes and culture

___ 8. Among the restraining forces in a force field analysis for the automobile industry of the 1970s is:
a. the rising cost of fuel
b. the quality of Japanese cars
c. changing customer values
d. the perceived lack of foreign threats
e. the increased acceptance of foreign products

___ 9. Which source of resistance to change occurs when the change process is not clearly presented, which results in people filling in the information gaps with rumors and speculation and often assuming the worst in terms of personal impact?
a. uncertainty and insecurity
b. perceptual differences
c. threats to vested interests
d. cynicism and lack of trust
e. lack of understanding

___10. Which of the following is a feature of organizational development (OD)?
   a. OD deals with a single function within a system.
   b. OD uses computer-systems or operations-research types of change approaches.
   c. OD involves planned change in the more rigid sense of organizational planning.
   d. OD focuses on the people processes almost exclusively.
   e. OD focuses on improving organizational effectiveness, in terms of both productivity and quality of work life.

Fill in the Blank

11. The difference between an organization's desired and actual performance levels is called its ____________________ ____________.
12. At one end of the continuum that describes the extent to which organizational change is planned is *reactive change;* at the other end is _______________ *change.*
13. At one end of the continuum that describes the degree of change is *incremental change;* at the other end is ______________ *change.*
14. The period during which the organization learns the behaviors needed to reach the desired future state is called the _______________ state.
15. Manipulation occurs when information and decisions are selectively distributed to control the perception of change. __________________ involves having resistant individuals join the change team—specifically to reduce their power to resist, rather than to truly participate.

Matching

Place the corresponding letter of the following OD interventions with each definition or description. Each answer can be used only once.

   a. survey feedback
   b. process consultation
   c. intergroup team building
   d. techno-structural redesign
   e. grid OD

___16. A large-scale intervention that involves redesigning the organizational structure to better address environmental contingencies and better utilize information and process technologies

___17. A six-phase organization intervention that comprehensively and systematically attempts to enhance personal management style, team functioning, intergroup organizational functioning, and the organization's ability to improve its method for solving problems, resolving conflicts, and making decisions

___18. A technique in which a consultant focuses on the dynamic task-related processes and assists the client organization in diagnosing how to enhance these kinds of processes

___19. The gathering of data through questionnaires and/or personal interviews and the return of that data to employees in a structured form to facilitate discussion and problem solving

___20. A set of activities designed to facilitate functioning between two or more groups by helping the groups understand and deal with areas of conflict

Short Answer/Discussion Questions

21. Describe the three phases of Lewin's model for implementing change.
22. Name several important implications of the systems approach to diagnosing and implementing change that the congruence model of change provides.
23. List the three major activities that are required during the transition.
24. What can managers do to sustain the momentum for change?
25. Name the areas, besides psychology, that provide the foundation for organizational development.

ANSWERS TO REVIEW QUESTIONS

Text page numbers where the answers can be found are included in parentheses.

1. False (561)
2. True (563)
3. False (564)
4. True (567)
5. True (570)
6. a (556)
7. c (559–560)
8. d (562)
9. e (566)
10. e (573)
11. performance gap (556)
12. reactive (557)
13. quantum (558)
14. transition (570)
15. co-optation (568)
16. d (577)
17. e (577)
18. b (576)
19. a (575)
20. c (577)
21. (a) unfreezing—the disruption of forces maintaining the existing state (state A) or level of behavior; (b) moving—the transition period (state B) during which the behaviors of the organization or department are shifted to a new level (desired state C); and (c) refreezing—the phase in which the organization is stabilized at a new state of behavioral equilibrium (state C). (562)
22. (a) Managers need to recognize that changes in one area may cause unintended changes in another, as the overall system seeks to regain equilibrium. (b) Because systems tend to seek equilibrium, managers can expect that some changes may be resisted or even nullified by a lack of change in the rest of the system. (c) For significant change to occur, managers may have to intentionally change all or a number of the transformational processes simultaneously and in support of one another so that the new configurations work in harmony to exact improved outputs. (564)
23. activity planning, commitment planning, and management structures (571)
24. Managers can provide resources, develop new competencies and skills, reinforce new behaviors, and build a support system for those initiating the change. (571–572)
25. behavioral sciences, organizational theory, strategy development, and social and technical change. (573)

STUDENT EXERCISE

Making a Change

You will recall the discussion in this chapter of Kurt Lewin's model of change, which includes the three phases of

unfreezing ➔ moving ➔ refreezing

This exercise will allow you to apply Lewin's model of change to a personal behavior or attitude that you want to change. Going through the steps in this process should help you to:
- more thoroughly understand the model of change
- see how difficult it is to change a behavior or attitude
- relate your experience to the difficulties organizations face when implementing change

Directions

You will step through the phases of change by completing the three sections below. In italics in each section, you will be provided with an example of how to apply each of the steps. Use the example provided to help you work through the behavior or attitude you have selected to change.

1. UNFREEZING

   Select a personal behavior or attitude where a performance gap (the difference between your desired and actual performance levels) exists. *(I haven't been exercising for the past three months; I want to establish a regular habit of exercising [swimming, rollerblading, jogging, bicycling, etc.] 30 minutes a day four times a week.)*

   ____
   ____
   ____

   List the ways you will benefit by making this change. *(I will have more energy. I will feel better physically. It's a good way to relieve stress.)*

   ____
   ____
   ____
   ____

2. MOVING

   What new behaviors, values, and attitudes will I need to develop? *(I will set the alarm 30 minutes earlier than normal on Mondays, Wednesdays, Fridays, and Saturdays and will __________ [rollerblade, swim, etc.] 30 minutes each day. In case of inclement weather, I'll ride my indoor exercise bike for 30 minutes. Since tomorrow is Wednesday, I will begin tomorrow morning.)*

3. REFREEZING

   After two weeks of practicing your new behavior or attitude as you have outlined above, answer these questions:

Do you perceive that the change is working in your favor?

If the answer is yes, list how it's working for you. *(I feel better, have more energy, and it's helping me feel fewer effects from the stress in my life than before I started my physical fitness program.)*

____

____

____

____

If the answer is no, list why it's not working for you. *(When the alarm goes off some mornings, I just don't want to get up, and I've missed four of the eight times I was supposed to go during the past two weeks. Because I'm not being consistent with the behavior change, I am not really experiencing the benefits that I had hoped to realize by changing my behavior.)*

____

____

____

____

Identify ways that might help the change be more effective for you. *(Consider trying different days of the week or different times of the day to exercise. Choose several physical fitness activities to rotate among. Try to find a partner to make me accountable for getting up; I couldn't just roll over and go back to sleep if I knew my friend were waiting to play tennis with me. Find a walking or jogging partner and select a scenic route. Listen to a CD or the radio on my Walkman during my physical fitness activity.)*

____

____

____

____

Did you successfully implement the change in your personal life?
❐ yes ❐ no

If the answer is yes, how long did it take you?

Are you ❐ better off *or* ❐ worse off as a result of your change effort?

Application

When you consider how hard it is to change our own attitudes and behaviors, we can better appreciate the challenge organizations face in implementing change that affects many people. We have all experienced the many personal barriers to making a personal behavior change—whether it's trying to improve our study habits, to lose weight, or to be more patient and understanding with others; and that's in situations where we have chosen to make the change.

In organizations, change is less a matter of personal choice and more a matter of being told by someone else what to do. Getting people to change established patterns of behavior that have become comfortable and predictable, just because someone tells them they have to, has a great potential for failure. That's why the principles and techniques presented in this chapter can be helpful in dealing with one of a manager's greatest challenges: implementing change successfully.

Sources: Corinne Livesay, *Management and Organizational Behavior Student Exercise Book*, Austen Press. © 1994, Richard D. Irwin, Inc., pp.158-160.

chapter twenty

Managing Operations and Increasing Productivity

LEARNING OBJECTIVES

- Define operations management and identify the activities associated with it.
- Determine the elements involved in planning and designing an operations system.
- Specify some of the techniques that managers may use to manage inventory.
- Assess the importance of quality in the operations management process.
- Define productivity, explain why it is important, and propose ways to improve it.
- Evaluate operations issues in a franchise operation.

CHAPTER OUTLINE

Introduction

The Nature of Operations Management
- The Transformation Process
- Historical Perspective
- Operations in Service Businesses

Planning and Designing Operations Systems
- Planning the Product
- Designing the Operations Processes
- Planning Capacity
- Planning Facilities

Managing Inventory
- Purchasing
- Inventory Control
- Routing and Scheduling

Managing Quality
- Establishing Standards
- Inspection
- Sampling

Managing Productivity
- Measuring Productivity
- The Importance of Productivity
- Improving Productivity

CHAPTER RECAP

Note: Boldface words are major chapter headings.

Introduction

Within an organization, the operations function is responsible for ensuring that the firm uses resources as effectively and efficiently as possible.

The Nature of Operations Management

Operations management—the development and administration of the activities involved in transforming resources into goods and services—is the "core" of most organizations because it is responsible for the creation of the organization's products.

The transformation process. At the heart of operations management (OM) is the transformation process through which *inputs* (resources such as labor, money, materials, information, energy) are converted into *outputs* (goods, services, and ideas). The transformation process combines inputs in predetermined ways, using different equipment, administrative procedures, and technology to create a product.

Historical perspective. Historically, operations was known as "production management," or "manufacturing," with a focus on the manufacture of physical goods. The change from "production" to "operations" represents a broadening of the discipline to include the increasing importance of service organizations. Therefore, manufacturing and production relate to those activities and processes used in making tangible products, whereas operations is the broader term used to describe those processes used in the making of both tangible and intangible products.

Operations in service businesses. Manufacturers and service providers differ in five areas:

- Nature and consumption of their output
- Uniformity of inputs
- Uniformity of their output
- Amount of labor required to produce an output
- Measurement of productivity for each output provided

Planning and Designing Operations Systems

1. **Planning the product.** This step begins with market research to determine what consumers want and follows with the designing of a product or service to satisfy that want. In addition, operations managers must plan for the types and quantities of materials needed to produce the product, the skills and quantity of people needed to make the product, and the actual processes through which the inputs must pass in their transformation to outputs.
2. **Designing the operations processes.** Before beginning production, a firm must first determine the appropriate method of transforming resources into the desired product.
3. **Planning capacity.** Capacity refers to the maximum load that an organizational unit can carry or operate at a given point in time. Efficiently planning the organization's capacity needs, whether for the long or short run, is an important process for the operations manager.

4. **Planning facilities.** Manufacturers must make decisions on the following factors:
   - Facility location
   - Facility layout (three basic options: fixed-position layout, process layout, and product layout)
   - Technology
   - Computer applications (CAD/CAM, monitoring transformation process, and flexible manufacturing)
   - Robotics

Managing Inventory

Three basic types of inventory are finished-goods inventory, work-in-process inventory, and raw materials inventory.

Purchasing is the buying of all the materials needed by the organization; it is also known as procurement.

Inventory control is the process of determining how many supplies and goods are needed and keeping track of quantities on hand, where each item is, and who is responsible for it. Approaches to inventory control include economic order quantity (EOQ), just-in-time (JIT) inventory management, material-requirements planning (MRP), and manufacturing-resource planning (MRPII)—all of which are defined in the Key Terms section that follows.

Routing is the sequence of operations through which a product must pass **and scheduling** is the assigning of work to be done to departments or to specific machines or persons. Two popular scheduling techniques are the Program Evaluation and Review Technique (PERT) and the Gantt chart, both of which are defined in the Key Terms section that follows.

Managing Quality

Because defective products can quickly ruin a firm, quality, like cost, is a critical element of OM. Therefore, quality control is the activity an organization undertakes to ensure that its products meet its established quality standards.

Establishing standards. Product specifications and quality standards must be established so the company can create a product that will compete in the marketplace.

Inspection. Inspection reveals whether a product meets quality standards. Organizations normally inspect purchased items, work-in-process, and finished items.

Sampling. By using principles of statistical inference, management can employ sampling techniques that assure a relatively high probability of reaching the right conclusion—that is, rejecting a lot that does not meet standards and accepting a lot that does.

Managing Productivity

One of the primary objectives of the operations function is to increase productivity by using resources efficiently.

Measuring productivity. Productivity is the measurement of the relationship between the outputs produced and the inputs used to produce them.

The importance of productivity. Productivity is important on three levels: (1) as it relates to the ability of departments and divisions within organizations to use their allotted resources as efficiently and effectively as possible; (2) at an organizational level, where it contributes to an organization's ability to stay competitive; (3) on the national level, where it is an important indicator of the economic strength and standard of living of a nation.

Improving productivity. Some key steps toward improving productivity are listed below:

1. Develop adequate productivity measurements.
2. Consider the "entire" or "whole" system when deciding on which operations to concentrate.
3. Develop productivity improvement methods (such as work teams) and reward contributions.
4. Establish reasonable improvement goals.
5. Make productivity improvements a management, particularly top-management, priority.
6. Publicize productivity improvements.
7. Use decision-support systems.
8. Link incentives with productivity increases.
9. Provide adequate training.

KEY TERMS

Text page numbers where terms are first defined are in parentheses.

operations management (OM) (588)—the development and administration of the activities involved in transforming resources into goods and services

inputs (588)—resources such as labor, money, materials, information, and energy that are converted to outputs in the transformation process

outputs (588)—goods, services, and ideas that are converted from inputs in the transformation process

manufacturing (590)—the activities and processes used in making tangible products; interchangeable with production

production (590)—the activities and processes used in making tangible products; interchangeable with manufacturing

operations (590)—those processes used in the making of both tangible and intangible products

capacity (593)—the maximum load that an organizational unit can carry or operate at a given point in time

fixed-position layout (594)—facility layout in which the organization has a central location for the product and brings all resources required to create the product to that location

process layout (594)—facility layout in which firms organize the transformation process into departments that group related procedures

product layout (594)—facility layout in which production is broken down into relatively simple tasks assigned to workers positioned along the line, and the product moves from worker to worker

computer-assisted design (CAD) (595)—a computerized approach in the operations function that links the design and manufacturing areas, making information readily available

computer-assisted manufacturing (CAM) (595)—a computerized approach in the operations function that links the manufacturing and design areas, making information readily available

flexible manufacturing (596)—a manufacturing process in which computers can direct machinery to adapt to different versions of similar operations

industrial robot (596)—a machine designed to move material, parts, tools, or specialized devices through variable programmed motions, for the performance of a variety of tasks

inventory (597)—all the materials a firm holds in storage for future use

finished-goods inventory (597)—those products that are ready for sale, such as a fully assembled automobile ready to ship to a dealer

work-in-process inventory (597)—those products that are partially completed or are in transit

raw materials inventory (598)—those materials that have been purchased to be used as inputs for making other products

purchasing (598)—the buying of all the materials needed by the organization; also known as procurement

inventory control (599)—the process of determining how many supplies and goods are needed and keeping track of quantities on hand, where each item is, and who is responsible for it

economic order quantity (EOQ) (599)—a popular approach to inventory control that identifies the optimal number of items to order while maintaining certain annual costs that vary according to order size

just-in-time (JIT) inventory management (600)—a concept that minimizes the number of units in inventory by providing an almost continuous flow of items from suppliers to the production facility

material-requirements planning (MRP) (600)—a planning system that schedules the precise quantity of materials needed to make the product

manufacturing-resource planning (MRPII) (601)—a computerized system that helps a company control all of its resources, not just inventory needed for production

routing (601)—the sequence of operations through which a product must pass

scheduling (601)—the assigning of work to be done to departments or to specific machines or persons

Program Evaluation and Review Technique (PERT) (601)—a scheduling technique in which managers identify all the major activities (events) required to complete a project, arrange the events in a sequence or path, determine the project's critical path, and estimate the time required for each event

Gantt chart (602)—a bar chart that shows the relationship of various scheduling activities over time

quality control (603)—the activities an organization undertakes to ensure that its products meet its established quality standards

productivity (606)—the measurement of the relationship between the outputs produced and the inputs used to produce them

partial productivity (606)—output relative to a single input or some combination of inputs

total productivity (607)—outputs relative to all the inputs used

REVIEW QUESTIONS

True/False

Indicate whether the following statements are true or false.

___ 1. Operations management is at the "fringe" of most organizations because the emphasis today is on providing quality service.

___ 2. Most organizations are a combination of service providers and manufacturers, with both tangible and intangible qualities embodied in what they produce.

___ 3. Long-term capacity-planning decisions tend to focus on the effects that variations in demand have on capacity, as with the fluctuating demand of a seasonal product.

___ 4. When managing quality, establishing standards precedes inspection.

___ 5. The repeated opening and closing of car doors to determine the life expectancy of hinges and latches is an example of a performance test.

Multiple Choice

Select the best answer for each question.

___ 6. Land, labor, and capital are examples of which component of the transformation process of operations management?
a. inputs
b. transformation or conversion
c. outputs
d. feedback
e. control standards

___ 7. Which of the following is a characteristic of a service provider?
a. a tangible product
b. uniformity of outputs
c. a high degree of automation
d. limited in working methods
e. a high degree of customer contact

___ 8. The first step in the production process is:
a. designing a product
b. determining consumer wants
c. obtaining the raw materials
d. hiring skilled workers
e. developing the right process

___ 9. When managing the materials that have been purchased to be used as inputs for making other products, a manager is managing the:
a. finished-goods inventory
b. flexible inventory
c. work-in-process inventory
d. raw materials inventory
e. MRPII inventory

___10. In the PERT scheduling technique, each completed activity is called a/an:
   a. path
   b. schedule
   c. event
   d. task
   e. critical path

Fill in the Blank

11. Planning the operational processes for the organization involves two important areas: capacity planning and ________________ planning.
12. The ________________ layout design requires that production be broken down into relatively simple tasks assigned to workers positioned along the line, and the product moves from worker to worker.
13. A machine designed to move material, parts, tools, or specialized devices through variable programmed motions for the performance of a variety of tasks is called a/an __________________ ________________.
14. Purchasing, also known as __________________, is the buying of all the materials needed by the organization.
15. A/An _____________ _______________ is a bar chart that shows the relationship of various scheduling activities over time.

Matching

Place the corresponding letter of each acronym associated with operations management next to each definition or description. Each answer can be used only once.

   a. CAD/CAM
   b. EOQ
   c. JIT
   d. MRP
   e. MRPII

___16. A concept that minimizes the number of units in inventory by providing an almost continuous flow of items from suppliers to the production facility

___17. A computerized system that helps a company control all of its resources, not just inventory needed for production

___18. A popular approach to inventory control that identifies the optimal number of items to order while maintaining certain annual costs that vary according to order size

___19. A computerized approach in the operations function that links the manufacturing and design areas, making information readily available

___20. A planning system that schedules the precise quantity of materials needed to make the product

Short Answer/Discussion Questions

21. Compare and contrast the terms *manufacturing, production,* and *operations.*
22. Give one example of *partial productivity* and one example of total *productivity.*
23. Name the three levels where productivity is important.
24. List three key steps toward improving productivity.
25. What are some ways to increase productivity through employees' attitudes?

ANSWERS TO REVIEW QUESTIONS

Text page numbers where the answers can be found are included in parentheses.

1. False (588)
2. True (591)
3. False (593)
4. True (603)
5. False (605)
6. a (589)
7. e (591)
8. b (592)
9. d (598)
10. c (601)
11. facilities (592)
12. product (594)
13. industrial robot (596)
14. procurement (598)
15. Gantt chart (602)
16. c (600)
17. e (601)
18. b (599)
19. a (595)
20. d (600)
21. Manufacturing and production are used interchangeably to represent the activities and processes used in making tangible products. Operations is a broader term used to describe those processes used in the making of both tangible and intangible products. (590)
22. partial productivity example:

$$\frac{\text{output}}{\text{labor hours}} = \text{output per hour}$$

total productivity example:

$$\frac{\text{output}}{\text{labor costs + machine costs + material costs}} = \text{output per total inputs}$$

(606–607)

23. departmental/divisional level, organizational level, and national level (607).
24. The three you listed should come from the following list of nine keys:
    - Develop adequate productivity measurements.
    - Consider the "entire" or "whole" system when deciding on which operations to concentrate.
    - Develop productivity improvement methods (such as work teams) and reward contributions.
    - Establish reasonable improvement goals.
    - Make productivity improvements a management, particularly top management, priority.
    - Publicize productivity improvements.
    - Use decision-support systems.
    - Link incentives with productivity increases.
    - Provide adequate training. (608–609)
25. Provide sufficient job training, increase job autonomy, provide financial incentives, and elicit and integrate employees' input on productivity issues. (610)

STUDENT EXERCISE

Examining Labor Productivity in the Service Sector

You learned in this chapter about the importance of productivity as it relates to the ability of departments and divisions within organizations to use their allotted resources as efficiently and effectively as possible. At an organizational level, productivity contributes to an organization's ability to stay competitive. Likewise, on the national level, productivity is an important indicator of the economic strength and standard of living of a nation.

The McKinsey Global Institute conducted a year-long research project[1] on economic productivity in the leading economies of the world (the United States, United Kingdom, Germany, France, and Japan), placing particular emphasis on the service sector (airlines, telecommunications, retail banking, general merchandise retailing, and restaurants). In this exercise, you will learn about the McKinsey Global Institute's findings as they relate to the retail industry (general merchandise retailing).

Research Findings

The labor productivity comparison of the five nations in this study revealed the following:

Table 20.1 Labor Productivity Comparison General Merchandise Retailing—1987

United States	100%
Germany	96%
United Kingdom	82%
France	69%
Japan	44%

Directions

Listed below are four statements taken from the research report that address specific factors listed in Table 20.2, Causes of Labor Productivity Differences. After each statement, write the number from Table 20.2 that this statement addresses, and identify whether the factor has an ●—Important; ○—Secondary; or X—Undifferentiating effect on explaining the causes of labor productivity differences among the five countries listed in Table 20.1.

1. The speed at which more productive store formats can replace less productive formats is constrained or spurred, as the case may be, by regulation. For example, governments in Germany, France, and Japan have enacted laws that limit opening of large-scale stores and regulate the number of days stores may be opened and the number of hours they may stay open each day. By contrast, the United Kingdom and United States regulate retailing store openings loosely and indirectly through land-use planning at the local level; and new stores have benefited from a bias to allow openings in both countries. The United States is the only country among the five that has no restrictions on opening hours. ("Retailing," *Service Sector Productivity*, p. 7)

   ______ Number from Table 20.2

   ______ ●—Important; ○—Secondary; or X—Undifferentiating

[1]McKinsey Global Institute, *Service Sector Productivity* (Washington, DC: McKinsey & Company, Inc., 1992). Used with permission.

2. The most important difference reflects how managers respond to the environment. Competitive intensity powerfully influences management behavior. Thus, the reason for the higher U.S. productivity levels in the service industries studied in this research project (airlines, telecommunications, retail banking, general merchandise retailing, and restaurants), indicates that the effect of competition on management behavior is the likely principal cause. Competitive pressures on companies operating in the United States are greater than in the other countries. ("Introduction," Service Sector Productivity, p. 3)

______ Number from Table 20.2

______ ●—Important; ○—Secondary; or X—Undifferentiating

3. There is much more formal training for sales clerks in France than in Britain or the United States. However, the technical burdens placed on the bulk of retail workers, especially in the stores, are relatively simple. This is not to belittle the importance of training as a key to commercial success, or the quality of labor as a key determinant of labor productivity. ("Retailing," Service Sector Productivity, p. 10)

______ Number from Table 20.2

______ ●—Important; ○—Secondary; or X—Undifferentiating

4. The issue of capital in retailing is more complex than in other service industries, because there are three fundamentally different types of capital involved: information technology (IT) assets, real estate assets, and inventory. However, none of these have been found to explain differences in labor productivity. ("Retailing," Service Sector Productivity, p. 9]

______ Number from Table 20.2

______ ●—Important; ○—Secondary; or X—Undifferentiating

5. Based upon what you know about the retail industry, fill in the remaining numbers on Table 20.2; then check your answers at the end of the exercise.

Table 20.2 Causes of Labor Productivity Differences
General Merchandising

○—Important
●—Secondary
X—Undifferentiating

EXTERNAL FACTORS	
- Market conditions	
• Demand factors	1. _____
• Relative input prices/factor availability	2. _____
- Policy and regulation	
• Competition rules and concentration rules	3. _____
• Government ownership	4. _____
• Labor rules and unionism	5. _____
↓	
MANAGEMENT BEHAVIOR	6. _____
↓	
PRODUCTION PROCESS	
- Output mix, variety, quality	7. _____
- Economies of scale	8. _____
- Capital (intensity and vintage)	9. _____
- Skill of labor	10. _____
- Organization of labor	11. _____
↓	
LABOR PRODUCTIVITY	

ANSWERS TO STUDENT EXERCISE

1. 3 ●
2. 6 ●
3. 10 X
4. 9 ○
5. See chart that follows:

EXTERNAL FACTORS	
- Market conditions	
• Demand factors	1. ●
• Relative input prices/factor availability	2. X
- Policy and regulation	
• Competition rules and concentration rules	3. ●
• Government ownership	4. X
• Labor rules and unionism	5. X

↓

MANAGEMENT BEHAVIOR 6. ●

PRODUCTION PROCESS	
- Output mix, variety, quality	7. ●
- Economies of scale	8. ○
- Capital (intensity and vintage)	9. ○
- Skill of labor	10. X
- Organization of labor	11. X

LABOR PRODUCTIVITY

chapter twenty-one

Managing Information Systems

LEARNING OBJECTIVES

- Explain why managers need information and the characteristics of useful information.
- Describe a management information system and explain its role in management.
- Specify the basic factors that determine an organization's information management needs.
- Determine how computers can be used in management information systems.
- Distinguish among the basic types of management information systems.
- Summarize the impact of information technology on people, organizations, and information.
- Critique a business's implementation of a management information system.

CHAPTER OUTLINE

Introduction

Information and Management
- The Role of Information in Management
- Characteristics of Useful Information

Management Information Systems
- How an MIS Works
- Determining Information System Needs
- Characteristics of Effective MIS Development, Implementation, and Usage

Using Computers in Management Information Systems
- Hardware versus Software
- Computer Networks
- Communicating with Computers
- Integrating Information Technologies

Types of Information Systems
- Transaction Support Systems
- Decision Support Systems
- Executive Information Systems
- Expert Systems and Neural Networks

The Impact of Information Technology
- The Effects of Information Technology
- Information System Limitations

CHAPTER RECAP

Note: Boldface words are major chapter headings.

Introduction

The technological revolution has greatly influenced the ways that business is conducted, as well as the activities and responsibilities of managers. Nowhere is this impact more evident and important than in the area of information management.

Information and Management

Obtaining, analyzing, and understanding information about the business environment are important activities in any business.

The role of information in management. Data are unorganized facts, statistics, opinions, and predictions gathered from various sources inside and outside the company. Data must be sorted and logically organized to produce relevant information—data that are relevant for a specific purpose.

Characteristics of useful information. All managers require accurate, timely, complete, and relevant information.

Management Information Systems

MIS is a system that organizes past, present, and projected data from both internal and external sources and processes them into usable information.

How an MIS works. The major task of an MIS, typically with the aid of computers, is to gather, store and update, analyze, and report data.

Determining information system needs. Every organization has its own unique set of information needs that must be clearly understood before it can design and implement a system to satisfy those needs. To understand them, the designer of the information system must consider both organizational factors (environment, size, and level of organizational diversity) and managerial factors (related to characteristics of individual managers, degree of interaction between functional units, and manager's level within the organization).

Characteristics of effective MIS development, implementation, and usage. Generally, an MIS investment should enable the firm to create new business processes; a successful MIS may depend on external systems experts; and the system must be "user/worker-friendly."

Using Computers in Management Information Systems

Many companies, regardless of size, rely on computer-based information systems to organize, manipulate, and distribute information.

Hardware versus software. Hardware is the basic physical components of a computer; software is a computer program or set of commands that instructs a computer to perform various operations, such as reading, analyzing, or storing data in a specified location.

Computer networks. Computer networks are the systems that permit different computers to communicate with each other. A local-area network (LAN) is a network in which computers are linked together directly within one building or one plant, while a wide-area network (WAN) is a network in which computers are linked by telephone lines or long-range communications devices.

Communicating with computers. Three forms available for communicating with computers are electronic mail (E-mail), electronic bulletin boards, and computer conferencing.

Integrating information technologies. One increasingly popular form of integrating information technologies is telecommuting— using telecommunications technology, such as a fax, modem, and computer, to work from home or other places outside the traditional workplace.

Types of Information Systems

1. **Transaction support systems**— an information system that handles routine, repetitious business transactions, such as credit card purchases, scanners at store checkout counters, and automated teller machines (ATMs).
2. **Decision support systems**—an information system that aids managers in decision making by helping them anticipate the possible outcomes of alternative actions.
3. **Executive information systems**—an easy-to-use DSS designed for executives who have limited experience using computers but need access to the firm's database.
4. **Expert systems**—decision support programs that mimic human decision-making processes by using a collection of thousands of "if-then" rules to solve complex problems—**and neural networks**—training the computer to think like the human mind by presenting it with repeated examples of information for use in forming patterns of logic with which to make future decisions.

The Impact of Information Technology

The effects of information technology fall into two general categories: (1) organizational effects, such as replacing workers with technology, while at the same time hiring more temporary workers to handle programming, data entry, and other MIS tasks; and (2) performance effects, such as helping companies retrieve information faster and more conveniently, which helps companies improve performance.

Information system limitations are classified as (1) performance limitations, which can be caused by such things as computer viruses, bugs in computer programs, and system crashes; (2) behavioral limitations, which can be caused, for example, by information overload; and (3) health risks, such as exposure to low-level radiation emitted by CRTs.

KEY TERMS

Text page numbers where terms are first defined are in parentheses.

data (618)—unorganized facts, statistics, opinions, and predictions gathered from various sources inside and outside the company

information (618)—data that are relevant for a specific purpose

management information system (MIS) (619)—a system that organizes past, present, and projected data from both internal and external sources and processes them into usable information

database (620)—a collection of related data—past, present, and projected—organized for convenient access

hardware (625)—the basic physical components of a computer

software (626)—a computer program or set of commands that instructs a computer to perform various operations, such as reading, analyzing, or storing data in a specified location

computer networks (626)—systems that permit different computers to communicate with each other

local-area network (LAN) (626)—a network in which computers are linked together directly within one building or one plant

wide-area network (WAN) (626)—a network in which computers are linked by telephone lines or long-range communications devices

electronic mail (628)—the exchange of "letters" or messages from computer to computer; also called E-mail

telecommuting (629)—using telecommunications technology to work from home or other places outside the traditional workplace

transaction support system (TSS) (630)—an information system that handles routine, repetitious business transactions

decision support system (DSS) (631)—an information system that aids managers in decision making by helping them anticipate the possible outcomes of alternative actions

group decision support system (GDSS) (631)—a special set of computer systems designed to aid group decision making

executive information system (EIS) (631)—an easy-to-use DSS designed for executives who have limited experience using computers but need access to the firm's database

artificial intelligence (632)—programs that seek to make computers able to work—to "think"—as much like the human mind as possible

expert systems (632)—decision support programs that mimic human decision-making processes by using a collection of thousands of "if-then" rules to solve complex problems

computer viruses (637)—computer programs concealed inside legitimate programs that change or destroy data kept on a computer; can damage or even cripple a system

bug (637)—an error in a software program

crash (637)—a system service failure

REVIEW QUESTIONS

True/False

Indicate whether the following statements are true or false.

___ 1. Data are information relevant for a specific purpose; information is unorganized facts, statistics, opinions, and predictions gathered from various sources inside and outside the company.

___ 2. The more uncertain and complex a company's competitive and technological environment, the greater will be its requirements for accurate, timely, complete, and relevant information.

___ 3. The information needs of each department must be considered in isolation because each functional area has unique informational needs.

___ 4. A management information system requires the use of a computer.

___ 5. There is a growing consensus that investments made in information technology pay for themselves in terms of organizational performance gains and returns on investment.

Multiple Choice

Select the best answer for each question.

___ 6. Which of the following is **not** a characteristic of useful information?
a. accurate
b. timely
c. complete
d. relevant
e. cost-effective

___ 7. Which of the following is **not** an example of a computer peripheral device?
a. CPU
b. CD-ROM
c. keyboard
d. modem
e. mouse

___ 8. Training the computer to think like the human mind by presenting it with repeated examples of information for use in forming patterns of logic with which to make future decisions is called:
a. DSS
b. EIS
c. expert systems
d. neural networks
e. TSS

___ 9. Which of the following is **not** an example of how information technology commonly affects internal organization structures?
   a. increasing emphasis placed on the marketing function
   b. creating a new position of chief information officer (CIO)
   c. reducing staff
   d. hiring consultants
   e. hiring temporary workers

___10. Which is an example of a behavioral limitation related to information systems?
   a. The information generated by an information system may not be as accurate, timely, complete, or relevant as needed.
   b. Too much information can overwhelm employees, cause stress, and even slow decision making.
   c. Computer use is limited in situations where highly personal or sensitive information is involved.
   d. Information technology is not suited for all tasks or problems.
   e. Computers and information systems are a tool for decision making, not a crutch.

Fill in the Blank

11. A collection of related data—past, present, and projected—organized for convenient access is called a/an ________________.
12. Many networks are centered on a mainframe or a minicomputer, also called a/an ______________, that stores databases and other information vital to all parts of the network and is thus the heart of a firm's MIS.
13. When employees use telecommunications technology to work from home or other places outside the traditional workplace, they are ________________.
14. ________________ ______________ are decision support programs that mimic human decision-making processes by using a collection of thousands of "if-then" rules to solve complex problems.
15. Two health risks associated with using computers are ________ radiation exposure and _______, a painful disorder in the hands and wrists caused by repetitive movements on a computer keyboard. (Use acronyms only in filling in both blanks in this question.)

Matching

Place the corresponding letter of the acronyms associated with management information systems with each definition or description. Each answer can be used only once.

a. **LAN**
b. **WAN**
c. **TSS**
d. **DSS**
e. **EIS**

___16. A network in which computers are linked by telephone lines or long-range communications devices

___17. An information system that aids managers in decision making by helping them anticipate the possible outcomes of alternative actions

___18. A network in which computers are linked together directly within one building or one plant

___19. An easy-to-use DSS designed for executives who have limited experience using computers but need access to the firm's database

___20. An information system that handles routine, repetitious business transactions

Short Answer/Discussion Questions

21. Name the two factors that a designer must consider before designing and implementing an information system.
22. Name five activities to which managers must attend in order to minimize system user resistance and frustration.
23. List three ways people can communicate with each other using computers.
24. Describe the "virtual corporation."
25. Compare and contrast a computer virus, bug, and crash as they relate to performance limitations of information systems.

ANSWERS TO REVIEW QUESTIONS

Text page numbers where the answers can be found are included in parentheses.

1. False (618)
2. True (621)
3. False (622)
4. False (624)
5. True (635)
6. e (619)
7. a (625)
8. d (633)
9. a (634-35)
10. b (637)
11. database (620)
12. server (627)
13. telecommuting (629)
14. expert systems (632)
15. CRT (cathode-ray tubes housed in computer monitors) and CTS (carpal tunnel syndrome) (639)
16. b (626)
17. d (631)
18. a (626)
19. e (631)
20. c (630)
21. organizational factors and managerial factors. (621–622)
22. (a) Carefully test new systems and introduce them in stages. (b) Involve those who will actually use the system in all stages of MIS development. (c) Clearly communicate business objectives and how MIS usage helps meet these objectives to system users. (d) Teach employees system usage by helping them improve their performance. (e) Don't ignore the generation gap. (624)
23. E-mail, electronic bulletin boards, and computer conferencing. (628)
24. A virtual corporation involves a temporary alliance of several independent companies—suppliers, customers, and even traditional business rivals—linked by information technology for purposes of exploiting an opportunity. Each company contributes only its specific expertise to the alliance to form an "ideal organization" for the task at hand. Once the venture has been completed, more likely than not, the group effort will be discontinued. (634)
25. All three of these problems originate in the computer software—and not in the computer hardware. Computer viruses are computer programs concealed inside legitimate programs that change or destroy data kept on a computer; they can damage or even cripple a system. A bug is an error in a software program, which can result in a crash —a system service failure. (637)

STUDENT EXERCISE

Assessing and Increasing Your Computer Literacy

As you read the following information, answer these two questions:

- What percentage of companies now require their managers and supervisors to be computer literate? ________
- How much more do computer-literate employees earn compared to their noncomputer-literate counterparts? ________

> A nationwide survey of 1,481 management information systems executives conducted by The Olsten Corp., in Westbury, New York, found that 71 percent of companies now require their managers and supervisors to be computer literate—up 36 percent from just three years ago. In addition, computer-literate employees generally earn 15 to 20 percent more than those without such experience.[1]

To help you assess your own level of computer literacy, complete the following questionnaire and score yourself using the answer key at the end of the exercise.

COMPUTER LITERACY QUESTIONNAIRE

Matching

Each set of three questions has five possible answers. Choose the correct answer and write the letter in the space provided in the left-hand column. A response may be used only once or not at all.

1.	Has four functional parts: input, processing, storage (programs and data), and output.	A.	Arithmetic/logical unit
2.	Performs the mathematical operations and any comparisons required.	B.	Computer system
3.	Physical parts of a computer.	C.	CPU
		D.	Firmware
		E.	Hardware

4.	Standard method of representing a character with a number inside the computer.	A.	Alphanumeric
5.	The base 2 numbering system that uses digits 0 and 1.	B.	ASCII
6.	Number system that uses the ten digits 0 through 9 and the six letters A through F to represent values in base 16.	C.	Binary
		D.	Hexadecimal
		E.	Numeric data

[1] "Tech Watch," *Black Enterprise* (May 1993), p. 45.

7.	Smallest part of a display screen that can be controlled.	A.	Cluster
		B.	Dvorak
8.	Standard keyboard arrangement.	C.	Light pen
9.	Uses position of light on a computer screen to record information.	D.	Qwerty
		E.	Pixel

10.	Technique for opening folders.	A.	Double-clicking
11.	Technique for moving an icon with a mouse.	B.	Dragging
		C.	Highlighting
12.	Pointer similar to arrows.	D.	I-beam
		E.	Scroll bar

13.	A read-only memory whose contents are alterable by electrical means.	A.	Access
		B.	Clockrate
14.	Internal memory that is erased when the computer's power is shut off.	C.	Memory
		D.	PROM
15.	Time it takes to find data stored externally.	E.	RAM

16.	Number of characters printed per horizontal inch of space.	A.	Font
		B.	Kerning
17.	Set of characters in one typeface, style, and size.	C.	Leading
		D.	Pitch
18.	Narrows the spacing between letters.	E.	Points

19.	Arrangement where each device is connected to a single communication cable.	A.	Bus network
		B.	Parallel
		C.	Ring network
20.	A group of computers usually connected by less than 1,000 feet of cable.	D.	Serial
		E.	Local area network (LAN)
21.	Sends data one bit at a time.		

22.	Operator that describes the quality that connects two data or expressions such as greater than, less than, or equal to.	A.	Commands
		B.	Distributed
		C.	Execute
		D.	Multitasking
23.	Messages the user sends to the computer that makes it perform specific operations.	E.	Relational operator
24.	The ability to run more than one program at one time without interrupting the execution of another program.		

25.	Place to enlarge or shrink a window.	A.	Active window
26.	Place documents are saved.	B.	Dialog box
27.	Place you are typing.	C.	Folders
		D.	Record box
		E.	Zoom box

28.	A term that refers to memory in which data or software is lost when the computer is turned off.	A.	Crash
29.	Program that moves the read/write head to a section of the disk that has no data.	B.	Erasable
30.	Read/write comes into contact with the disk's surface.	C.	Pack
		D.	Park
		E.	Volatile

31.	First line of a paragraph that prints by itself at the bottom of the page.	A.	Block
32.	Text aligned flush with the left or right margins.	B.	Orphan
33.	Series of adjacent characters, words, sentences, or paragraphs.	C.	Pasted
		D.	Ragged
		E.	Widow

34.	Number of times per second that a transmitted signal changes.	A.	Baud
35.	Sends or receives data, but not both simultaneously.	B.	Half-duplex
36.	Process of sending prearranged signals specifying the protocol to be followed.	C.	Handshaking
		D.	Modem
		E.	Simplex

37.	Prints italics characters.	A.	Daisy-wheel
38.	TV-like device that gives users of microcomputer equipment video feedback about their actions and the computer's actions.	B.	Dot-matrix
39.	Repeats the phone number twice when you call information.	C.	Monitor
		D.	Scanner
		E.	Voice synthesizer

40.	The smallest piece of data that can be recognized by computers.	A.	Bit
41.	Basic unit of measure of computer's storage.	B.	Byte
42.	Placed in a microcomputer to take the burden of manipulating numbers off the CPU.	C.	Chip
		D.	Control unit
		E.	Coprocessor

43.	Program that translates the mnemonics and symbols of low level language into the opcodes and operands of machine language.	A.	Assembler
44.	Software that translates a whole program into machine language.	B.	Compiler
45.	Language designed so that machines and human beings can interact easily.	C.	Interpreter
		D.	Natural
		E.	Pascal

Source: Based on the "Computer Literacy Questionnaire" developed by Floyd Brock, Wayne E. Thomsen, and John Kohl, College of Business and Economics, University of Nevada Las Vegas. Used with permission.

ANSWERS TO STUDENT EXERCISE

1. B	16. D	31. B
2. A	17. A	32. D
3. E	18. B	33. A
4. B	19. B	34. A
5. C	20. E	35. B
6. D	21. D	36. C
7. E	22. E	37. B
8. D	23. A	38. C
9. C	24. D	39. E
10. A	25. E	40. A
11. B	26. C	41. B
12. D	27. A	42. E
13. D	28. E	43. A
14. E	29. D	44. B
15. A	30. A	45. D

Indications from Score

Although there are no hard and fast cut-off scores to provide a completely accurate assessment of your computer literacy level, the following breakdown can give you a general idea of where you fall based on your performance on this computer literacy questionnaire:

Number of Correct Answers	Computer Literacy Level
40–45	High
33–39	Above average
26–32	Average
19–25	Below average
0–18	Very low

Attaining and Maintaining Computer Literacy

Most colleges and universities offer a basic introductory computer course that is a good start toward your becoming computer literate; however, nothing beats hands-on experience with your own computer or a computer you can use on your job. Even if you're satisfied with the level of computer literacy you exhibited on this assessment, you won't be able to rest on your laurels for too long. In the rapidly evolving world of computer systems and software, it is very easy to lose your literacy status in a short period of time.

Here are some ideas to help you keep pace with the rapid changes in computer technology:

- Enroll in additional computer-related classes where you can learn more about specific software applications (word processing, spreadsheets, etc.).
- Use the wizards and other "help" features that accompany many of the newer software packages.
- Join a computer club or specific users' group.

- Access electronic bulletin boards and other computer information forums on on-line services such as CompuServe, America Online, Prodigy, or the newest service, the Microsoft Network—all of which provide access to the Internet.
- Read computer-related periodicals.
- Talk to your friends whom you consider computer literate, and ask them what they do to keep up-to-date.

chapter twenty-two

Management Control Systems

LEARNING OBJECTIVES

- Define management control and explain why it is necessary.
- Examine the process through which managers develop and implement control.
- Distinguish among the various forms of control.
- Summarize the elements of effective control.
- Determine why control is sometimes met with resistance and how managers may overcome this resistance.
- Assess an organization's control program.

CHAPTER OUTLINE

Introduction

Control in Organizations
- The Importance of Control
- Responsibilities for Control
- The Link between Planning and Controlling

The Control Process
- Establishing Performance Standards
- Measuring Performance
- Comparing Performance against Standards
- Evaluating Performance and Taking Corrective Action

Forms of Management Control
- Organizational Control
- Operations Control
- Strategic Control
- Financial Control

Managing the Control Process
- Developing the Control Process
- Understanding Resistance to Control
- Overcoming Resistance to Control
- Signs of Inadequate Control Systems

CHAPTER RECAP

Note: Boldface words are major chapter headings.

Introduction

The challenge to managers when managing the control function is to understand both the purpose and importance of control and to use it so that it does not infringe on employees' personal freedoms but it does maximize organizational performance.

Control in Organizations

Management control includes all of the activities an organization undertakes to ensure that its actions lead to achievement of its objectives. A management control system is a planned, ordered scheme of management control.

The importance of control. Control is an essential part of effective organizational management because it helps an organization adapt to changing conditions, limits the magnifications of errors, assists in dealing with increased complexity, and helps minimize costs.

Responsibilities for control. Traditionally, managers have been responsible for the control process. Today, however, more emphasis is being placed on sharing the responsibility for control activities with lower-level employees.

The link between planning and controlling. For control to be effective, it must be integrated with planning so that managers can compare actual results with planned projects. Also, the ability to control activities must be considered during the planning process.

The Control Process

The control process consists of four basic steps:

1. **Establishing performance standards.** Performance standards are targets set by management against which actual performance is compared at a future date. Without such standards, managers cannot accurately gauge the effectiveness of the company's efforts.
2. **Measuring performance.** Managers must measure actual performance in the context of the specific activities that they wish to control.
3. **Comparing performance against standards.** After comparing measured actual performance against the standards established in step one, management must decide how much deviation from the standards will be tolerated before considering corrective action.
4. **Evaluating performance and taking corrective action.** Before responding to deviations between performance standards and actual performance, managers in charge of control must determine the reason(s) for the deviation. Was the plan properly implemented and failed to work, or was the plan not implemented properly? Three options include: correct the deviation, change the standards, or maintain the status quo.

Forms of Management Control

There are three levels of control:

1. **Organizational control** is a broad-based form of control that guides all organizational activities and oversees the overall functioning of the whole firm. The two dominant forms of organizational control are bureaucratic control (an attempt to control the firm's overall functioning through formal, mechanistic structural arrangements) and clan control (the regulation of overall organizational functioning through reliance on informal, organic structural arrangements).
2. **Operations control** regulates one or more individual operating systems within an organization. The three basic forms of operations control that most companies use simultaneously to effectively achieve control of operating systems are: (a) preliminary (or feedforward or steering) control, which monitors deviations in the quality and quantity of the firm's resources to try to prevent deviations before they enter the system; (b) screening (or yes/no or concurrent) control, which regulates operations to ensure that they are consistent with objectives; (c) feedback (or postaction) control, which monitors the firm's outputs, the results of the transformation process.
3. **Strategic control** ensures that the organization effectively understands and responds to the realities of its environment.
4. **Financial control** techniques include (a) budgetary control, which allows companies to anticipate and control financial resource needs by using operating and capital budgeting, developed by either top-down budgeting, bottom-up budgeting, negotiated budgeting, or zero-based budgeting (ZBB); (b) analysis of financial statements, such as the balance sheet and income statements, by using ratio analysis; and (c) financial audits—a periodic and comprehensive examination of a firm's financial records.

Managing the Control Process

Here are several areas requiring attention when managing the control process:

Developing the control process. Effective control systems are typically well integrated with planning and are flexible, accurate, timely, and objective.

Understanding resistance to control. Common reasons for resistance to control include overcontrol, inappropriately focused control, control that rewards inefficiency, and the creation of enhanced accountability.

Overcoming resistance to control. The challenge to managers is to exercise control so that employees understand the need for control but are not unduly inconvenienced by it. In general, there are four things managers can do to overcome resistance to control: create effective control, encourage employee participation, use management by objectives, and use a system of checks and balances.

Signs of inadequate control systems. Following are some indicators of possible control-related difficulty:

- A high incidence of employee resistance to control.
- A unit meets control standards but fails to achieve its overall objectives.
- Increased control does not lead to increased or adequate performance.
- The existence of control standards that have been in place for an extended period of time.
- Organizational losses in terms of sales, profits, or market share.

KEY TERMS

Text page numbers where the key terms are first defined are in parentheses.

management control (646)—all of the activities an organization undertakes to ensure that its actions lead to achievement of its objectives

management control system (646)—a planned, ordered scheme of management control

performance standards (649)—targets set by management against which actual performance is compared at a future date

organizational control (652)—a broad-based form of control that guides all organizational activities and oversees the overall functioning of the whole firm

bureaucratic control (652)—an attempt to control the firm's overall functioning through formal, mechanistic structural arrangements

clan control (653)—the regulation of overall organizational functioning through reliance on informal, organic structural arrangements

operations control (654)—the regulation of one or more individual operating systems within an organization

preliminary (or feedforward or steering) control (654)—a form of operations control that monitors deviations in the quality and quantity of the firm's resources to try to prevent deviations before they enter the system

screening (or yes/no or concurrent) control (654)—a form of control that regulates operations to ensure that they are consistent with objectives; also called yes/no or concurrent control

statistical process control (SPC) (656)—an alternate form of screening control that employs "control charts" to continuously track performance variation over time

feedback (or postaction) control (657)—a form of control that monitors the firm's outputs, the results of the transformation process; also known as postaction control

strategic control (658)—a form of control whose purpose is to ensure that the organization effectively understands and responds to the realities of its environment

budgeting (658)—the process of establishing formal, written plans to control the availability and cost of financial resources

budgets (658)—the formal, written plans for future operations in financial terms

operating budgeting (658)—budgeting that deals with relatively short-term financial control concerns, such as having sufficient cash on hand to cover daily financial obligations, including routine purchases and payroll

capital budgeting (658)—budgeting concerned with the intermediate and long-term control of capital acquisitions such as plant and equipment

top-down budgeting (658)—control budgeting in which top managers establish financial plans and hand them down to middle- and lower-level managers for review and implementation

bottom-up budgeting (659)—financial planning by those employees more directly engaged in the actual tasks being covered and in which information flows up from the lower levels of an organization for review by top management

negotiated budgeting (659)—the give and take between both upper and lower levels of management in developing the most appropriate form of budgetary control for a given situation

zero-based budgeting (ZBB) (660)—a method of budgeting in which managers thoroughly reevaluate organizational activities to determine their true level of importance

balance sheet (660)—a snapshot of the organization's financial position at a given moment, indicating what the firm owns and what proportion of its assets are financed with its own or borrowed money

income statement (660)—a statement of an organization's profitability over a period of time—a month, a quarter, or a year

ratio analysis (660)—a method used by managers to take information from balance sheets and income statements in order to measure a company's efficiency, profitability, and sources of finances relative to those of other organizations

financial audit (661)—a periodic and comprehensive examination of a firm's financial records

REVIEW QUESTIONS

True/False

Indicate whether the following statements are true or false.

___ 1. Recent developments in management practice have resulted in greater sharing of responsibility and increased employee empowerment.

___ 2. Increasing control and control-related responsibilities at lower levels decreases the need for more controls.

___ 3. Performance standards can be expected to vary widely internally within a particular organization with respect to different products or markets.

___ 4. The final step in the control process is to evaluate actual performance relative to standards and then take appropriate action.

___ 5. In practice, most companies employ one form of operational control at a time in order to achieve control of operating systems.

Multiple Choice

Select the best answer for each question.

___ 6. The advantages of management control include all of the following **except:**
a. it enhances management motivation
b. it limits magnification of errors
c. it helps to minimize cost
d. it assists in dealing with complexity
e. it helps adaptation to changing conditions

___ 7. Which of the following is a characteristic of an effective control system?
a. overcontrol
b. inappropriate focus
c. rewards for inefficiency
d. timeliness
e. subjectivity

___ 8. Which of the following is a common reason for resistance to control?
   a. The control system is well integrated with planning.
   b. The control system creates enhanced accountability.
   c. The control system relies on accurate information.
   d. The control system provides unbiased information.
   e. The control system allows the company to respond to changes in the business environment.

___ 9. Which of the following is **not** a strategy managers can use to overcome employee resistance to control?
   a. Establish effective control.
   b. Encourage employee participation.
   c. Reward inefficiency.
   d. Use MBO.
   e. Use a system of checks and balances.

___10. Which of the following is **not** a sign of an inadequate control system?
   a. The existence of control standards that have been in place for an extended period of time.
   b. Increased control does not lead to increased or adequate performance.
   c. A unit meets control standards but fails to achieve its overall objectives.
   d. A high incidence of employee resistance to control.
   e. Organizational gains in terms of sales, profits, or market share.

Fill in the Blank

11. Rigid hierarchical structure, strict rules, formal controls, a reward system focused on individual employee compliance, and limited employee input are characteristics of ______________ control.
12. __________________ ratios indicate an organization's ability to meet short-term debt obligations as they come due.
13. __________________ ratios allow a company to assess its ability to meet long-term obligations.
14. A _____________ _____________ is a periodic and comprehensive examination of a firm's financial records.
15. ________ is a management philosophy based on converting organizational objectives into individual objectives.

Matching

Place the corresponding letter of the terms related to budgetary control with each definition or description. Each answer can be used only once.

a. operating budgeting
b. capital budgeting
c. bottom-up budgeting
d. negotiated budgeting
e. zero-based budgeting

___16. Budgeting that deals with relatively short-term financial control concerns, such as having sufficient cash on hand to cover daily financial obligations, including routine purchases and payroll.

___17. Financial planning by those employees more directly engaged in the actual tasks being covered and in which information flows up from the lower levels of an organization for review by top management.

___18. Budgeting concerned with the intermediate and long-term control of capital acquisitions such as plant and equipment.

___19. The give and take between both upper and lower levels of management in developing the most appropriate form of budgetary control for a given situation.

___20. A method of budgeting in which managers thoroughly reevaluate organizational activities to determine their true level of importance.

Short Answer/Discussion Questions

21. List the four steps of the control process.
22. What three options do managers have after evaluating the firm's performance?
23. Provide all the names associated with each of the three forms of operations control.
24. Discuss statistical process control (SPC).
25. Describe how managers can analyze financial statements.

ANSWERS TO REVIEW QUESTIONS

Text page numbers where the answers can be found are included in parentheses.

1. True (648)
2. False (648)
3. True (649)
4. True (651)
5. False (657)
6. a (646-647)
7. d (663)
8. b (664)
9. c (665-666)
10. e (667)
11. bureaucratic (652)
12. liquidity (660)
13. solvency (660)
14. financial audit (661)
15. MBO (666)
16. a (658)
17. e (660)
18. c (659)
19. b (658)
20. d (659)
21. establishing performance standards, measuring performance, comparing performance against standards, evaluating performance, and taking corrective action. (649)
22. Correct the observed deviation, change the performance standards, or simply maintain the status quo. (651–652)
23. (a) preliminary (or feedforward or steering) control, (b) screening (or yes/no or concurrent) control, and (c) feedback (or postaction) control. (654-657)
24. SPC is a key TQM tool used to explain the variation that inevitably occurs in every production process. SPC employs "control charts" to continuously track performance variation over time. The charts provide employees with readily accessible information with which to monitor their work and predict when they are about to exceed control limits and possibly waste organization resources. SPC serves to determine whether work processes can effectively be brought under control or if they should be left alone, as well as when manager intervention is necessary. (656–657)
25. Using ratio analysis, managers take information from the balance sheet and the income statement so that they can measure the company's efficiency, profitability, and sources of finances relative to those of other organizations. Ratio analysis allows an organization to determine its levels of liquidity and solvency. (660–661)

STUDENT EXERCISE

Applications to Operations Control

You learned that most companies practice three basic forms of operations control:

- *preliminary (or feedforward or steering) control*—a form of operations control that monitors deviations in the quality and quantity of the firm's resources to try to prevent deviations before they enter the system
- *screening (or yes/no or concurrent) control*—a form of control that regulates operations to ensure that they are consistent with objectives
- *feedback (or postaction) control*—a form of control that monitors the firm's outputs, the results of the transformation process

Figure 22.1 illustrates how these three forms of operations control relate to one another.

Figure 22.1
Control at All Stages of Operation

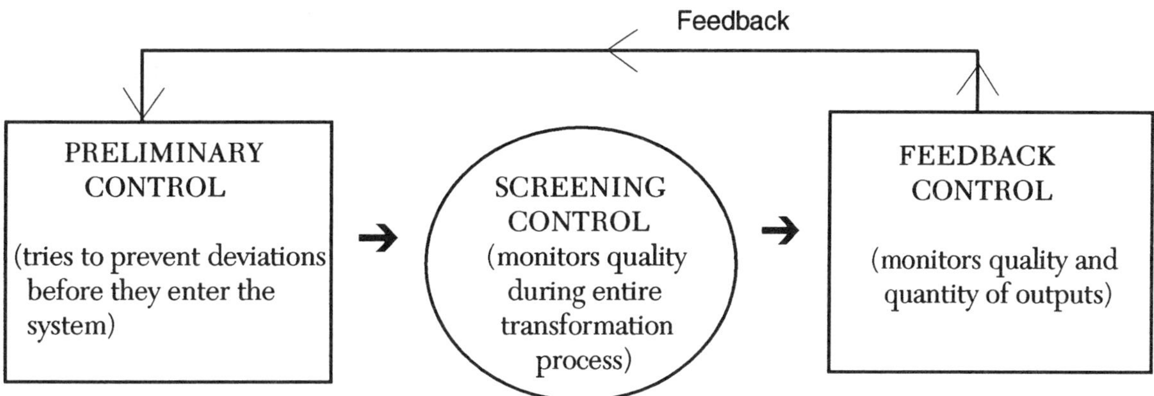

Directions

Identify each example provided below as:

a. preliminary control
b. screening control
c. feedback control

___ 1. One international fast-food restaurant has a supplier in Bavaria that cranks out some 2.5 million patties a day. Computers mix ground beef to ensure that the fat content meets the company's world standard, 20 percent or less. The specs and production demands are exacting, and, with monthly evaluations, the pressure for quality is constant.

___ 2. An automaker runs extensive, around-the-clock, seven-day-a-week test schedules, putting its test vehicles through 100,000 miles of the most stringent weather conditions, ranging from the grueling heat of Death Valley to the icy conditions of Ontario.

___ 4. At an industrial equipment company, statistical process control data are collected, analyzed, and used to control the processes.

___ 5. A pharmaceutical firm conducts procurement planning that emphasizes a market analysis of key suppliers' ability to manage costs, conform to raw material specifications, maintain production, and ship reliably.

___ 6. An aerospace company conducts quality system audits for suppliers to evaluate their commitment to continuous quality improvement.

___ 7. A leading overnight delivery carrier uses an on-package computer tracking system, combined with advanced telecommunications, to monitor the status of each shipment as it moves through key handling points in the system en route to its final destination.

___ 8. An executive at a Malcolm Baldrige Quality Award winning company makes the statement: "Education and communication were cornerstones at the foundation of our success. Education and communication were critical for instilling in every team member an awareness of the importance of a total quality system. Education built an understanding of the necessary tools, techniques, and approaches to achieve that system."

___ 9. Bank executives employ "mystery shoppers" to open accounts and use various services at the bank's branch locations. The "mystery shoppers" then report back to the bank executives their experiences and their assessment of the quality of the service they received from the tellers and other bank personnel.

___10. A chemical company checks final product quality and conformance to customer requirements through product sampling and by testing against sales specifications and customer requirements.

ANSWERS TO STUDENT EXERCISE

1. b
2. c
3. a
4. b
5. a
6. a
7. b
8. a
9. b
10. c